T

Kohima○

Imphal○

Mogaung○ ○Myitkyina

C H I N A

○Mandalay

B U R M A

FRENCH
INDO-
CHINA

ab○

RANGOON○

S I A M

00 miles
60 kms.

Gulf of
Martaban

GW00982754

H.J.B.

PRISONERS OF HOPE

PRISONERS OF HOPE

by

MICHAEL CALVERT

A NEW EDITION

with a foreword by
MAJOR-GENERAL DEREK TULLOCH,
C.B., D.S.O., M.C.

and a new postscript by
MICHAEL CALVERT

LEO COOPER

First published in 1952 by
Jonathan Cape

First published in this edition, 1971, by
Leo Cooper Ltd.
196 Shaftesbury Avenue, London, W.C.2

Printed in Great Britain by
Cox & Wyman Ltd.,
London, Reading and Fakenham

CONTENTS

ILLUSTRATIONS

MAPS

FOREWORD

Specially written for this edition by
MAJOR-GENERAL DEREK
TULLOCH, C.B., D.S.O., M.C.

Chief of Staff, Special Force (3rd Indian Division),*
The Chindits

Michael Calvert is one of the most distinguished fighting soldiers produced by the British Army in this century. In this book he describes the operations carried out by the 77th Infantry Brigade, under his command in Burma in 1944.

His brigade was one of the five Chindit Brigades of Wingate's Special Force which operated against the Japanese in 1944.

The history of Special Force operations, as a whole, has not been produced up to now. It is a sad story, for Wingate was killed only three weeks after the 'Fly-in' operations commenced and when his Force was in position to carry out his strategic design. After his death the Japanese Commander, General Mutaguchi, regained the initiative and for a number of reasons Wingate's plan was abandoned, the chief of which was, possibly, the divergent aims of the three Allies concerned in these operations as a whole – the British, the Americans and the Chinese.

Calvert's own task was never altered. This was to cut the communications of the Japanese divisions facing Stilwell and Chiang Kai-shek, though the force employed for the second task was put directly under Special Force Headquarters half-way through the operations. How well he succeeded in this task can be seen from this book. The effect of the stranglehold that he imposed on the Japanese 18th Division facing Stilwell, failed to produce immediate

* '3rd Indian Division' was a cover name designed to confuse and delude the Japanese Intelligence.

results because Chiang Kai-shek refused to allow the Chinese divisions under Stilwell's command to advance until the situation at Imphal was cleared. Under little pressure, the 18th Division subsisted on the supplies and ammunition they already possessed. Two months later, when Stilwell's advance was resumed, the 18th Division quickly ran short of ammunition, petrol and food and the results of Calvert's blockade were felt at once.

Wingate's Plan B, which was to position his two reserve brigades on the communications of the Japanese divisions attacking Imphal, was abandoned on 9 April, 1944, Wingate having been killed on 24 March, just when one of these brigades, the 14th, was moving into position. The late Field-Marshal Viscount Slim said, in retrospect, that he considered the cancellation to have been a grave mistake.

Subsequently Special Force were ordered to give up all the ground they had captured and were directed to act solely in aid of Stilwell. The Force became unbalanced, and bad weather and sickness affected the course of operations now of a type never envisaged or intended by Wingate.

It is greatly to the credit of the leadership qualities and the personal bravery shown by Michael Calvert himself that his brigade fought on to the bitter end, decimated as they were by casualties and disease.

Our own official military historians and the military hierarchy generally have 'written down' the operations of Special Force and indicated that its operations had little or no effect on the campaign. The Japanese Commanders involved, on the other hand, blame their failure to capture Imphal (and the subsequent defeat of their armies in Burma) almost entirely on the effect of Wingate's operations, both in 1943 and 1944.

Meanwhile, this story of how a brigade fought and adapted itself to the problems which faced it shows how British and Gurkha soldiers can face up to any problems if they have confidence in the officers who lead them. It is, basically, a story of courageous endeavour under exceptionally trying circumstances and, as such, is an important part of the history of British warfare.

DEREK TULLOCH
RUSHALL,
HANTS.

INTRODUCTION

When I first met the author of this book he was a subaltern in the Royal Engineers. It was in the summer of 1940;
France had just fallen.

He was sitting at a table in a corridor of the War Office;
this table acted as a sort of ante-room to the overcrowded
office occupied by one of the less orthodox sections of the
Military Intelligence Directorate. As I came along the corridor the man with me said:

'That looks like your Sapper.'

The stocky, crouched figure (Calvert has not got what I
should call a natural seat on a chair; you get the feeling that
he means to gallop it into the ground if necessary) rose to its
feet with simian grace and we shook hands warily; I was one
rank senior to him, but he was a regular soldier. As we
started to discuss, in the usual pleasantly chimerical way, the
special duties for which we had been selected, neither of us
was aware that he had found a close and (as far as we can
tell) a lifelong friend.

Ever since – I think – the campaign whose events are
recorded in these pages, Mike has been known to the popular
Press as 'Mad Mike', but I have never heard any of his
friends use the sobriquet. 'Mad' is in point of fact far from
being the *mot juste* for an unusually imaginative and vigorous fighting commander. Perhaps, like most brave men, he
has a streak of recklessness in him; but, although the
methods by which he assesses risks are not always the
obvious ones, I would say that his assessments are sound. It
may well be that it is his sense of humour which has earned
him his aura of lunacy; and if in moments of peril he had not
so often giggled he might not live in the popular imagination
as a sort of hare-brained tiger.

The youngest of four brothers who all served in the same
corps, Mike first heard shots fired in anger during the
Shanghai fighting in 1937. Early in the war he volunteered

for service with a skiing battalion which was being formed to fight the Russians in Finland. Nothing came of this project, and Mike went to Norway instead. After that he and I laid the unsure foundations of a guerrilla movement designed to harass the *Herrenvolk* if (it looked more like 'when' at the time) they occupied Kent, before he went off with Freddie Spencer Chapman – who later wrote *The Jungle is Neutral* – to teach commando methods in Australia and New Zealand.

He and I met again during the retreat from Burma in 1942, where he was commanding a scratch battalion of odds and sods, including several lunatics and deserters. The following year he was back in Burma, leading with great distinction a column of Wingate's first, experimental, expedition and winning the first of two D.S.O.s. The year 1944 is dealt with in this book. After Burma he went to Europe to command the Special Air Service Brigade throughout the closing stages of the war.

After that he went, via the Staff College, Trieste and Hong Kong, to Malaya, where he raised and commanded the Malayan Scouts, the 22nd Special Air Service Regiment, an anti-guerrilla force designed to beat the bandits on their own ground. But a tropical disease with a very long name intervened. Mike was sent home on sick leave and at the moment he is back with his own corps, the Royal Engineers, as a lieutenant-colonel building works and fortifications in Germany. His book is about fighting, a subject of (unfortunately) considerable importance and one which he thoroughly understands. The operations which he describes bear, in their conception, the stamp of Orde Wingate's questing and audacious mind, and there is much to be learnt about the arts of war from the man who, although he did not succeed Wingate in command of Special Force, was unquestionably thought of by Wingate as the heir to his doctrine and tradition.

PETER FLEMING
NETTLEBED
1951   OXON.

PROLOGUE

In this book I try to tell the story of the actions of 77 Infantry Brigade, General Wingate's old brigade, during the operations in Burma in 1944 when the allied forces turned from the defensive to the attack. I tell it from my own viewpoint, giving my hopes and fears, feelings of elation and disappointment – but fully realizing that throughout the pyramid of command from commander to man, there are other points of view both from those above and those below me. I tried first to write this account objectively and dispassionately but it did not come easy, so I have told it personally as a story as I saw it. The details are drawn from a 60,000-word narrative report written immediately after the operation and from the reports of my own officers.

In 1943 Brigadier Wingate (as he then was) carried out his deep penetration through the north of Burma with his brigade consisting of the 13 King's (Liverpool) Regiment, 3/2 Gurkha Rifles, the Burma Rifles and attached troops. This operation can be compared, for its success and failures, with the Dieppe operation in that it paved the way both technically and in the hearts of men for the final offensive and the overthrow of the enemy. Its greatest achievement was the final proof that airpower in the form of air supply could, as General Wavell said as long ago as 1927, give back to the ground forces mobility and freedom of manoeuvre without being tactically tied to ground communications. As with seapower, the influence of airpower could mean that an army was free to strike anywhere as long as it had superiority of the air and a sufficient air merchant fleet to bring in the goods direct to the fighting man. A formation supplied by air needs very few vehicles and appendages; therefore there is an enormous saving in manpower and in supplies necessary for the fighting line. But the formation must have complete trust in air support to supply them, and must not temporize with supply vehicles as well.

This first operation proved that the European soldier, as of old, can shake off the shackles of his civilized neuroses and inhibitions and live and fight as hard as any Asiatic, and, because of his intrinsic sounder constitution and basic health due to good feeding, better the Asiatic in overcoming hard conditions. Most Europeans do not know what their bodies can stand; it is the mind and willpower which so often give way first. Most soldiers never realized that they could do the things they did, and hardly believe it now. One advantage of exceptionally hard training is that it proves to a man what he can do and suffer. If you have marched thirty miles in a day, you can take twenty-five miles in your stride.

There were many equipment, medical, signals and other lessons learnt, the development of which benefited all.

We had singed Tojo's moustache and a curious and unexpected result was the attack on Imphal and Kohima which the Jap Army commanders had hitherto thought impossible. As General Numata, Chief of Staff Japanese Southern Army, said on interrogation: 'It was found, as a result of the Wingate campaign of 1943 and the Japanese operations in opposition thereto, that the terrain in north Burma was favourable for guerrilla warfare by small bodies of crack troops, but it was very difficult to defend the territory because the enemy could not easily be engaged; therefore, under the circumstances, it would be best to give up defensive tactics and resort to an offensive to destroy the enemy's bases for counter operations, such as Imphal, Kohima, Tinsukia, etc.' These operations failed through lack of airpower.

At a time when America and Australia and New Zealand were fighting hard in the Pacific we had shown an offensive spirit. This example of what airpower could do had a direct influence in the obtaining from America of a very substantial air merchant fleet, in the form of Dakotas, without which the conquest of Burma by land was impossible. Air superiority in itself achieves little unless there is an air merchant fleet available to take advantage of it and free the ground forces of earthbound communications.

I had been interested in this subject since 1940, when with the encouragement of General Holland, I wrote a paper at the War Office called 'The operations of small forces behind the enemy lines supplied and supported by air'. This, with the interest in guerrilla warfare awakened in me by General Sir Andrew Thorne, and the founders of Lochailort Special Training Centre in 1940 – Colonel Coates, Lord Lovat, Bill and David Stirling, Jim Gavin and others, led me first to Kent and Sussex helping Peter Fleming organize the beginnings of the Guerrilla Defence of Great Britain; thence to Australia and New Zealand, under Colonel Mawhood, and later Colonel Scott and my great friend and hero Major Stuart Love, D.S.O., where we helped raise and train the Independent Companies of Australia and New Zealand which did so well in the Pacific War. It was in this school, and as part of the mission, that I made a great friend of Freddie Spencer Chapman. He taught me as much about fieldcraft and tracking as my insensitive nature would allow.

From Australia I went to Burma in late 1941 as part of 204 Mission to China. The object of the mission was to raise the efficiency of the Chinese guerrillas from 1 per cent to 2 per cent by teaching them technical methods of destruction and thus tie up another 100,000 troops in China and deflect Japs away from thoughts of Pacific conquest. The American Volunteer Group (AVG) of airmen were the more glamorous air counterpart.

From Australia I went first as Chief Instructor and then Commandant of the Bush Warfare School in Maymyo, Burma, a cover name for the Guerrilla Warfare School, to teach the instructors of the Chinese. When the Jap war broke out the various training cadres of instructors consisted of a few officers and N.C.O.s called 'Commandos' to confuse everybody, under the commands of – amongst others – Lieut.-Col. Brocklehurst, Count Bentinck from Abyssinia, Lieut.-Col. Johnston from India, Lieut.-Col. Munro Faure from China, Lieut.-Col. Musgrave from Aden with their British and Australian officers and N.C.O.s. Soon after the Jap war started they moved off to their appointed tasks in China, or new tasks in the eastern borders of Burma.

It was whilst at this school that I met Brigadier Wingate. He had been sent out by General Wavell to take charge of all guerrilla and kindred activities in Burma. Once having met him there was no further need to struggle for one's ideas. He would do the fighting and I would follow. Any ideas that I had I could safely give to him, confident that they would be assessed and then fought for if necessary. Wingate drew the best from his subordinates.

He himself toured around Burma, met Lieut.-General Slim, visited Chiang Kai-shek in Chungking, but matters were too far gone and there were too many officers involved in the guerrilla warfare business in Burma for him to be able to organize anything in time. So he returned to India to report to General Wavell.

It was the remnants of the Bush Warfare School, coupled with a new, specially picked Commando draft from home, which eventually formed his training team for the first 77 Brigade. Captain Lord, my adjutant, became his staff captain, and, later, Colonel in charge of all supply-dropping in the 1944 operation. Two of us commanded columns in the first operation – George Dunlop and myself. Some others missed the 1943 operation, for illness or other reasons, but returned in 1944. The thread ran on.

In 1943 in Burma there were two British offensive-movements before the monsoon, one in the Arakan and the other the Wingate Operation. They both returned to base.

During the monsoon June–October 1943, and during the winter, both sides were building up their forces whilst the R.A.F. and U.S.A.A.F. were obtaining complete superiority in the air. General Stilwell was licking many Chinese divisions into shape and refitting them with American equipment. The Americans in the Pacific were advancing step by step to cut all Jap sea communications to Singapore and the West. Yet the Japanese Army still gambled on a major victory in Asia with a revolt in India and therefore built up their strength in Burma from about six divisions in early 1943 to nine or more in 1944. The planners of Great Britain and India firmly stated that there could be no British Burma offensive before 1945 and then it would be by sea. They had not yet learned the Wingate lesson, that air communication for armies in the field should be a direct sequence to the securing of the freedom of the air.

A few days before we went in, a G.H.Q. planner said to me: 'Of course this operation will never take place as we have never planned it.' From then on till the capture of Rangoon the planners rarely caught up with events.

Lord Louis Mountbatten arrived in India soon after the Quebec conference in the autumn of 1943. Air Transport

14

increased and airfields multiplied as one result.

The Japanese made an abortive attack in the Arakan in early 1944. It was held. With reliance on air transport, it did not matter if ground communications were cut.

By March 1944 General Stilwell had slowly advanced down the Hukawng valley in spite of floods and supply difficulties. The Chinese armies in the east remained immobile, remembering the direful result of their previous essay into Burma in 1942. In the west at Imphal the 4th Indian Corps were building up their strength, administration and, above all, roads. Behind in Assam the six brigades of General Wingate's Special Force – 14, 16 and 23 British, 77 and 111 Indian, and the West African brigades – were getting ready to strike into the centre of north Burma. Under Bernard Fergusson 16 Brigade was already on its arduous way from the north on foot to the scene of operations. A total of seventeen British, five Gurkha and three West African battalions, coupled with the ever-necessary Burma Rifles and Burma Intelligence Corps and ancillary arms, comprised the force. This was the force which, according to the Jap Army Commander in Burma on interrogation, had a final decisive influence in the battle of Kohima by cutting communications and preventing stores reaching their 31 Division at the front. These results were not obvious to the man in the line, but were as effective as air interdiction or strategic bombing in its help in his fight. Later, when the Special Force was broken up after Wingate's death and after the end of its series of successful operations, Lord Louis Mountbatten wrote to me: 'It was the most distasteful job in my career to agree to your disbandment, but I only agreed because by that time the whole Army was Chindit-minded and therefore there was no need for a Special Force as such.'

The Japanese were on the move too. If the British could move from Imphal to Burma in 1943 so could His Imperial Japanese Majesty's ever-victorious army, in the reverse direction.

The immediate role of General Wingate's Special Force, as laid down at Quebec, was to cut all communications leading north to the Japanese opposing General Stilwell and to assist in the capture of the airfields of Mogaung and Myitkyina. This would allow a road and oil pipeline from

Assam to be built to link up with the Burma road to China; thus giving mainly moral and some material aid to China, relieving the air transport over the 'hump' to China, and keeping China in the war. A subsidiary role was to help 4th Corps at Imphal by severing two out of three of the Japanese communications to that front. The role of 77 Brigade in these operations was to land and make an air base, then cut and keep cut the main road and railway north to Mogaung, whilst the other brigades harassed north and south and towards the Chindwin. This is the story of how 77 Brigade tried to carry out that role. A force, at first under command of 77 Brigade, had the task of cutting the Bhamo-Myitkyina road and of helping to raise the Kachins in revolt in that area. But this force soon became a separate command, and its achievements are hardly touched on here.

I repeat that this is the story of 77 Brigade, which played a pivot part in the plan; but the achievements of the other brigades which did as well must be remembered throughout. We were all part of one force and our roles were interlinked in the general plan. We were a well-balanced fighting force, 20,000 or more men, all potential Jap-killers and no hangers-on, going to the hub of the situation in order that we might cut some of the spokes. Then with pressure on the rim, the whole structure might break down. Thus Special Force in itself was only part of a grander design.

I found myself in command of 77 Brigade in this manner.

In 1943 I was on leave in the swimming pool in Calcutta, realizing from water blisters on my lips, a sure sign for me, that I had a recurrence of malaria, and listening to the woes of an ex-Commando officer who had been sent on a three weeks' fire-fighting course, on how he had had to stand a one and a half hours' lecture on a bucket, and three-quarters of an hour on the nozzle of a hose that morning – when Geoffrey Lockett, my column Commando officer, sought me out with an urgent message from Wingate. It was a scribble:

'I am off to England. You will be second in command 77 Brigade as full Colonel and will probably command it.'

Then a list of instructions:

'Get fit and get fat as you will have a lean hard winter's hunting ahead of you. ORDE WINGATE.'

I was aged 30 at the time and the advancement in rank was a shock to me. Within two months I was a Brigadier.

Then followed the return to Delhi; the reconnaissance and choice of a training centre at Orccha in the Central Provinces; the formation of a new Brigade H.Q.; the fight for the fourth battalion; the arrival of the first three battalions, 3/6 Gurkha Rifles, 1 King's (Liverpool) Regiment, and 1 Lancashire Fusiliers. The construction of the camp during our occupation added to our difficulties. I was in bed with a temperature of 103 on my first conference with my C.O.s. I told them: 'You have eight weeks to put your house in order and weed out the unfit while I form and train the Brigade H.Q., and then we start full training. Target date for operations January 1st, 1944.'

There followed long arduous training, marching, watermanship, mules, air supply, jungle shooting; air support with live bombs; digging, column marching, column bivouac, patrols, R.E. and Signal exercises, medical and veterinary tests. Three or four C.O.s, ten or more years senior to me, were found too old and unfit for operations. Their help in training, loyalty, support and courtesy to me, so many years their junior, is an example for all elderly officers to follow when put under command of someone younger than them. What bitterness and disappointments they had they kept from me and their troops so as not to make our task the harder.

The fight for better rations for those who had no access to the luxuries of a N.A.A.F.I. so that training did not wear them out and so that they entered operations sleek, healthy and fit for war, lasted a long time. This fight went finally as far as General Auchinleck, C. in C. India, who was always our helper. Always we enjoyed the benign and fatherly influence of General Wilcox, G.C.O. Central Command.

Then came the return of Wingate from Quebec as a Major-General with a host of new officers collected in Britain and with the news of three more brigades to be formed; and the arrival of my fourth battalion, 1st South Staffordshire Regiment, fresh from Tobruk and adept at defensive warfare. My fortunate choice of Col. Rome as my second in command and Bobbie Thompson as my R.A.F. Sqn. Leader; talks and new plans; our introduction to Merrill's Marauders, and Cochrane's new Air Commando

(Dakotas, Mitchell medium bombers, Mustang fighter bombers, gliders and light aircraft); glider training and airfield construction; the receipt of new weapons and equipment and its adaptation to our needs – all this before the final fifteen days' test exercise under the eye of Wingate. Then away from the jungle for a week, to the trams and bright lights of Bombay.

Wingate's typhoid, and return after being pulled through by Matron McGreary; packing up and move to Assam; further air training, planning, and, for our new role – fourteen days digging, wiring and mining exercise in anticipation of 'The White City'; airborne planning, test loading and the making out of glider and Dakota load manifests.

Then the final talks: 'Our victory is already half won, thanks to our training, superb equipment, good communications and singleness of purpose. Now we must put our teaching into action and show that we can beat the Japanese wherever he may be. There will be no rest, no leave, no return until the battle has been won.'

Chindit Order of Battle in North Burma

This list shows the fighting arms, without the artillery, engineers, signals or medical and service units. (Units which came under command 77th Indian Infantry Brigade are shown at right.)

14th Infantry Brigade (Brigadier Tom Brodie)
Ist Bedfordshire and Hertfordshire Regt.
7th Leicestershire Regt
2nd Black Watch
2nd York and Lancaster Regt

Under command 77th Bde
One column for counter-attack battle, White City. One platoon in White City

16th Infantry Brigade (Brigadier Bernard Fergusson)
51st 69th Field Regt, RA (as infantry)
2nd Queens' Royal Regt (West Surrey)
2nd Leicestershire Regt

45th Reconnaissance Regt

Brief period during 77 Bde counter-attack at White City.
Counter-attack force.

77th Indian Infantry Brigade (Brigadier Michael Calvert)
1st King's (Liverpool) Regt
1st Lancashire Fusiliers
1st South Staffordshire Regt
3/6 Gurkha Rifles
3/9 Gurkha Rifles

4/9 Gurkha Rifles

One column 3/4 Gurkha Rifles

To 111th Brigade for Blackpool

To 111th Bde at Blackpool
To Morrisforce, 6 May
To Morrisforce, 6 May

111th Indian Infantry Brigade (Brigadier Joe Lentaigne)
1st Cameronians
2nd King's Own Royal Regt
One column 3/4 Gurkha Rifles

3rd West African Brigade (Brigadier Gillmore)
6th Nigeria Regt
7th Nigeria Regt
12th Nigeria Regt

Under command at White City

For counter-attack
Under command at White City

PART ONE

CHAPTER ONE

GOING IN

In quietness and confidence shall be your strength.
                                        ORDE WINGATE

The two gliders gathered speed along the runway and
soon took off behind the tug plane. We were off. The invasion of Burma had started in earnest at last. The Dakota
tug plane took most of the runway before it cleared the
ground, with the two heavily loaded gliders on tow in
echelon behind. We were the fifth and sixth gliders to take
off. Lieut.-Col. Scott (Scottie), Commanding 1st King's
(Liverpool) Regiment, and Colonel Alison, U.S.A.A.F., were
in the first two. The other two contained some of Alison's and
my own advance parties. We were to mark out the landing
lights and establish our glider landing ground in a clearing
which we had named Broadway, 150 miles into the heart of
Burma, in preparation for the reception of the main body.
The date was March 5th, 1944.

The main body in gliders consisted of the remainder of the
King's Regiment, and a company of the 1st Battalion Lancashire Fusiliers under the command of Major Shuttleworth. Twenty-four hours later, having constructed a
Dakota strip, the rest of my brigade and other brigades
would follow by plane.

We circled slowly under the brilliant full moon to gain
height to cross the 7000-feet hills surrounding Imphal. Our
Dakota was chugging along slowly just above stalling speed
as our two Waco gliders had been overloaded to 7000 lb. in
order to get the necessary number of men and gear into the
first lift.

Originally my plan had been to land my brigade on two

clearings, 'Piccadilly' and 'Broadway', in order to get the maximum number of men in the first night before any Jap reaction took place. General Wingate had ordered that no reconnaissance planes should fly over our proposed landing places, once we had chosen them, until the last afternoon. As we were preparing to emplane, watched by General Slim, Air Marshal Sir John Baldwin and other Generals and Air Marshals, Colonel Gatey, U.S.A.A.F., came over with the photographs of the two landing grounds. Piccadilly had been blocked by a covering of tree trunks.

There was an immediate huddle. After some argument, General Wingate came over to me and said, 'Are you prepared to go into Broadway and Chowringhee?' (this last another possible landing ground east of the Irrawaddy). 'If we don't go now I don't think that we shall ever go as we should have to wait for the moon, and the season is already late. Slim and the airmen are willing to go on now that everything is ready. What do you think? I don't like ordering you to go if I am not going myself. At the moment, I have told them that I will consider it because I wanted to hear your views.' I had discussed the possibilities with Colonel Claude Rome, my second-in-command, who was to look after the India end while I was at the receiving end. I said, 'I am prepared to take all my brigade into Broadway alone and take the consequences of a slower build-up as I don't want to split my brigade either side of the Irrawaddy. This will mean rebriefing of the crews, but I think that that can be done in time if we send those we have briefed on the Broadway route first.' Colonel Cochran, U.S.A.A.F., who was under command of Wingate, with an excellent American 'Air Commando', and was his air adviser, agreed with me. Wingate was still not quite happy and General Slim came over and asked my opinion. I told him that any new split of my brigade would spoil my plan for the attack on the railway which was the real object. I did not think that there would be any trouble. If the air force could land us we should be all right from there. Slim turned away silently, and remained silent. He left Wingate, and Wingate alone, to decide that the operation should go on.

After some further discussion and being wished 'Good luck' by General Slim and Wingate, we went back to the four rows of gliders to sort the matter out. Thanks to excellent teamwork by Cochran, Alison, Claude Rome and the Dakota and glider crews, the advance party was ready in a short time. This change of plan, however, unsettled crews and passengers: gliders were not reloaded with due care in the dark, which was understandable, and this accounted for many of the casualties that night. As I sat nervously in the glider I wondered how the plan would work out.

It was not due to any personal bravery that I had said that we ought to go in that night. Scott and Alison were prepared to go on with it without any question. We had five or six nights of good moon to land three brigades of 12,000 men and 3,000 mules, A.A. guns, stores equipment, barbed wire, etc. Our concentration of gliders must soon be noticed by the Japs. If we hesitated we were lost, and there were a great many senior officers who either did not believe in the operation or did not want it to go on. We could never wait for another moon. A Jap offensive was in the offing and, once that started, we would have lost our opportunity, and the attack on Burma would be delayed another year – which was what the Whitehall and Delhi planners wanted. We were all so eager to put Wingate's ideas and plans into action, and we all so much believed that these ideas were the keys to the defeat of the Japs, that in spite of our – certainly of my – nervousness, we knew that we had to go. We could never again be keyed up to such a pitch morally, physically or materially. The collection of aircraft alone had been one of our greatest difficulties, overcome only by the enthusiasm and unselfish co-operation of Sir John Baldwin and Major-General Old, U.S.A.A.F., and the truly admirable American belief that any enterprise which savoured of the attack was right.

This belief in Wingate's ideas and the determination to put them into effect kept us going through most of the campaign when otherwise we might have cracked up. We were 77 Brigade, Wingate's Brigade, and we had to do our stuff.

We were now nearing the mountains and my thoughts turned from these high ideals straight to the pit of my stomach, as we bumped and swayed, huddled together with our luggage, in that flimsy wooden glider. Old Lees, the American glider pilot, was sitting there unconcernedly chewing gum. Cochran had asked me whom I wanted as a pilot, and as I had seen Lees, a Scandinavian, unshakable type of

American, in earlier trials, I had asked for him. We could not afford to have co-pilots as there were not enough to go round. Lees had chosen a compatriot to sit beside him. I was glad as I looked into space that I had chosen Lees. Most of the Dakota crews were members of Cochran's No. 1 Air Commando and had experience in towing gliders, but double towing is not so easy as towing a single glider, especially at night over hills 7,000 feet high. About one-third were R.A.F. crews taken off other duties and having had little or no experience in towing, except for two or three days' training before the operation.

Through my peephole I saw the Imphal plain and then more mountains. We crossed the Chindwin. This was my fourth crossing – two by swimming, one by boat with the Japs in pursuit. Perhaps this was a better way to go back. I knew the route fairly intimately, having walked it a few times, and I watched the ground, so that I might know where we were in case we made a forced landing. The others in the glider were mostly asleep, putting their trust in their commander and their countries' air forces.

On we went over the Zibyutaungdang Range – over the railway where Bernard Fergusson and I had been blowing bridges exactly a year before – on to the Irrawaddy near Katha. Someone said, 'There's some A.A. fire.' I could only see sparks from the Dakota's exhaust. I shivered at the high whistling of the wind around the glider as we lost height. I remembered the finish of General Wingate's Operational Instruction to me: 'In quietness and confidence shall be your strength.'

I tried to recount the whole of it to myself.

MOST SECRET
adv. H.Q. 3 Ind. Div.
16 ABPO
28 Feb. '44

3rd Indian Division Operation Instr. No. 3
To: *Brigadier* J. M. CALVERT, D.S.O.,
Commanding 77 Ind. Inf. Bde.

1. INFORMATION
   Same as in Operation Instruction No. 2.

2. INTENTION

You will cut all rail, road and river communications of the Japanese 18 Division between the parallels 25° and 24°.

3. METHOD

You have 3 lines of communication to consider:

    (i) The road and railway Naba–Mogaung.

    (ii) The river Katha–Myitkyina.

    (iii) Road Bhamo–Myitkyina.

To deal with these you are supplied with the following forces:

  (a) 77 Ind. Inf. Bde.

      Bde. H.Q. including Gurkha Defence Company. Hong Kong Volunteer Squadron. Royal Corps of Signals. Medical, etc.

      Coy. Royal Engineers.

      1st Bn. The Lancashire Fusiliers.

      1st Bn. King's (Liverpool) Regiment (81 and 82 Columns).

      1st Bn. The South Staffords (38 and 80 Columns).

      3/6 Gurkha Rifles (36 and 63 Columns).

      Two companies The Burma Rifles.

  (b) 49 and 94 Columns (111 Bde.) under command.

  (c) Dah Force under command 49 Column.

  (d) 3/9 G. R. (Stronghold Battalion).

  (e) R Troop 160 Field Regiment (25-pdrs.) Stronghold Artillery.

  (f) 267/69 Troop Light A.A. Regiment (Bofors).

These forces will be put down by air on the three landing grounds on the line of longitude 96°40′, two to the north of Okkyi and the third to the south of Shweli, longitude 96°25′.

Dah Force with 49 and 94 Columns will be put down south of the Shweli, to proceed north-east with a view to blocking the northward communications to Myitkyina.

In the first place, 49 and 94 Columns should establish blocks on the road Siu-Bhamo, while Dah Force sees to the Kachin areas to the east and north of Bhamo.

At a later stage, 49 and 94 Columns will move north-east to join Dah Force and select a stronghold.

The possible employment of the Force Stronghold Battalion in this area will be borne in mind.

Sima Pa is a possible site for this stronghold, but Loiwing would be greatly preferable if and when abandoned by the Japanese.

Kachin Raising

No Kachins will be raised on the understanding that our forces are going to remain in the area south of the 24th parallel. Any Kachins which are employed by Dah Force south of the area which we intend to occupy permanently will be warned of this fact. In general, it is not desirable to start any Kachin revolt to the south of Sinlum Kaba because the enemy will be able easily to crush such revolt if it does not have our close protection. The organization of Kachins should therefore take place to the north of this line and not to the south of it. There is, of course, no harm in using agents and introducing wireless sets into the south, as has already been done by the various secret organizations.

Stronghold

Your stronghold will be organized in Map Square SH 53 or nearby area.

You should investigate the possibility of establishing a monsoon site on the Samapum, SH 5543.

The forces under your command will remain in these areas until the monsoon is broken, when it is hoped to carry out their progressive relief.

Aircraft

Apart from the light plane force at your disposal, you will consider the possibility of operating fighters from your stronghold strip, or other strips, from time to time.

'In quietness and in confidence shall be your strength.'

(*Sgd.*) O. C. WINGATE,
Major-General,
Comdg. 3 Ind. Div.
Imphal 28/2

Our job was to cut all the communications of the Japanese divisions facing General Stilwell to help his advance south. I would be aged 31 in a few hours' time, I hoped.

26

I remembered my 'intention' paragraph in order to the battalions

My intention is, after the introduction of 77 Brigade by air into the Kaukkwe valley:

(i) To form a stronghold with an air strip at the south landing ground which will be held until the Japs have been driven from northern Burma.

(ii) To establish and maintain a block on the road and railway between Mawlu and Hopin.

(iii) To deny the Japs the use of the Irrawaddy and road Bhamo–Myitkyina as an L. of C. to the north.

(iv) By the cutting of his L. of C. and by inflicting as much damage as possible on his men and material, to gain such moral and material ascendancy over the Japanese in this area that he will be forced to withdraw his remnants south of parallel 24° in defeat and rout.

Well, here we were now where the mouth of the Kaukkwe meets the Irrawaddy. We turned north. I saw Piccadilly lovely in the moonlight. What would be our reception at Broadway? I did not care a damn now as long as I could get on to dry land, on to the country I knew, and out of the glider. I woke the others and told them to hold tight. I told Sgt. McDermott who was beside me to hold on to the stanchion behind me. L/Cpl. Young opposite cheered me with some remarks about 'a bush in the hand is worth two in a bird!' He was my batman, who had escaped wounded from Hong Kong. Major Taffy Griffiths, my Burma Rifles officer, remained inscrutable behind his great moustache.

We caught up one of the other tows. I was watching Lees. I could see Broadway below. We cut. There was a sudden tremendous silence. We banked steeply and made towards the ground. There was a big bump and we took off, nose in the air. Lees was still chewing gum. A crash, a stanchion hit me in the small of the back and we were down. Sgt. McDermott who was next to me shouted that his hand was jammed between the stanchions. I gave the order to deplane, while my Air Force officer Sqn. Ldr. Bobbie Thompson and I tried to lever the sergeant's hand free. We broke a rifle in doing so and wasted valuable time. His hand was crushed.

I went out to get bearings. I established my H.Q. at the

27

place that I had decided on the air photograph. I saw why we had vaulted into the air. The glider in front of us had had its undercarriage taken off in a ditch. Lees, with excellent presence of mind, in the dark of the surrounding trees, had managed to jump over it.

I joined Alison, who was putting out the petroleum flares to guide the main body of gliders down. Scottie with his party was patrolling around to see all was safe. The snags were that there were two lone trees in the centre of the main runway whose area was 500 yards by 2,000 yards. Across the runway were one or two ditches – drag paths along which, in the monsoon, elephants dragged timber to the river. In the dark it was difficult to see the extent of the runway. Apart from the fact that the fire licked your face, if you held the petroleum flares in order to place them in line, you could see nothing further, and it was very difficult to line the flares to indicate an area where there were no obstacles. Alison was shouting to me and others, and we were trying to do his bidding. I wished that I had had my pony, Jean, with me. She was coming in with Colonel Fleming in the advance party, but had inadvertently put her foot through the glider. She was relegated to a Dakota. I had, in previous rehearsals, found her invaluable when trying to help organize such a large area as an airfield. Next to a jeep, which we could not carry in our small overloaded Waco glider, a well-trained pony is the best vehicle for initial airfield control.

We were still trying to circumvent the obstacles and to pull the crashed gliders clear (all six had landed but at least three could not be moved by our small force), when to our horror, the first wave of the advance party started to come in. The first few landed safely, avoiding obstacles, but many of them became ditched and immovable. Alison's plan for the landing had been one which we had practised successfully by moonlight in India. This was to lay three sets of lights. The planes would come in low. At the first set of lights gliders would cut. At the next they would touch down. At the third they should stop and the crews wheel them out of the way. The two hidden ditches, concealed from us on the air photos by grass, upset this plan. Landing gliders crashed into stationary gliders. Landed gliders left their wing lights on to show their position but confused later pairs. Some of the Dakotas travelled too fast, or misjudged the correct height. A few gliders tried to make a second turn, some successfully, others crashing into the trees. We did our best trying to haul gliders out of the way, but were continually run down by more gliders. At last one glider came roaring at me, landed and went straight between two trees where there was an awful crash. I could not believe there were any survivors. There was silence, broken only by the cries of the wounded and the shouts of the helpers. Scottie and his men were doing valiant work all this time setting up a dressing station, collecting the wounded, hauling gliders away, and, like true Chindits, making the best of a bad situation. The crescendo of gliders and tumult reached its peak and died down. The first wave had landed.

By this time I was exhausted and dispirited. I was unnecessarily rude to Alison. I went along to his excellent unruffled wireless officer. He had managed to get through to Silchar and Wingate was on the line – Wingate, who had sat a night-long vigil, wondering whether his plans were working, and being powerless to do anything about it – first tasting the real horror of high command.

General Slim sat at a table with Wingate's Chief of Staff, Brigadier Derek Tulloch, and my second in command, Colonel Claud Rome, who was organizing the take-off. Claud told me Slim was a tower of strength – absolutely calm, absolutely in the picture and worth a guinea a minute to the staff whose nerves became badly shaken as they realized how badly astray some of the gliders were going.

I was very tired, and the last few months of arduous training, planning and exhortation, culminating in the last few days, had worn my nerves thin. At first sight the scene appeared worse than it turned out to be. It always does. I had arranged a code with Brigadier Tulloch, Wingate's Chief of Staff. If things were going badly I would send 'Soya Link' in clear – if well, 'Pork Sausage'. Some of those who served may understand the significance. I knew that many of the first wave had not turned up at all. I sent 'Soya Link' at about 0400 hours, March 6th, my birthday. From alarmist reports by some pilots it was thought at Silchar that we were being attacked on the ground. All that in fact occurred of this nature was that one rather overwrought glider pilot had started firing aimlessly into the trees. I stopped him. It was rather dangerous.

I flopped down exhausted next to War Correspondent Vandervelt, who comforted me with some cocoa. Alison sat down beside me, and after a few sentences we were asleep. We were woken by the now familiar shout of 'Gliders', as two more gliders appeared from nowhere and landed safely. I was too tired to worry. But soon I was woken again in the grey dawn by a figure, with a monocle, and thirty men all correctly in place. 'Major Shuttleworth and thirty men of the 1st Battalion The Lancashire Fusiliers reporting for orders, sir.' If only people knew what a welcome sound that is to a harassed commander! Alison and I got up and surveyed the scene. Shortly we were startled to hear the sound of an engine from the region where I had seen the glider crashing into the jungle like a charging elephant. Soon emerged U.S. Army Engineer Lieut. Brocket on a bull-dozer.

He and his pilot had had an alarming experience. A Waco glider has the pilot and co-pilot's seat attached to the part which opens upwards, like a bonnet of some cars. The bull-dozer was secured to their rear. Brocket was sitting in the co-pilot's seat and there were no other passengers. The glider flew over all the wreckage as there was little room to land, and the pilot had chosen to land – by luck or good judgment – so that each wing hit a tree with the body going between. As they hit they were swung into the air in their seats, the bulldozer rushed out under them, and then they swung back again, unhurt, into an otherwise empty glider. They set out to retrieve their bulldozer, got it going, and proudly chugged out into the open to the admiring gaze of, at any rate, Alison and myself.

We had a look round and counted our assets and losses. Our total losses on the ground amounted to about thirty killed and twenty-one wounded, including aircrews and U.S. engineer personnel. We had U.S. engineers because Alison had wanted them, and British and Indian engineers had said that the project was not practicable. I had available about 350 all ranks under command. Of the fifty-four gliders that took off, thirty-seven had landed at Broadway, six fell into Japanese-occupied territory in Burma, the remainder forced-landing in Assam. About 50 per cent of the passengers and crews of the gliders which forced-landed in Burma returned safely either to Broadway or to India. One glider load, under command of Lieut.-Col. Peter Fleming, landed near a Jap H.Q., but he led his party back over about 100 miles to India, losing only one man in the crossing of the Chindwin. His is one example of how so many of these fine men of the King's got back to fight again. All who got back to India came straight on to Broadway and rejoined their battalions. Peter Fleming's account of his journey is given in Appendix I.

Brocket found that, besides his two bulldozers, he had one jeep and scraper and about seven men. His other officers and men were killed. A further officer and party had been killed in practice in a glider a few days previously. Brocket stated that he had enough equipment and labour, with the help of the King's, to make a Dakota strip by evening. Both Alison and myself rather doubted this but, on the strength of it, I sent a cheerful 'Pork Sausage' to India and later spoke to General Wingate. I was still perturbed by the number of missing gliders, but was told that some had landed in India, not being able to get over the mountains. One keen officer took off three times in different gliders, but each time either crashed or landed near by. One glider load landed near a British H.Q. and its passengers and crew had kept them all at bay till dawn, thinking they were in Burma.

Sixty-six officers and men were missing and did not return. Some of these may have been taken prisoner, but I have no figures. One consolation that they may have is that the land-ing of gliders all over North Burma thoroughly confused the enemy, and it was not for some time that he knew our where-abouts and our strength.

I was still a bit dejected but was morally supported by Alison and Scott. Alison got on with the job of preparing for the Dakotas next night while Scott sent out patrols in all directions to contact any possible enemy. There were nil reports.

We had found no water, and Brocket and his men, with Scott's labour parties, toiled in the heat and dust of the day, dragging away gliders, levelling ditches and cutting down one or two trees. Others went in search of survivors of the gliders in the trees and brought back some wounded, some unhurt, but most were dead. One glider was not found for three days, and, in spite of Brocket's desire to give a decent burial to his chaps, I had to insist, with Alison's support, having seen them, that they be burnt with their glider in a fitting funeral pyre.

I established my Brigade H.Q. under Taffy Griffiths, who had been my right-hand man the year before. I then went out to find a suitable site for our projected stronghold. I found what I thought was a perfect place which dominated the whole area and which had a nice stream running through it. Water was obtained for the workers and the wounded.

During the day twelve light planes arrived under command of Major Rebori, U.S.A.A.F. I was worried over our wounded, whom we could not possibly carry if we were attacked. I was still doubtful whether the construction of the Dakota strip would be finished that night. We were at least 180 miles from the nearest Allied troops and had only three mules for the carrying of a R.A.F. wireless set, under command of F./Lt. Lloyd George. We had about seven days' rations each. I was very anxious to get the wounded evacuated, for their sake as well as ours, as I had laid down that we would never leave wounded behind. I did not, at the time, realize the full strain of flying twelve unarmed light planes in broad daylight across 200 miles of enemy territory. After persuasion, however, Rebori very gallantly offered to fly the wounded back – 400 miles of daylight flying for the first time over enemy territory, by pilots who had never seen Burma before. It was a very gallant action and was tremendously heartening to us all. By skimming the trees and setting a clever course over wild country, they succeeded without casualty.

This was our first experience in the field of those very gallant pilots. Later perhaps we took their gallantry too much for granted.

Brocket and his men worked without cease till dusk. I was pacing about with anxiety and worrying Alison, who was setting up a control tower. An hour after dusk, Brig.-General Old, U.S.A.A.F. landed (from the wrong direction) with the first load. Sixty-three more Dakotas landed that night under the excellent control of Alison and his staff.

Advance parties for all battalions had already come in on the gliders. All ranks and mules deplaned quickly and quietly, and were led to their collecting points and thence to their concentration areas around the field. Our training in this at least could not have been bettered.

Next morning I showed Lieut.-Col. Noel George, Commanding 3/9th Gurkha Rifles, the area I had chosen for the stronghold which he was to command. We selected sites for the field and anti-aircraft artillery which was coming in the next night.

The King's were still patrolling widely. An average of 100 Dakotas were coming in each night. We were visited by Air Vice-Marshal Williams. There were no accidents, no enemy air activity, no reports of enemy patrols. Sqn. Ldr. Bobbie Thompson, my senior R.A.F. officer, sent back a message to Cochran: 'La Guardia has nothing on us. Can take over 100 a night.'

General Wingate landed the first night, went around and went away comforted.

In those next nights parts of the 111th Brigade also landed at Chowringhee, south and across the Irrawaddy.

In a few days we had 12,000 men, 2,000 mules, masses of equipment, anti-aircraft and field guns all established behind the enemy lines. We have been criticized by the knowalls and the perfectionists for our casualties on the first night. There would have been many more casualties if we had had to march through or wait until aircrew, pilots and ourselves reached a peak of perfection, in which case Burma would not have been invaded that year. At least one result was that it put Burma on the map in the eyes of the British and American public, and from then on that front had most of the planes it wanted. Without them, perhaps, Imphal and Kohima might not have been held.

In my opinion it was a very fine achievement by Alison, Brocket, Thompson, Brig.-General Old, and all R.A.F. and U.S.A.A.F. involved, and even more so by Wingate and Cochran who conceived the idea. As in any airborne operation, we soldiers were the tools brought to the site to carry out our job. It was now up to us.

CHAPTER TWO

BROADWAY

Turn ye to the Stronghold, ye prisoners of hope.

ZECHARAIAH, IX, 12

Broadway, our stronghold, was established. Claude Rome landed with rear Brigade H.Q., and, with Lieut.-Col. George, 3/9th Gurkha Rifles, dug and wired an impregnable position in the area I had reconnoitred. Broadway was to remain our light plane base until the monsoon. It was well stocked and we could receive replenishment from there by light plane if weather stopped the Dakotas from India. A hospital was set up to look after our wounded, who would be flown in by light plane and flown out to India by Dakota. It was a centre of influence throughout the whole area, bounded by the mountains to the west and the Irrawaddy to the south and east. Burma Rifles and Burma Intelligence Corps established a far-reaching network of intelligence. Shops were set up to barter goods with the inhabitants and to obtain intelligence.

Major David Monteith of the Lancashire Fusiliers was sent south to the Irrawaddy and stopped all traffic on the river. A dummy gun emplacement was erected and, by means of explosive, was made to appear to fire. Later, Scottie, with the two columns of his battalion, became 'floater' battalion of the stronghold. This meant that it roamed around the stronghold to spread its influence and to attack in the rear any enemy attacking it. One column ranged far and wide up to the bank opposite Bhamo, and the other remained close at hand.

I issued an edict to the Burmese that no boat would be allowed to use the Irrawaddy unless flying the Union Jack. This order was enforced by Monteith and Scottie.

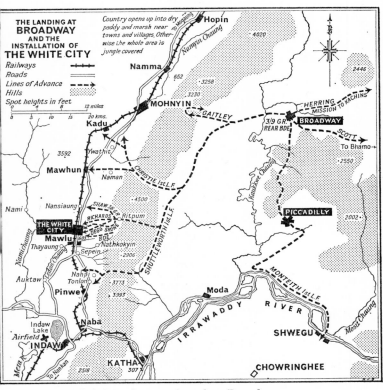

THE LANDING AT
BROADWAY
AND THE
INSTALLATION OF
THE WHITE CITY

Railways	+++++
Roads	=====
Lines of Advance	---
Hills	
Spot heights in feet	

Country opens up into dry paddy and marsh near towns and villages, Otherwise the whole area is jungle covered

Later a Spitfire wing was based on Broadway.

A chicken farm was set up and crops planted. Any visitor was received and conducted to adequate shelter and given all hospitality. Broadway was made to fulfil all that Wingate envisaged and desired in his famous training memorandum 'The Stronghold'. It is such a fine piece of tactical writing and shows so well the nature of the man and the General that I have placed the first part of it in Appendix II to this book.

I quote here some extracts from Wingate's 'Report on Operation of 77th Indian Infantry Brigade in Burma February to June 1943'.

(a) *Unity*

Ignorance is our main weakness. This is not realized. Long Range Penetration will prove a dismal failure unless it is conducted from one centre, with one plan, one doctrine, one training and one control in the field.

(b) *The Time Factor*

Assuming the improved Long Range Group we are able to produce, it should be capable of twelve weeks' marching and fighting. After that it must come into harbour. With an adequate follow-up this can be arranged without devoting several weeks to getting out.

The campaigning season in Burma lasts from December to June. This means that relays of Long Range Groups are required. If three are in use from December, three more must be ready by March.

(c) *Quality*

The quality of existing Infantry is bad. At the same time the types required do exist in the Army, even in this theatre of war, in amply sufficient quantities, and for the most part in other arms. From these, therefore, they ought to be extracted; the more so in that these other arms cannot conceivably be used to anything like the normal extent in the war against Japan. As the Chinese soldier said to Major Gilkes, 'This war will be won by the infantry and the air forces.' Those qualified to judge who have had the requisite experience in fighting the Japanese at close quarters, and observing his methods, think the same.

(d) *Use of Surviving Personnel of 77th Brigade*

Of the total of 2,200 available, at least 1,600 are of the wrong type and should probably not be sent in again. Perhaps 30 per cent of the whole will not be fit for rigorous marching for many months. But the remainder constitutes a core of personnel qualified beyond all others for command, training and general use in connection with the expansion required. Among the officers who have reached India are two capable of commanding brigades, and nineteen possible column commanders. To use these officers again as subalterns, etc., is a waste of material which is needed and does not exist elsewhere.

Set up at once a command and staff to control Long Range Penetration in all its phases. This must be the centre of doctrine, training, planning and, later, control in the field.

Take, at once, measures to raise not less than six Long Range Groups out of the proper materials. (The strength of each Group should be in the neighbourhood of 3,000 all ranks.)

The date by which the first Groups must be ready for the field must decide the tempo, but need not affect us otherwise.

A copy of General Wingate's report was read by Mr. Churchill. Wingate was recalled to England. Still in his tropical clothing, he was taken to see Churchill, who said, 'You are coming with me straightaway to the conference at Quebec.' 'What about my wife, sir?' 'Bring her along as well.' They sailed.

At that time, on the Burma front, all efforts to advance into Burma and the Arakan had failed. The war there had been conducted from Delhi. General Stilwell was training his Chinese divisions for an advance down the Ledo road into Burma. China was on her last legs and the Americans were doing their utmost to keep her in the war by flying supplies in from India over the 'hump', but with great loss due to high mountains, long hauls and bad weather.

At Quebec it was decided to appoint a Supreme Commander to command and control all forces fighting on the Western Front of Burma. India would be the supply base, training area and reservoir of new manpower.

At that time, guided by their planners, the British Chiefs of Staff were most reluctant to embark on an invasion of Burma, except by sea to Rangoon. There were not enough landing craft available, so they advised that there should be no advance before 1945. This reluctance was understandable. We had had our Dunkirks, Norways, Greeces, Cretes, etc., where we had advanced with too little strength and had been hurled into the sea. Britain was most concerned with the war in Europe and did not want to take her eye off the ball. The Indian Army's morale had not yet recovered from its recent series of defeats in the East.

The Americans, however, were anxious to have an offensive – any sort of offensive – which would tie up Jap troops. There were only two men in Burma who appeared to want to attack – Stilwell and Wingate. General Slim had been given the job to clear up the results of the débâcle in Arakan and was not yet in a position to put his offensive ideas into practice. The Americans offered Stilwell as Supreme Commander or, failing that, Wingate's name was mentioned. Finally, the brilliant, versatile Lord Louis Mountbatten was chosen. Wingate talked with him many days, and Lord Louis liked his ideas and improved on them, with such ideas as a light plane force, use of gliders, etc.

It was finally decided at Quebec that operations in Burma would be confined to the capture of the airfields and towns of Mogaung and Myitkyina, with a sufficient depth southwards to the 24° latitude as a cushion to prevent their recapture.

14th Army, now just formed, would assist with a limited offensive to help Stilwell forward. If conditions were favourable 14th Army would extend across to the area of Indaw. Wingate would be appointed Major-General in command of a special force of five Long Range Penetration Brigades each of four battalions, and with all necessary ancillary troops. The brilliant American flyer Colonel Cochran would form an air commando of Mustangs, Mitchell medium bombers, Dakotas, 100 light planes and a number of the light Waco gliders. They would operate in support of General Wingate's Special Force. The role of this Special Force was to assist General Stilwell forward by landing in the rear of the forces opposing him and cutting, and keeping cut, their communications. An American Ranger regiment, later known as 'Merrill's Marauders', was originally formed to operate under Wingate's command, but later it was thought best for them to go to Stilwell to give an example to his Chinese forces. This regiment was the only American fighting regiment in Burma at any time. General Stilwell had a number of magnificent engineer regiments who, with the aid of Indian engineer and pioneer regiments, would continue to build airfields and the Ledo road to Mogaung. At least one of these engineer regiments fought gallantly at Myitkyina, but I emphasize that the United States had only one purely fighting regiment in Burma.

It is necessary to state the above plan because so many people thought that we were dropped in to help forward the 14th Army in the Imphal plain. This was not, and was never meant to be, the object. Later certain brigades were deflected west for this role and did a lot of marching and counter-marching, but that was after Wingate's death and before General Lentaigne was fully in the picture of Wingate's opportunist plans.

For this operation the Americans reinforced the Dakota squadrons in India. They were meant to be available for those who attacked and not for formations who, through no fault of their own, were compelled to stay stationary. At that time there was a nucleus of Special Force (later known as 3rd Indian Division as a cover name, although no purely Indian units formed part of it) in 111th Indian Infantry Brigade, which had been formed on similar lines to Wingate's first 77th Brigade, and was in training, and the slowly re-forming 77th Brigade. When Wingate left for Britain and thence for Quebec he obtained permission, very much to my surprise, for me to be appointed his successor, to command his brigade.

The main principle on which the Long Range Penetration (L.R.P.) Brigade was based was above all versatility. Versatility of manoeuvre due to air supply and air casualty clearance. Versatility of power in that such a brigade could penetrate through every type of country in eight columns of about 400 men each, like the fingers of one's hand, and then concentrate in bringing the fingers together to clutch at the throat of the enemy when his attention had been duly scattered, or so strike a blow with a clenched fist at an important objective. When the brigade was concentrated in battle it re-iormed into a more normal brigade of three or four battalions reinforced by artillery, heavy mortars, hospitals, engineer stores, etc., brought in by air. This turned it from a series of marauding columns into a homogeneous-co-ordinated brigade. Above all we placed our reliance on air. Close air support was practised in training so that with the help of R.A.F. officers with columns on the ground, a column, battalion or brigade commander could call up support at very short notice and deliver a very great weight of explosive at ranges from 100 yards to 300 yards of our own troops. Without this essential arm the troops on the ground could never have succeeded.

Entire reliance was placed on the use of wireless. It is difficult, if not impossible, to transmit a wireless message when the set is moving on a mule. Therefore halts had to be made to pass messages. But at that time the projected recipient may also be on the move. Therefore, we established a great battery of high-powered stations in India which could pick up the weaker messages from the troops in the field, and re-transmit these messages strongly to the intended recipient when he opened up. If the brigade was fighting a concentrated brigade battle the more normal method of radio-telegraphy and line were used.

Another great feature of this brigade was that more than 90 per cent of those in the field were potential Jap killers. Nearly all our supply and quartermastering staff were held back at base in India to look after the supplies required for the brigades. If a long-drawn-out concentrated brigade battle was to take place, it was easy to fly any such staff required into the brigade in the field along with the necessary guns, mortars, ammunition, barbed wire, etc.

Observers in India criticized the large staffs visible there, but if one took away all the distributing staffs of any normal brigade or division the size of staff left behind would be even greater. For instance, all our mule-drivers were also trained infantry soldiers and were interchangeable with the men in the infantry companies, and were thus interchanged. Having such a short tail the power of manoeuvre was wonderfully enhanced.

Another false conception of Wingate's Special Force, or as he named them 'the Chindits', was that they were all volunteers and thus milked other units in India of their best men. This is a completely erroneous conception. About 5 per cent were volunteers or selected men from depots. Normal infantry battalions were selected for the role. A certain amount of weeding out of the unfit was done, the unfit being replaced from depots and only a very few from formed units.

In all there were seventeen British battalions, five Gurkha battalions and three West African battalions in Special Force. No Indian battalions were used, owing to the difficulty, at that time, of special feeding, cooking, camp followers, etc., insisted upon by the Indian Army, whereas all the battalions in Special Force could, and did, eat any type of food, although certain special provisions were sometimes made for the Gurkhas.

In general the column consisted of an infantry company of four platoons, a commando platoon (including engineers), a reconnaissance platoon (mostly Burma Rifles), a support platoon (two medium machine guns, two 3-inch mortars), Animal Transport platoon and Column H.Q.s including R.A.F. detachment, Intelligence Section, Signals, medical detachment, etc. It was homogeneous, of one race, and thoroughly versatile and adaptable. Each man carried, on an average, about fifty-five lbs including his weapons.

Brigade H.Q., in my case, was slightly more complicated. Besides the brigade staff, there was the brigade commander's personal mounted guard which protected him when riding from battalion to battalion if there was a chance of opposition en route, a fairly large signal unit of both Army and R.A.F., a company of Gurkhas, and a Hong Kong Volunteer platoon which was used to protect the wireless operators, and would act in liaison when we came across the Chinese.

I had been in Hong Kong before the war and had been in charge of the Chinese Royal Engineers, and had helped increase their numbers from seventy to 250, all of whom were selected by myself with the aid of the Chinese Sgt.-Major Yip Fuk. Later the Hong Kong coast and anti-aircraft artillery had followed suit and, later, a Chinese battalion was in the process of being formed. Beside that there were the Hong Kong Volunteers who had various British, Chinese and Portuguese units. Shortly before our campaign I found about 100 of these men, many of whom I knew, kicking their heels in a transit camp at Deolali near Bombay, well looked after, but feeling disconsolate and forgotten. They had escaped from Hong Kong after its fall, and had trekked the thousands of miles from Hong Kong to India in order to fight for their King and Country, and now felt that they were not wanted. I asked them if they would join me and go into action. The answer was a shout of 'Yes'.

I obtained permission to take them in with me, and we gave them some hurried training. One party went with Lieut.-Col. Herring, Commander Dah Force, to assist in the

Kachin rising near Bhamo, where there were already Chinese guerrillas operating. One platoon went to Claude Rome at Broadway. There were one or two bad N.C.O.s in that party, and they affected some of the others, so Claude Rome sent them back to India, much to the sorrow and loss of face of the others who really did want to fight. We had mixed them up, and told them that we would have to have Portuguese, Chinese, Portuguese Chinese, Anglo-Chinese, and one or two Filippinos all in one unit. The Portuguese with Rome did not like this lumping together with Asiatics and it was this which was the cause of the trouble.

My Chinese platoon, although at first the bane of my brigade major's existence, later did quite well and was invaluable when we joined forces with Stilwell's Chinese later on. Lieut.-Col. Herring's party in the hills also did very well.

At one time my brigade major, Francis Stuart, had to compete with seven different races in Brigade H.Q., comprising British, Indian, Burmese, Karens, Chinese, West Africans and Gurkhas. People have often asked how it worked. I can only point out that it was due to the excellence of my staff, and that every soldier in the British Empire understands the same words of command.

Of course this did not always work perfectly. I might give out my orders complete with signs and play-acting: 'Follow the path by that milch cow there,' and I would trudge wearily and then milk frantically at an imaginary udder – 'Over that hill', and I would slow up, lean forward, and point – 'Down again', and I would slip and slide, leaning backwards – 'Up again, over a stream in the fir trees' – conventional sign portrayed by a series of short sweeping motions of the hand, coupled with a noise of babbling brook – 'to that lone tree on the hill', and I would look forlorn and lonely – 'There is your objective!' and I would make motions to dig in madly. I now know why cosmopolitan races gesticulate.

This usually worked, but at times, of course, it didn't and the platoon commander in Brigade H.Q. would use his own judgment and take absolutely the right, but quite a different, hill, confounding the Japanese. I would alter my plan instantly to conform, and, with an accompaniment of 'but, sir,' might win a famous victory and get the credit.

Trust your own judgment but always use unexpected

events as a stepping stone to success before the enemy does.

I must mention here some of the leaders in this campaign.

Of my own staff, there was Claude Rome, my second-in-command, an excellent, loyal, painstaking, long-suffering, courageous soldier, all of which he had to be to carry out that most difficult job of being second in command of a brigade to a very much younger commander.

Lieut.-Col. Skone commanded that famous battalion, the 3/6th Gurkha Rifles. He was a solid, robust, enthusiastic soldier, much older than I. One might say he was married to his regiment – a grand chap who would march miles in agony, because he had a spur bone growth in his heel, without complaint or loss of efficiency. He was a very wise counsellor to me, and a very good infantry soldier; a quiet, self-effacing man who was loved by his own troops.

His other column commander was Major Freddie Shaw.

Lieut.-Col. Richards commanded the 1st Battalion, the South Staffords. He had been with the Malaya Regiment in the fighting in Singapore, and was one of the last to escape. An experienced infantry soldier, he was a broad, quiet type who liked a joke.

His other column commander was Major Ron Degg, Staffordshire ex-coalminer who had risen from the ranks to Sgt.-Major, and on. He was a very fine, solid, unshakable type, which the South Stafford Regiment appears to breed.

Lieut.-Col Scott of the King's (Liverpool) Regiment, a man with great strength and *goodness* of character, was painstaking in planning and prepared to take all risks in attack.

His other column commander was Major Gaitley who had been second in command of the first British Parachute Battalion in India, and has since been killed in Kenya.

Lieut.-Col. Hugh Christie had only recently joined us from the Arakan. A delightful character, completely and disarmingly truthful and courageous, he was dogged by sickness, but continued to the end, having seen his battalion do great things. Major Shuttleworth was his second in command. He also had two fine officers in Majors Monteith and

Butler from the Guides Cavalry who had been lent to us, the Guides having at that time had little to do, and many of their officers were pining for action.

I met Francis Stuart on a short leave in Simla. He had been in the Western Desert with Auchinleck, and he was always giving me most valuable advice. He was a poet and a soldier, and possessed a positive 'goodness' factor, in the best sense of the word, which helped him overcome his physical infirmities. He was mad keen on the L.R.P. idea, and shortly turned up as company commander in the Lancashire Fusiliers, although he himself was a Sikh officer. Later when my previous brigade major, just before the start of the campaign, could not go in with us I chose Francis to be my brigade major.

Sqn. Ldr. Bobbie Thompson was the R.A.F. officer in my column in 1943. He had been an extremely brave, brilliant young colonial administrator in Malaya. He fought for six weeks in Hong Kong as one of the stay-behind parties, and then made his way across to India. He possibly did more than anyone else to develop and perfect the technique of close air support as applied to Burma

Major Taffy Griffiths was my mainstay in 1943. Strong, silent, with a huge bushy moustache, he worked in Burma in forestry for years, and was one of the first of that fine body of officers of the Burma Rifles whom Wingate considered the best set of officers, without exception, that he had met in any unit in the world. I agree with him. Taffy, when asked his opinion whether we should attack, would always say, 'Well, why not? That is what we are here for. I expect the Japanese are frightened.' A most comforting officer.

My D/Q was Major Gordon Hodgson. He was a Q staff officer who had volunteered to do the most arduous job, that of looking after an independent brigade in a Special Force, with all its special equipment and establishments. He did this with a devotion to duty which resulted in his death when he had offered to help the supply-dropping crews during a very nasty period of weather, and when we, in the field, were very short. The plane crashed and he died in order to show all staff officers and their staff that it is the duty of a staff officer to serve his units and not to be a jack-in-office. You may imagine what a difficult and hard-working time he had before and during the campaign, serving

44

under a young and harassing brigade commander.

Very few of the soldiers or officers had seen or tasted action. The South Staffords were the best off in this respect as many of them had been in Tobruk.

On General Wingate's return he soon obtained permission to form the number of four-battalion brigades he required. We had insisted on the four-battalion and four-platoon basis instead of three-battalion and three-platoon organization at that time in use in the British Army. In such warfare as we were to fight there are no safe flanks. If you were ordered to take a Japanese-occupied town or position, the ideal procedure would be first to harass the enemy over a wide area to make him spread his forces. Then rapidly seize a base as close as possible to the objective, but one out of range of his artillery and A.A. guns. This base should include a light plane strip and a supply dropping zone, and if possible a potential Dakota strip. One battalion having seized the base, the other three battalions concentrate rapidly. In the meantime Brigade H.Q will have asked for a large supply of offensive weapons and ammunition, such as 4.2-inch mortars, 25-pounders or 75-mm. guns, flame-throwers, and if possible the heaviest armoured vehicle which can be deposited by glider. It will also need barbed wire, telephone line, picks and shovels, and other stores which are not normally carried when in column. To cover this concentration, the enemy is kept on the defensive by fighting patrols, deception, and other alarums and excursions. Then having transformed the brigade from a brigade of eight light mobile columns to a homogeneous hard-hitting force, the attack is due to start. Whilst one battalion guards the base, collects and distributes supplies and assists, if possible, in short-range flank protection, the other three battalions under a tactical Brigade H.Q. advance to the attack. If the attack is unduly prolonged any one forward battalion can be relieved. The danger always is an attack by the enemy in the flank as a counter-measure. The only protection against this is by information. Around the flank and to the rear is spread what Wellington called 'a cloud of skirmishers' whose duty it is to give information of any flanking movement and then cause the maximum delay to this movement, until such time as the brigade can redeploy to face the threat. In our case the 'cloud of skirmishers' would be the Burma Rifles thickened up with Kachin levies raised on the spot. Once the objective is taken it can be held by more regular troops who can be flown in. The special weapons of the L.R.P. Brigade can be flown out, and the brigade can then revert to an eight-column basis for speed and penetration and go on to the next objective where the procedure is repeated. In the same way a company can form a base protected with one platoon, and attack with the remainder.

CHAPTER THREE

WHITE CITY

The boldest measures are the safest.
PITT

The brigade, less the King's and 3/9th Gurkha Rifles (an extra battalion given to me for protection of Broadway), moved fanwise towards the railway in preparation for the establishment of a semi-permanent block between Hopin and Mawlu where the road and railway to the north run side by side. We had reconnoitred the area in a Mitchell medium bomber some weeks before the operation started. This reconnaissance was invaluable, especially to those battalion commanders who had not seen the country before. We were escorted by three Mustangs.

The first time I went out with Colonel Gatey, U.S.A.A.F., we had been told to pretend that we were on a normal bombing operation; so after having chosen two likely places, Gatey asked me what I would like to bomb. I remembered some Jap barracks we had come across when campaigning the previous year. They were well hidden in the trees, and, if we could find them, would be an ideal target, as the Japs could not expect us to know of their existence. The Japs had long since ceased to dwell in towns or villages after we had obtained air supremacy. I was very glad when I did find these barracks; they could only just be seen and then only if you knew they existed. We put one cluster of bombs there. I next remembered that the Japs were building a diversion around a blown railway bridge over the Mesa river. So we bombed that and undid quite a lot of good work. Gatey then decided to show me how the 75-mm. gun mounted in the Mitchell would work. We had various shots at the diversion, but it was a difficult target, and we only scored one hit. We

47

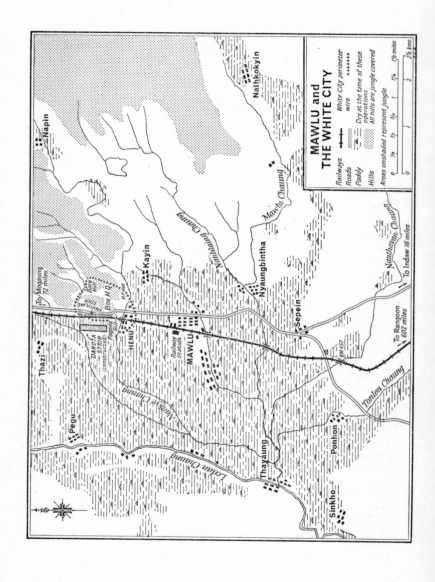

MAWLU and
THE WHITE CITY

Railways
Roads
Paddy
Hills
Areas unshaded represent jungle

White City perimeter
wire
Dry at the time of these
operations
All hills are jungle covered

Napin

To Mogaung
72 miles

Thazi

Pegu

Kayin

Nyaungbintha

Nathkokyin

Mawlu Chaung

Nanthadwin Chaung

Sepein

To Indaw 16 miles

To Rangoon
602 miles

BM 457

Tonlon Chaung

Ponhon

Sinkho

Thayaung

Ledan Chaung

Mahie Chaung

MAWLU

Railway
Station

HENU

DAKOTA
STRIP
(constructed)

Boe H.Q.

Pagoda

Barb
Wire

Nanthadwin Chaung

then decided to beat up the area around Indaw. I did not like this very much as, in order to fire the gun, we had to come very low, 200 feet, and we kept circling over Indaw's deserted airstrip. Eventually we went home, and on our return found one bullet hole in the plane. The crew found the bullet and kept it as a souvenir, as this was their first action. I reported that there must be at least one Jap in north Burma.

Having the opportunity to make such a reconnaissance and join in some bombing was a tremendous advantage; it made one see the airman's view and one tended afterwards not to ask him to take on absurd targets. I have seen ridiculous requests, such as 'bomb ten miles of the west bank of the Irrawaddy between X and Y, three Mitchell bombers required'!

On our next trip we showed the battalion commanders concerned their objective. General Wingate told me that all Army officers should get up in the air at least once a month as otherwise they tend to get an earthbound mentality.

My plan for the installation of the block was fairly flexible. One Lancashire Fusilier column under Hugh Christie would harass communications and blow bridges just south of Mohinyin, and slow up any enemy advancing from there. Another column, under Shuttleworth, would do the same between Indaw and Mawlu. I had heard Mawlu had a garrison of about 500, but I expected that many of them might be Lines of Communication troops and therefore not very efficient.

The alternative sites for the block were at Nansiaung and Henu. I favoured the first as it was farther away from Mawlu. The South Staffords and one column of 3/6th Gurkhas would initially establish the block, while Brigade H.Q. and the other Gurkha column would remain with me in reserve.

We pushed forward fairly fast. Brigade H.Q. Column went faster than the rest mainly because we were more experienced and we risked walking along tracks. I had gained valuable experience in fieldcraft from Freddie Spencer Chapman, the best man at all forms of fieldcraft that I know. The jungle in the Kaukkwe valley was of the real story-book type – dark, dank, primeval growth with enormous creepers. Shuttleworth's column got left behind. Hugh Christie's

49

column went fast and was the first to draw blood by blowing up the Kadu bridge. He had Capt. H. N. F. Patterson, R.E., with him, one of my sapper officers, who later became one of my best patrol officers.

I could classify the jungle by types, as follows, starting with the most dense:

1. 'Limpopo type': dark, green, greasy, situated along rivers and marshes.

2. 'Technicolour type': slightly more friendly than Limpopo with fewer prickles; definitely 'primeval'.

3. 'Midsummer Night's Dream type': sylvan glades, crystal clear babbling brooks surrounded by fairly honest, reasonable types of trees and bushes.

4. 'Tall timber type': dry teak or 'indaing' forest with little or no undergrowth between the tall straight trees – similar to a pine forest. Very easy going.

In our area of operation, type 4 occurred around Indaw, and in places west of Mawlu. Elsewhere one found type 3 on the hills and foothills, degenerating to type 2 in the plains and type 1 in the Kaukkwe and Mogaung valleys and in the lesser valley bottoms leading to the rivers.

Brigade H.Q. arrived first on the hilltop, which was what I had intended so that I could cast around for information and, if necessary, change the plan. This became necessary as we heard that there were 300 Japs at Nansiaung. I altered the plan so that Freddie Shaw's column would put in a holding attack at Nansiaung, and then return to me in reserve, whilst the two South Stafford columns and Skone would establish the block at Henu.

Degg was on the railway line first and asked for the consolidation supply drop consisting of barbed wire, picks and shovels, much ammunition and food. Unfortunately the planes dropped it right up on the hillside near us, and it was not until a week later that I could retrieve it by means of a team of elephants we had appropriated. Degg was rapidly joined by Skone and Richards, and they started to dig in with what they had. I heard Freddie Shaw putting in his attack, and after receiving all the reports by wireless, I left the hillside, where wireless reception was good, and entered the valley to meet Freddie next morning at our rendezvous. Freddie's column came in the following morning rather shaken. It was their first fight; it was at night and the enemy

50

had opened up on them first. They exchanged shots and Freddie mortared the area and, in fact, did his job by holding the enemy there while Degg and the others got installed.

I felt in great form that day. I went around Freddie's Gurkhas but they would hardly smile at me, which was unusual. However, my own crack Gurkha Brigade H.Q. company, which I had always insisted should be the best fighting unit in the brigade, was in great form. They had a wonderful young Canadian Gurkha officer who had fought with me in 1942, and whom I had especially asked for, and got. This officer, Ian Macpherson, was one of the finest men I have met. Skilful, fearless, quiet, with tremendous energy and endurance, he was a proud and worthy soldier.

I heard more firing at the block and so decided to move forward to it with six platoons. Bobbie Thompson, Cpl. Dermody, L/Cpl. Young, my Anglo-Chinese orderly and one or two others accompanied us. As we moved nearer the sound increased in volume; it seemed that quite a battle was taking place.

From the map I had planned to attack the Japanese in the flank or rear. The difficulty was to find out where everyone was. Plunging forward fairly rapidly, as we did not wish to miss our first action, we at length came across a clearing leading to a stream. We cautiously crossed the clearing and hesitated before mounting the high bank on the other side. The battle seemed very close now. I was determined that we must win our first engagement. All else would follow. Eventually we took the plunge and mounted the bank. Here we found a few bullets whistling about. I shouted for Ron Degg, but got no answer; so we advanced along the ridge holding in front of us a long bamboo with a coloured handkerchief map, which was our recognition sign, tied to the top. I felt rather foolish walking along in front into battle with this banner with a strange device.

After we had progressed awhile, chanting that we were coming, one of the more sane officers, who viewed the whole proceeding with alarm, had a more sensible idea. He tried to get in touch with Degg on a walkie-talkie and succeeded. I talked to Degg. However, he was well imbued with security and doubted that it was me. So I told him what he had done one night at the Jhansi Club, and that convinced him. He guided us by voice along the ridge until we suddenly saw the Japs milling around a small pagoda on top of a little knoll over-looking the paddy.

We got down and had some quite nice shooting. However, I saw some of Degg's chaps across the little valley in a very exposed position. I told Freddie Shaw to give us covering fire while Bobbie and I contacted them, and then to conform with whatever we did. Bobbie, Paddy Dermody, L/Cpl. Young and myself ran across the valley, actually behind quite a number of Japanese who had penetrated between Degg's and Hubert Skone's position. As we scrambled up the other side we were greeted with, 'Thank God you've come, sir.' I saw quite a number of dead and wounded. Someone quickly gave me the situation. They were attacked at dawn before they were properly dug in. The Japs had infiltrated between Degg and Skone's columns. The Japs appeared to be based on Pagoda Hill and the village of Henu. The enemy had nothing more lethal than mortars.

I saw something had to be done pretty quickly, so I shouted to Freddie that we were going to charge. I then told everyone that we were going to charge the Pagoda Hill. There were reinforcements on our left flank who would charge as well. So, standing up, I shouted out 'Charge' in the approved Victorian manner, and ran down the hill with Bobbie and the two orderlies. Half of the South Staffords joined in. Then looking back I found a lot had not. So I told them to bloody well 'Charge, what the hell do you think you're doing.' So they charged. Machine-gunners, mortar teams, all officers – everybody who was on that hill.

By this time I was not in front. I had not reckoned on a sunken road, which reminded me of Waterloo. However, the gallant South Stafford officers and men were across the road, and climbing up the other side with us close behind. At the top the Japs, entering into the spirit of the thing, got up and charged us. This definitely was not in the book. There, at the top of the hill, about fifty yards square, an extraordinary mêlée took place, everyone shooting, bayoneting, kicking at everyone else, rather like an officers' guest night. In front I saw Lieut. Cairns have his arm hacked off by a Jap, whom he shot. He picked up the sword and carried on. Finally we drove them back behind the Pagoda. Paddy Dermody and

L/Cpl. Young had been doing valiant work while protecting me, with L/Cpl. Young shouting, 'Be careful, sir. Be careful, sir,' as he shot Japs.

Then there was an intermission while both sides lobbed grenades over and around the pagoda. You could see them curling their way into the air, falling and rolling – then a loud bang. Fortunately the Jap grenade is a typical Oriental grenade – all bark and very little bite. Freddie's boys had also charged down the valley and were hacking about with their kukris. While I was wondering what the next move was, the blessed Freddie came up to me, saluted and said, 'I have two platoons here at your disposal, sir.' Someone shouted, 'We are short of ammunition.' I immediately thought that if we were short, the Japs must be shorter as they had been fighting longer. The Japs were yelling at us in English, 'You dirty hairy bastards,' etc., so I shouted, 'We will retreat as fast as possible in that direction' – pointing towards the enemy – 'Staffords right, Gurkhas left. When I say the word "Now".' Up all the unwounded jumped, and tore around the pagoda. By the time I was around, the hill was ours, and we were pursuing them into the village of Henu. There the Gurkhas and South Staffords went into them with their manpack flame-throwers, burning up at least a dozen more Japs in dug-outs. The remnants fled across the paddy, and the day finished up with our taking pot shots at them as they ran or crawled away. A few of the Japs who had infiltrated and were cut off tried to make a dash for it, and were soon seen off.

Then there was the anticlimax. We succoured the wounded, counted the dead. Freddie's men took over the Pagoda Hill. I saw a young Gurkha turn over with his foot an even younger-looking Jap with glasses on, and I saw the expression on his face: 'Are these the supermen whom they depicted in those frightening posters in India? Are we meant to be frightened of them?' He gave the corpse one more kick and walked away. The fighting had been not unlike that depicted in scenes from ancient battles in the closeness of the hand-to-hand grappling before the Japs finally broke. In spite of our casualties, we all had that elation of the winners of a battle, especially of a bayonet charge. Our casualties are a good indication of the number of officers who led the way. Fourteen officers of all arms took part in the charge.

53

Killed: 3 British officers, 20 other ranks.
Wounded: 4 British officers, 60 other ranks.

I spoke to Lieut. Cairns before he died. 'Have we won, sir? Was it all right? Did we do our stuff? Don't worry about me.' Five years later His Majesty graciously awarded Lieut. Cairns the Victoria Cross.

Included amongst those of the South Staffords who charged were Major Jefferies, Capt. Stagg, Lieut. Scholey, Lieut. Day, Lieut. Cairns, Lieut. Wilcox. All were killed later in the campaign, except Lieut. Wilcox, who was wounded four times and still carried on.

Scholey was awarded an immediate M.C. for his part in the charge, Sgt. Perry an immediate D.C.M.

Many of the British had been killed before our charge. It was a grievous loss but it set a standard for the brigade. After that the Brigade never looked back, and all tried to emulate the example. That is the real fruit of victory, that it lays seeds in the minds of others for further victories.

We counted forty-two Jap dead, including four officers. More were shot and killed or wounded by our machine guns as they struggled across the open paddy, with the Japs giving them some covering fire from Mawlu 800 yards across the paddy on to Pagoda Hill.

Documents showed that the attackers consisted of about two companies of a Railway Engineer Battalion. We had been fortunate to be blooded against comparatively untrained, although gallant troops.

Direct air support had helped to keep the Japs' heads down in Mawlu both the previous day and this day, while we hurriedly dug in.

The block was now established, but still insecure owing to the lack of entrenching tools, wire and ammunition. On the night of March 18/19th, however, much of this was dropped to us, and I signalled General Wingate that our position was much more secure.

The block was ideally situated around a series of wooded 'mole' hills about thirty to fifty feet high with numerous little valleys in between, with water at the north and south extremities. We brought the village of Henu into our defended area and also a slightly higher hill – we called it O.P.

Hill – which had a grand view over the surrounding countryside. The cover from fire and view afforded by the little hills decided me to bring in all the mules and establish Brigade H.Q. in the block.

This was done on the 19th. Digging and wiring, booby trapping and mining proceeded apace. Patrols reported at least 300 enemy in Mawlu, but they were probably only Line of Communication troops. They were well bombed by Cochran's planes.

Hugh Christie's column in the north had blown a bridge at Mawhun, and had a couple of affrays with the Japs, honours being about even. David Monteith was established with 100 men on the Irrawaddy, stopping all traffic. Shuttleworth's column had at last reached the road at Pinwe. He had got into such dense jungle in the Kaukkwe valley that he had plaintively asked for a path to be dropped to him. On reaching the road he just had time to ambush some trucks whose destruction was completed by some Mustangs who were flying over and whom he directed on to them. Many casualties were inflicted. These trucks belonged to the battalion which later on attacked the block. Mines were laid with quite good effect south of Mawlu by one of the Gurkha commando platoons.

On the nights 18/19th, 19/20th and 20/21st, the Japs' reconnaissance patrols made probing attacks on the block, inflicting one or two casualties. We collected some of the dead for identification, but they had no documents or badges. These probing attacks helped us to rectify mistakes in the defences.

On the 21st, probing attacks in daylight from north and south were severely dealt with. In the south a Jap patrol walked blatantly across the paddy from Mawlu to within 300 yards of our machine guns and mortars. Very few returned. That day we lost one killed, five wounded, and estimated at least five Japs killed and thirty wounded.

When the patrol sought refuge in the dried bed of a stream, F/Lt. Harte in a light aircraft stirred them out again by dropping hand grenades on to them.

It was obvious that trouble was brewing up. Every platoon and company post was wired in; telephone lines were laid and buried; water was stored; mortar and machine-gun fire plans co-ordinated and perfected; all section posts were well

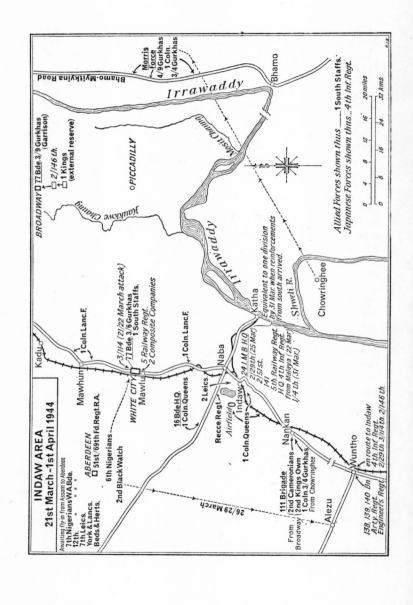

**INDAW AREA
21st March - 1st April 1944**

Awaiting fly-in from Assam to Aberdeen
7th Nigerians W.A.Bde.
12th. " " "
7th Leics. " " "
York & Lancs. " " "
Beds.& Herts. " " "

ABERDEEN
51st/69th Fd.Regt.R.A.

6th Nigerians

2nd Black Watch

Kadu

1Coln.Lanc.F.

Mawhun

3/114 (21/22 March attack)
77 Bde. 3/6 Gurkhas
1 South Staffs.

WHITE CITY
Mawlu
5 Railway Regt.
2 Composite Companies

1Coln.Lanc.F.

16 Bde H.Q.
1 Coln.Queens

2 Leics.

Naba

Recce.Regt.
Airfield

Indaw

24 I M B.HQ.

1 Coln.Queens

Nankan

111 Brigade
2nd Cameronians
2nd Kings Own
1 Coln.3/4 Gurkhas
From Chowringhee

Alezu

From
Broadway

Wuntho

en route to Indaw
4th Inf.Regt.
2/29th.3/114th.2/146th.

138, 139, 140 Bn.
Arty.Regt.
Engineer's Regt.

2/29th.(25 Mar)
2/51st.
141.
5th.Railway Regt.
H.Q 4th.Inf.Regt.
from Malaya (22 Mar)
1/4th.(31 Mar)

Katha

Equivalent to one division
by 31 Mar when reinforcements
from south arrived.

Shweli R.

Chowringhee

Mohsi Chaung

PICCADILLY

Kaukkwe Chaung

BROADWAY 77 Bde. 3/9 Gurkhas
(Garrison)

2/146 th.
1 Kings (external reserve)

Irrawaddy

Irrawaddy

Bhamo-Myitkyina Road

Morris
Force
4/9 Gurkhas
1 Coln.
3/4 Gurkhas

Bhamo

Allied Forces shown thus ——— 1 South Staffs.
Japanese Forces shown thus ... 4th Inf. Regt.

0   4   8   12   16   20 miles
0   8   16   24   32 kms.

26/29 March

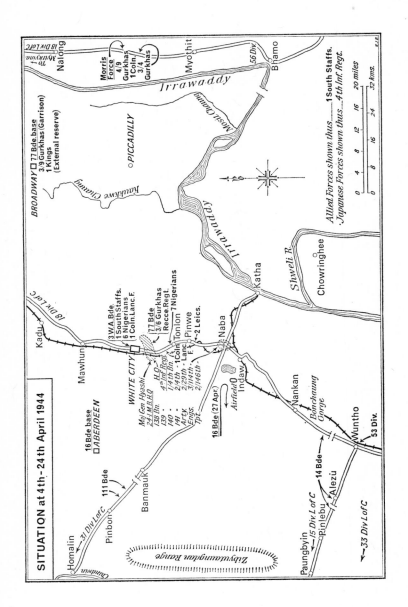

SITUATION at 4th – 24th April 1944

Allied Forces shown thus .... **1 South Staffs.**
Japanese Forces shown thus ..... *4th Inf. Regt.*

Homalin
Chindwin
Pinbon
31 Div L of C
111 Bde
Banmauk
Paungbyin
15 Div L of C
Pinlebu
Alezu
14 Bde
33 Div L of C

Zibyutaungdan Range

16 Bde base □ ABERDEEN

Kadu
Mawhun
3 W.A. Bde.
1 South Staffs.
6 Nigerians
1 Coln. Lanc. F.
WHITE CITY
Maj. Gen. Hyashi
24 I.M.B. H.Q.
138 Bn.
139 –
140 –
141 –
Arty.
Engs.
Tpt.

H.Q.
4th Inf. Regt.
1/4th Bn.
2/4th – 1 Coln.
2/29th – Lanc.
3/114th – F.
2/146th –

77 Bde
3/6 Gurkhas
Recce. Regt.
Tonlon – 7 Nigerians
Pinwe
2 Leics.
Naba
18 Div L of C

Indaw
Airfield (27 Apr)
16 Bde (27 Apr)
Nankan
Bonchaung
Gorge
Wuntho
53 Div.

Katha
Shweli R.
Chowringhee

Irrawaddy
Mosit Chaung

PICCADILLY
Kaukkwe Chaung

BROADWAY □ 77 Bde. base
3/9 Gurkhas (Garrison)
1 Kings
(External reserve)

Nalong
To Mogaung
Myitkyina
18 Div L of C

Morris Force
4/9 Gurkhas,
1 Coln.
3/4 Gurkhas
Myothit
56 Div.
Bhamo

0 4 8 12 16 20 miles
0 8 16 24 32 kms.

stocked with grenades and ammunition. We were preparing for a siege.

A light plane strip had been made between the railway embankment and Pagoda Hill, and all our wounded had been evacuated to Broadway, and thence to India by the nightly Dakotas.

White City, as we named the block, because of the shrouds of white parachutes draping the high trees which could be seen for miles around, was in the form of a rectangle, about 1,000 yards long and 800 yards wide. The south side overlooked a stream and open paddy. The western defences were dug fairly high into our highest hills, and overlooked the railway and the open paddy beyond. To the north there was a small open valley about twenty yards across, culminating in a wooded knoll. Beyond this valley was a hill which just overlooked us. To the east the line ran along the tops of several little densely wooded hills where visibility was down to ten yards. At the south-east corner was O.P. Hill, from which the Gurkhas had made their charge on to Pagoda Hill.

The garrison consisted of the South Staffords manning the northern and eastern sectors of the perimeter, and the 3rd/6th Gurkhas the southern and western. One company was detached as 'floater company' in touch by wireless with the block, to attack in the rear any enemy attacking the block. This was a nerve-racking job, and the company was frequently relieved. Brigade H.Q. was installed in the centre with its wireless sets, etc. Ian MacPherson's Brigade Defence Company manned the place of honour, isolated O.P. Hill. The mules and ponies were protected by walls of parachute containers filled with earth. The main dressing station was near the northern end in a small concealed re-entrant. Opposite this on the perimeter was 'Bare Hill', a knob where all the trees had been cut down and lay as logs all over it.

The reserves consisted of the commando platoons with their flamethrowers and the reconnaissance platoons of the battalions.

The Lancashire Fusilier columns, from secure bases at the edge of the hills, harassed enemy communications in an area ten to twenty miles north and south of the block.

Within the block our main armament, later increased, was eight 3-inch mortars, and up to eleven Vickers machine guns firing along the wire, which at that time was only about six to eight feet in depth.

Our greatest defensive fire power during the day was Cochran's Mustangs, which could be obtained at about two and a half hours' notice. Supply dropping went on nearly every night, the planes dropping to our lines of fires on the top of the western ridge. Some replenishments could also be brought by day from Broadway by the light planes evacuating casualties.

CHAPTER FOUR

THE JAPS ATTACK

The motto of the Stronghold is 'No Surrender'.
WINGATE

I had given orders that at night everyone was to stay in his foxhole, whatever happened. Anyone moving about was liable to be shot.

At about 1845 hours on the night March 21st/22nd a fusillade of grenades and shouting on the northern sector was the first warning of an attack. The enemy rushed the forward sections shouting 'Tik Hai [O.K.] Johnny,' 'Cease Fire', 'O.K. Bill', 'Stand down now', etc. This did have a momentary effect of holding our fire, but not for long.

The enemy got a foothold in two platoon positions in Colonel Richards's sector, suffering very heavy casualties both from close-quarter fighting and 3-inch mortar fire. We laid down our co-ordinated barrage of mortar fire when we were given the SOS. We thought the Japs were using explosive bullets fired from the hill to the north. These gave the impression, when they exploded nearby, that the Japs were right in the block. However, Richards all night kept me informed on the phone of the true situation.

After a while there was a lull, during which we could hear the Japs chattering to each other. Capt. Paddy Ryan, my Japanese-speaking Intelligence Officer, asked me if he could go and find out what they were saying. In view of my orders about movement I was reluctant to let him go, but eventually he persuaded me. He came back and said that they were arguing whether they should retire or push on with the attack. All their officers were killed, and they did not know what to do. Finally they decided to push on, their orders being to clear the block and take prisoners.

Very confused close-quarter fighting started up again, in which many more were killed. Another attack in the neighbourhood of Bare Hill was completely broken up by about 100 rounds of 3-inch mortar fire. Fighting continued all night with continual jabbering by the Japs, who by now had established two light machine guns within our lines. Richards asked me for two platoons for counter-attack. I sent two commando platoons with flame-throwers which crept along the western ridge to join him. At dawn Richards put in a whirlwind counter-attack led by himself, and drove out or killed the lot, he himself being wounded in the chest. The remainder of the enemy were driven across our wire. I contacted our floater company and they put in a further counter-attack. They hit strong opposition where the Japs were licking their wounds, and Major Jefferies, the company commander, was shot dead by a sniper from up a tree. I then called the counter-attack off.

I went up to see the results. The Japs had reached our dressing station where Capt. Cheshire and Capt. Thorne, R.A.M.C., were valiantly caring for our wounded, but they did not interfere.

As Paddy Dermody, L/Cpl. Young and myself went on to Bare Hill, which was supposedly clear of the enemy, Paddy shouted 'Get down!' and gave me a push, he himself falling, wounded in the groin. There was a wounded Jap the other side of the tree trunk, so I emptied my revolver into him, and then Young and myself carried Paddy down to the dressing station which was about thirty yards away. Paddy Dermody bore the pain of his wound with great fortitude while we were manhandling him down. I ordered the Gurkhas to clear Bare Hill. They killed eleven Japs there, some of whom were not even wounded, but were hiding awaiting their chance to get away, or to shoot an officer.

I visited the dressing station and spoke to Richards, who did not seem very bad. He was cheerful and told me with glee that he had killed seven Japs before they had got him.

Our Public Relations officer, a brave chap, who had taken part in the charge, was in mortal agony which no amount of morphia appeared to subdue. He held my hand, and I tried to comfort him. Cheshire and Thorne were working up to their elbows in blood, doing a magnificent job, with the padres giving comfort to the badly wounded.

61

We strengthened our defences and prepared for another attack. I had called air support on to the hills 200 yards to the north of us where the Japs were still in evidence.

At 1700 hours a squadron of R.A.F. Vengeances arrived and were directed on to the spot by mortar smoke. Later some of Cochran's Mustangs did the same. Their efforts blasted the Japs off the hills and valleys, causing many more casualties. One Jap was thrown into the air on to a tree. Other snipers' bodies were later found strapped to trees. Bombing had done them no good.

We counted our casualties, and they were high. There was the usual high percentage of casualties amongst officers which is bound to occur at the beginning of a campaign when individual leadership is most necessary.

Killed: 6 British officers, 26 British other ranks, 2 Gurkhas.

Wounded: 6 British officers, 36 British other ranks, 1 Gurkha missing.

Again the South Staffords had had to bear the brunt of the battle, and had fought magnificently under the fine leadership and example of Lieut.-Col. Richards.

We counted sixty enemy dead, and held four prisoners. There were many more corpses outside the perimeter which we could not count, and many wounded must have been taken away.

Captured enemy maps showed that we had been attacked by 7, 8 and 9 Companies of 3rd Battalion 114th Regiment, 18 Division, assisted by two Railway Engineer Companies.

We captured their adjutant, Lieut. Satrai, and their battalion flag. Satrai was absolutely disgusted with himself. He said that he came from a battalion where it was considered worse than death to be captured. He had been stunned by someone and was not badly hurt. He kept asking, 'Interrogate me, and shoot me.' He hated the sight of me, but would talk to Paddy Ryan. He said that they were a battalion from 18 division who had been sent to rest and refit near Mandalay after some hard fighting against General Stilwell's Chinese. They were rushed up by lorry to eject what they thought were not more than 300 guerrillas blocking the main line to the north. He said that their intelligence was to blame. They had not anticipated such opposition, and had thought that it would be a walkover.

62

From the marked map the enemy's plan was to drive us out from the north, on to the open paddy to the south and west, which was covered by Jap machine guns in Mawlu and in the wood in the paddy. From all interrogations it appeared that they had no idea of the size of the forces operating against their communications, and I signalled Wingate to that effect.

We collected a mass of diaries and documents which were sent back by the light planes evacuating the wounded. I am afraid that many of these valuable documents were retained as souvenirs by some of the pilots and crews.

The important lessons learnt from this engagement can be summarized as follows:

(a) British troops, as ordered, stayed and died in their foxholes.

(b) Some of the British troops who were overrun stayed on shooting the enemy around them, and were recovered alive in the morning. I was told that one Bren gunner had been able to give a good account of himself all night, even though overrun, as a parachute container filled with armed Bren gun magazines had dropped close to him from the planes, which continued their supply dropping all night.

(c) Manpack flame-throwers again proved invaluable. Unfortunately one or two of our men who had remained in their trench became casualties of our own flame-throwers.

(d) Centralized control of mortar fire was very effective and completely broke up one attack near the north-east corner, where we found many more bodies some days later.

(e) Our wire was insufficiently thick. This was remedied during the next few days.

(f) Our booby traps were most effective. At that time warfare was all in. The Japs had not yet been beaten on the Burma front, and it was a life-and-death struggle, which we were determined to win. I could not afford to be genteel.

(g) Our positions were too high up on the hills. We reorganized them so that two platoons of a company were at paddy level, and two in support above them.

(h) The role of the floater company was very difficult. We found this out again later, and I abandoned the idea. The best role for the floater company is to find the enemy's base or gun area and attack that while his troops are away, but not to mix it in the immediate battle area.

(i) Telephones were of enormous assistance in controlling the battle.

The period from March 23rd to 27th was spent by the garrison energetically improving defences, thickening up the wire, and laying more minefields. Every night there was a supply drop of defence stores, ammunition and rations until White City was turned into a well-stocked secure fortress.

I asked a lot from my troops in extensive patrolling and 'jitter' raids against the Japs in Mawlu, and thus we thoroughly dominated No Man's Land and imposed our will on the enemy. Even though this meant a severe strain on the troops, it was well worth it, as we retained the initiative and I was kept well informed and ready for all eventualities.

The Lancashire Fusilier columns were maintaining the pressure north and south, and on the 24th Hugh Christie's column blew the rail bridge at Kadu, while to the south, Shuttleworth blew some small culverts and mined the road. We had further patrol clashes, and obtained identifications of 15 and 51 Division, but this turned out later to be 2nd Echelon troops working at Mawlu. In all, during this period, we wrote off thirty to forty Japs with practically no loss to ourselves.

General Wingate visited the block on March 24th, and I proudly showed him round. He made one or two wise suggestions, but on the whole was well pleased. I remember asking him what the policy was on the destruction of the railway line. He answered that General Stilwell did not want it 'destroyed' too much – he expected to move down it shortly from Mogaung.

He gave me a long description of the difficulties he was encountering in Assam. Soon after we had landed, three Jap divisions had attacked the area between Tiddim, Imphal and Kohima. He reminded me of what he had said in his first report, 'There is no answer to penetration except counter-penetration.' Everyone was in a flap, and they were trying to take our planes away from us. There was much uninformed criticism about our being put in too far away from the 4th Corps front, but they would not listen when he told them that the Chindits' object was primarily to help General Stilwell, as was laid down at Quebec, and not 4th Corps.

We had $3\frac{1}{2}$ divisions with armour in the Kohima-Imphal

area to hold off the three Jap divisions and had the equivalent of $5\frac{2}{3}$ moving to their support (9 in all), but he was
afraid that the policy would be to reinforce failure rather
than exploit success. If we took the Indaw area, there was
less chance now of getting 36 Division to garrison it,
which he had always hoped would happen.

Lentaigne's brigade had got split up crossing the
Irrawaddy, and one battalion had been directed to the
Bhamo-Myitkyina area to help the Kachin revolt.

He said that Stilwell was slowing up because the Jap thrust
towards Kohima was threatening his rail communications
and he did not want to involve himself too deeply 'in case
the Limeys ran away'.

Wingate had moved his headquarters out of the Imphal
plain – as he had previously anticipated that he would have
to – in order to reduce the number of mouths to feed, and
not get involved in somebody else's campaign.

He showed me messages of congratulations from Churchill and Roosevelt on his magnificent achievement. He had
sent back an immediate reply that, if he could have four
Dakota squadrons and sufficient replacements to keep them
up to strength, he could take the whole of north Burma in
the next three months. The message had been allowed to go
through, but was endorsed all the way up by higher command that they did not think this number of squadrons was
necessary. In actual fact the squadrons did arrive and made
logistically possible the conquest of north Burma within the
next six months.

He showed me his 'Forecast of Possible Developments of
Operation "Thursday" ' (this was the code name for the
whole Chindit operation), 'by Commander Special Force',
which he had sent to 14th Army. He said that General Slim
was taken with the idea, but that he was surrounded by
'doubting Thomases'.

The plan envisaged more brigades being installed, with
their airfields, south of Indaw to block further all routes to
Imphal.

When I remonstrated and said that surely we were going
beyond our object, which was to help get Stilwell along, he
smiled and said, 'We have got to help 14th Army. We are all,
including Stilwell, under 14th Army Command, and in spite
of my complaints at times, they have been very helpful on

the whole, even if they did doubt the practicability of this operation. Now, they are converted.'

He then became genial and insisted on walking along the railway line, kicking it: 'So this is 18 Division's rail communications.' I asked him whether we could not hold 'White City' and drive north from it up the backside of 18 Division. He said, 'Now you're getting away from the principle of L.R.P. Incidentally I told you that Broadway was much better than Piccadilly and you did not listen.' He then gave me a mild admonishment, indicating that because I had been successful I should not let success confuse my judgment.

He visited every part and chatted to everyone and asked many questions. He had sensible suggestions for everyone, whether it was the siting of a machine gun, the lie of a 3-inch mortar, a point of hygiene to the doctors, the means by which the Protestant and Roman Catholic padres could keep up morale, the places for burying the dead, or the siting of the wireless aerials, etc. He told me that I needed guns, and we discussed with Bobbie Thompson the construction of a Dakota strip in the paddy west of the block.

He finally bid me 'Be of good heart. I will see that you lack nothing,' and took off with his A.D.C., George Borrow, in a light plane to visit Bernard Fergusson, and then back to Broadway.

We had also talked about the glider landing and he told me of his long night vigil with the Generals and Air Vice-Marshals awaiting for news – then dismay at my first 'Soya Link,' and delight at my 'Pork Sausage'. I told him that it was through Alison that we succeeded. He said that Scott had got a D.S.O., and 'Oh, by the way you have a bar to your D.S.O. Let it go to your heart and not your head.' 'Yes, sir. Thank you, sir.'

We waved him off. It was the last we ever saw of him, but his dreams lived with us.

His visit had put new heart into all the garrison, and we looked for new worlds to conquer.

CHAPTER FIVE

CLEARING MAWLU

We will impose our will on the enemy

We had achieved three out of four of the objectives in the 'intention' paragraph of my orders.

First, we had formed our stronghold at Broadway.

Secondly, we had physically blocked the road and railway, the main communications to 18 Division facing General Stilwell, and there were no possible diversions in that corridor. It was a pity that fighting had ceased in the north, otherwise the Japs would have suffered more severely from our squeeze.

Thirdly, we had stopped all traffic on the Irrawaddy.

The fourth object of blocking traffic on the road from Bhamo to Myitkyina had not yet been fully achieved, and the Japs had diverted some supplies for 18 Division to this route.

In consultation with Lieut.-Col. Skone, Hugh Christie, Bobbie Thompson and Ron Degg, I had decided that the time had come to take the offensive and try to dominate the area. If we waited we would lose the initiative. So I decided on an an attack to clear Mawlu. We had, from patrols, a good idea of where the enemy were, and they had been repeatedly bombed, while Shuttleworth to the south had done much to prevent new supplies reaching them.

I had thought that the Japanese plan for attack on the block had been a good one, marred by the fact that it had been carried out by far too few troops. I decided to risk denuding the block and to put a battalion and a half, less heavy weapons, into the attack. It was no real risk, since if you are engaging the enemy you know, and patrols screen you from any enemy you do not know, what risk is there?

The gist of the plan was that Hugh Christie's column, which had joined the block from the north in order to receive further instructions, should set out in the evening and march five to six miles during the night to the east of Mawlu, and establish themselves with their machine guns, to the south-east of Mawlu, from where they could kill anyone retreating across the paddy to Sepein. Hubert Skone's column and Freddie Shaw's column would advance boldly just before dawn across the open paddy, gaining cover before first light, in the jungle north-east and north-west of Mawlu respectively, and then drive the Japs through Mawlu on to the waiting guns of Hugh Christie. I would move with Tactical Brigade H.Q. behind Skone.

Hugh Christie set off after dark. We heard a little firing about an hour later, which worried me. I was up very early and in a bad temper. The handover of positions in the dark had not gone smoothly. There was no strong sweet tea to cheer me, as I had forbidden fires before dawn. Freddie Shaw set off in time, but Hubert Skone was late, blaming the South Staffords. I was a bit short with him. We then marched in a long single file out across the paddy with the sky getting lighter all the time. As Tactical Brigade was at the end of the column I was increasingly apprehensive; we were only a few hundred yards, if that, from the Jap guns, and there was no cover. However, we just got to the jungle in time. Skone, possibly piqued by what I had said to him, got moving straight away, and very shortly there was a fusillade of shots, explosion of grenades, and a lot of shouting. At Brigade Francis and I first thought that it was the Japs shouting. We crept up nearer, and found Hubert Skone sitting down holding his knees and roaring with laughter. 'I have never heard them use such language before.' I said, 'Is everything all right?' He looked at me strangely: 'Of course it is when a Gurkha swears like that.' Quite a number of wounded were coming back, but they were all grinning. I could also hear, from a distance, Freddie joining in the fray. After even harder firing, the Gurkhas went off after the Japs into the town.

A lot of the enemy had run towards Freddie, who had inflicted heavy casualties, so they then turned to hurry, loaded with their belongings, along the railway towards Sepein. Unfortunately only Christie's advance guard saw them, and fired a few shots which did little else than make them hurry still faster. Christie's column had bumped against a patrol soon after leaving the block. The leading officer had been killed, and two other ranks wounded. This had delayed them. The country was difficult in the dark, as I was to find out myself at a later date, and they had failed to get there in time. It was a pity, because three or four hundred Japs were estimated to have fled. We found out later that Mawlu was a records centre.

The defenders appeared to be a company of a battalion of 113th Regiment. There were a few of the 3rd Battalion, 114th Regiment, also amongst the dead. Those running away were clerks, railway operators, administrative personnel, etc. The Gurkhas, who can ferret out anything, probed a few filled-in foxholes, and found masses of buried documents. We collected literally several hundredweight of these, and sent them to India where it must have pleased the 'I' boys and given them something to do. Amongst the documents was a complete record of the Indian (Traitor) National Army, and of other agents trained in Burma for India.

It was bad luck also that Shuttleworth had just removed an ambush on the road and railway when the Japs came hurrying through. A Burma Rifles havildar with his patrol saw them, and shot a few. The panic of the Japs spread to those who were in Sepein, who upped sticks and joined them. They did not stop till they got to Indaw, twenty-five miles away.

The Gurkhas had done very well. Their offensive spirit, combined with the determination and leadership of Lieut-Col. Skone, won the day. The Japs left much equipment behind, including very many cavalry swords. These were useful to give to light-plane, close air support, and transport pilots in recognition of their continued great service to us.

We found about thirty-three Jap bodies, some of whom may have been killed previously by bombing. Our casualties were:

Killed: 1 Lancashire Fusilier officer, 6 Gurkha other ranks.

Seriously wounded: 1 Gurkha officer. Wounded: 35 Gurkha and 2 British other ranks.

We now occupied the first sizable Burmese town to be retaken from the Japs.

After the victory at Mawlu, Hugh Christie returned to the Mawhun area in the north, and, after a few engagements, drove the Japs back to Kadu. The Japanese, expecting an attack on the large town of Mohnyin, collected every sort of unit for its defence, denuding the line to the north. About 2,000 troops, which they could ill spare, were reliably reported in that area; this was later confirmed from Jap diaries. It was a great pity that General Stilwell stopped his offensive just at that time when we were having the greatest successes on his enemy's communications.

We now had a comparatively quiet period from March 27th to April 6th. Constant patrolling was carried out, and columns in their turn came out to act as 'floater' and to stretch their legs. I also decided on a 'denial' policy south of Sepein. Although this was not fully carried out, mines were laid and obstacles with booby traps were placed across all routes from the south. Bridges blown on the railway by that time included one south of Pinwe, one south of Sepein, Mawlu bridge, Henu bridge, Nansiaung, Mawhun and Kadu bridges, and also a few small culverts. Our mines later took some toll of the unsuspecting Jap motor transports.

We had constructed a glider strip just west of the block, and two 2-pounder anti-tank guns were landed by glider. These were dug into formidable bunkers in the railway embankment and well camouflaged. In the block, defence work continued, wells were sunk, further minefields laid, telephone lines buried, more and more wire erected, overhead cover increased by use of railway sleepers and rails; the light plane strip was improved, and mules and every conceivable thing were 'dug in' and protected in anticipation of a siege.

During the quiet period we also improved our intelligence system and propaganda in the areas around. Capt. Musgrave Wood* of the Burma Rifles had started an excellent Kachin levy organization based on Naman which gave us, and the whole force, much valuable information. He had constructed a concealed light plane strip connected by telephone with his bandits' lair in the foothills. This lair was protected in every sort of way and was almost impossible to

---

* 'Emwood' the cartoonist.

find. Kachins were recruited according to the directions laid down by General Wingate.

In the south near Nahpi, Capt. Bell of the Burma Rifles had started a similar, although not so elaborate, organization. Our successes had boosted the morale of the Burmese and Shans in the valley as well as the unconquered Kachins in the hills. We sent out medical officers with the Gurkha Rifles to administer medical aid to the Burmese and Kachins, who flocked to obtain medicines. We started shops outside the block where we exchanged old parachute cloth for rice and green vegetables. Cloth was very short in Burma. I called on the head man of Mawlu and gave him Rs. 1,500 to distribute for the damage we had done to their property.

Bernard Fergusson's 16 Brigade was now establishing a stronghold at Mankhton sixteen miles west of White City. This was to be called Aberdeen in honour of General Wingate's home town. So at this period we had under our control an area eighty miles by a minimum of thirty miles from Mankhton to the Irrawaddy.

It was during this period that Taffy Griffiths organized some elephants which had recently arrived, to collect all the barbed wire and ammunition and other consolidation stores which had been dropped by mistake 3,000 feet up the side of the hills. I must say I like elephants; next to mules I think that they are the best animals I have met. I have been off dogs since I saw a cocker spaniel eating a man's face in Mandalay after our forces had retreated from there in 1942. Other 'officer type' dogs were eating other corpses of refugees killed by the Jap bombers.

I especially like to see a string of elephants head to tail, each with its separate sounding bell, as they syncopate off into the evening jungle. It is a poetry of motion and unorthodox rhythm which I wish someone could put to music. I remember one column in 1943 had an interesting experience with an elephant. They were with difficulty trying to cross the Chindwin. Eventually they chose as their crossing place a point where a sandy spit stretched three-quarters of the way across. 'There are shallows in them in which a lamb may wade, and there are depths in which an elephant may swim.' The mahout then took a loaded elephant (they had picked up the elephant somewhere), with its load of a battery-charging engine, and swam the beast casually to the other side. This gave the column commander an idea. He was having great difficulty in getting his column and stores across owing to the swift current and inadequacies of the boats. So he recalled the elephant and loaded it up, and it walked and swam over again. This occurred two or three times with ever increasing loads, until eventually, as the elephant stepped off into the deep water with its swiftly moving current, he missed his footing and capsized. He floated down stream, the load acting as a keel, with his four legs and trunk waving idly in the air. He could still breathe as long as he kept his mouth shut. A Canadian officer,* with great presence of mind, ran downstream, plunged into the water, sat on the elephant's belly, the elephant behaving correctly all the time, and cut the girth. The elephant then righted himself, spurted one long jet of water through his trunk, and made quietly for the shore, where he awaited his mahout. As Mackenzie, the Canadian officer, passed him, he gave one wink, and that was his only apparent sign of emotion.

I myself had a little incident with an elephant. After Bernard Fergusson and I had blown the railway that year, I waited for a supply drop. Unfortunately it was delayed for forty-eight hours, by which time all sorts of Jap parties started to chase us and close in on us. I had to use every single device and artifice taught me by General Wingate, as well as more than one of my own, to try and shake them off. To manoeuvre swiftly with a column of 400 men, 120 mules, 18 bullocks, 12 horses and an elephant is like trying to avoid arrest by the police in Soho while dragging along a hundred yards of fire hose. You are liable to get noticed, and it is extremely difficult to curl it all up in a hiding place before someone interfered with the other end, or it gets entangled in an Italian restaurant. So at one time I had plunged into some elephant grass, with my column following. The grass got higher and higher until it was about twelve feet tall, and two inches thick. I was exhausted, pushing my way through this, so I stopped the column and passed a message down, 'Bring on the elephant.' The elephant duly arrived. I put a trusted British corporal on top while I proceeded close behind with my compass. I would then say, 'Left, left' or

* Captain Mackenzie, attached 3/2 Gurkha Rifles

'Right, right, hold it' as one used to do with anti-aircraft searchlights. The corporal communicated this by taps on the shoulder to the mahout, who communicated it to the elephant in the way mahouts do.

This worked very well, and we proceeded apace. All was going well and I was feeling very pleased with myself, when the elephant stopped and stalled. I bumped into her. Unfortunately the elephant was a female. All the waters of the Irrawaddy, which we crossed that night, would not wash the odour off me. We had to stop and have another supply drop, or I walked alone. I do not know what the moral is. Perhaps, 'Never look a gift elephant in the tail.' I have never been treated like that even by the most senior staff officer.

Talking about compasses, I was amused to hear, later, various people lecturing on this subject. My compass had a bubble in it. The result was that when I set off from A to B sometimes the bubble made us veer one way and sometimes another, but over a distance the variations would compensate each other, and we would arrive unscathed at our destination. The result was that through three years' campaigning in Burma, I was never ambushed. I used to imagine the intense little Japanese noting which direction we had gone, guessing correctly our destination, organizing a beautiful ambush, and the mortification when through the guile and perfidiousness of the British they were circumvented, while we veered gaily to and fro under the influence of Archibald, my bubble. As General Wingate preached, 'You must be unpredictable to your foes, constant to your friends.'

In order to improve our communications with our patrols up and down the railway, I ordered the telephone wires to be mended and a link led into White City so that patrols could pass messages by telephone if their wireless was out of range.

To the surprise and delight of my Signal Officer, Major Pringle, he heard Japs talking down it. The Japs were using the telephone from Mogaung, via Hopin, to Mohnyin to pass over routine messages and situation reports. We now could hear what their situation was twice daily! Paddy Ryan was delighted and after we had given the good news to Force H.Q., General Stilwell flew to us two Nesei (American-born Japanese), whom he could ill afford, who kept watch day and night. We received a great deal of important information both from the situation reports, and from the telephone orderlies' chat.

This continued successfully for nearly ten days until, in rejoining a wire broken by shelling, one of our linesmen gave the show away. However, it was most useful as long as it lasted, as will be seen later.

Also during this time I rode around the villages wearing my red hat, with my mounted bodyguard under the command of my new groom Ginger, who had taken Paddy Dermody's place. Passing through on my white pony Jean, followed by my aides and escort, I benignly acknowledged the obeisances of the villagers in true nineteenth-century fashion. I liked the exercise, and I wanted to give the impression of calmness and security so that they would know who were the real conquerors, and therefore whom it was best to support and to give information. But in reality Taffy Griffiths and his Burma Rifles were quietly doing the real job of propaganda and intelligence.

I could never understand why my head would itch after these, and other, flag marches with my brigadier's red hat on, which I normally kept in my voluminous pack. It was months later before I found that the fold concealed a nest of very small, harmless, benign ants.

CHAPTER SIX

ATTACK ON BROADWAY

We wish, therefore, firstly to encounter the enemy in
the open and preferably in ambushes laid by us,
and secondly to induce him to attack us only in our
defended strongholds. Further to make sure of our
advantages, and in view of the fact that the enemy
will be superior in numbers in our neighbourhood,
we shall choose for our stronghold, areas inaccessible to wheeled transport.

WINGATE

Broadway had been left in the capable hands of Claude
Rome. Claude had all the characteristics of the Gay Cavalier
tempered by years of regular army and staff training and
experience.

Besides the garrison, as already described, there were such
necessary administrative or operational units as R.A.F. ser-
vicing, commando and ground staff for the airfield; packing
sections of an Air Supply Company, the light plane force
under Capt. Rebori, and a small casualty clearing station.

On March 12th, six days after the initial glider landing,
and before there had been any interference by the enemy,
six Spitfires were flown in to help protect the airfield against
enemy air attacks. One crashed on landing.

The following day the airfield was attacked by thirty
enemy fighters. The Spitfires were scrambled on warning
from the radar sets which had been flown in, and all five
serviced aircraft took off. They were quickly involved with
the top cover and some twenty enemy fighters attacked the
airfield, the light aircraft in their dispersal areas, and the
anti-aircraft guns, as they came into action. This attack
combined the dropping of 50 lb. anti-personnel bombs with

strafing by cannon and machine gun fire. The attack was singularly ineffective. Three or four light aircraft were damaged, the radar set was destroyed, and a large number of crashed gliders were set on fire. Our own aircraft shot down four certainties, and probably two more of the Zeros. Our anti-aircraft defence shot down one for certain. One Spitfire was shot down. Casualties to the garrison were only three Gurkhas wounded.

One very interesting point in the air battle was that the vastly out-numbered Spitfires, when in difficulties, flew low over our own light anti-aircraft Bofors guns in the stronghold. These engaged, with great accuracy, the pursuing Zeros on the tails of the Spitfires. The whole garrison was much elated at the magnificent display by the Spitfires and the gunners.

A few days later, the airfield was attacked again by some twenty enemy fighters. They flew in low from the east, and the new radar set picked them up only nine minutes' flying time away. Previous to their arrival the Spitfires had been scrambled four times during the day without making contact. As a result the squadron leader and one other aircraft alone took off, leaving the remaining three serviceable aircraft at immediate readiness on the strip. The two airborne Spitfires were quickly involved with one formation of the enemy, while another formation attacked and destroyed the Spitfires still on the ground. The squadron leader was shot down and, as a result of this action, the remaining Spitfire was recalled, and no fighters were ever again based on Broadway.

The warning system, although not perfect, was considered adequate. It was an understandable error on the squadron leader's part in not scrambling all his planes.

This venture was an experiment, and if it did nothing else, it drew off a comparatively large-scale air effort from what was becoming the crucial front, Kohima. The R.A.F. had shown their usual adaptability and gallantry, and their example again urged us all on to greater effort.

A few days after the Spitfires were withdrawn an enemy force of some twenty fighters and twelve bombers bombed the airfield and the stronghold itself. 50 lb. anti-personnel, incendiary and 500 lb. bombs were dropped in a pattern bombing attack, a typical 'Japanese all sorts'. The bombing was accurate, all bombs landing on the airstrip, or on the strong-hold. Much damage was done to the exposed light planes, stores and equipment, but only three or four light planes themselves were damaged. The craters on the airstrip were quickly filled in by bulldozers. There was, however, a serious consequence in that the light plane force personnel, with noticeable exceptions amongst some of the N.C.O.s, were much shaken, and dispersed into the jungle and refused to fly. It took a visit by General Wingate and Colonel Alison to restore their morale and get them into the air again. I have noticed this in many fronts. Aircrews who are wonderfully brave in the air can be shaken by comparatively minor dangers on the ground. The reverse is also true, and many a soldier who thinks he is brave finds his bowels turn to water when in the air.

After this episode all the pilots carried on their good work as before, and certainly we, in White City, had noticed nothing amiss.

After an interval of a few days, four Zeros attacked the strip, strafing the light plane dispersal area ineffectively, but unfortunately catching one light plane as it was taking off. Both the pilot and passenger were killed with little damage to the aircraft. This was the Japs' last air attack on Broadway until after our evacuation months later.

During all these attacks, our six Bofors light anti-aircraft guns shot down six for certain, and probably four more. These gunners later went to Myitkyina, and with the troop which operated at White City, their battery probably shot down more Jap aircraft that year than the rest of the Allied anti-aircraft defences of India and Burma put together. So it certainly pays to carry out aggressive defence and place your guns where they can shoot down aircraft, rather than using them as a sort of life insurance tucked away in a bank.

It was unfortunate that we had too many light planes at Broadway. There were nearly thirty of them, when eight to ten would have done. This exposed valuable machines to unnecessary destruction from air attack. In actual fact it was surprising how few were irreparably damaged, and most of them flew again. The pilots were their own mechanics.

All this information of the affair of Broadway I received from Claude Rome when I visited him, and from his report later. I will now digress and follow, for a while, the troubles

77

of a West African battalion en route from Broadway to Aberdeen, where Bernard Fergusson, after his stupendous march from Ledo, was establishing a stronghold.

The 6th Nigerian Rifles were landed at Broadway soon after 77 Brigade was complete. One battalion from III Brigade had also landed, Chowringhee having been occupied by the enemy. General Wingate had told me that 6th Nigerian Rifles would move to Mankhton, but that as I was engaged in establishing a block on the railway, I could route them to the best advantage of that operation. He never believed in a column marching from one place to another without making some effort to influence the enemy. As I had already routed my own columns like the outstretched fingers of a hand from Kadu to Pinwe in order to cause the enemy the maximum amount of dispersion before we clenched our fist and grasped their communications at Henu, I routed the Africans north of Mohnyin, hoping that their presence might delay the Jap garrison in Mohnyin from coming south to dislodge us. This appeared to have had a successful result. But possibly I had routed this African column slightly haphazardly, not taking into full account the difficult open valley that they would have to cross before reaching the shelter of the jungle and the hills on the other side.

The battalion advanced at commendable speed, and soon the mile-long column was crossing the railway at night. There they were surprised, and a confused engagement occurred. It says much for the leadership of the officers, the common sense and loyalty of the men, and the standard of training, that in spite of this incident they soon reformed at their rendezvous, and were a fighting unit again. However, a number of casualties were caused, and one or two were captured. We later captured the Jap interrogation reports on their African prisoners, to whose answers the Japanese gave nearly the highest degree of credence.

'Where have you come from?'

'We dropped from the sky.'

'How many are there of you?'

'Thousands upon thousands upon thousands, too many to count.'

'How did you come, by aeroplane, glider or what?'

'We just dropped.'

'Are you all parachutists?'

78

'Naturally. All Africans are parachutists.'

'When did you leave Africa?'

'It is so long ago. I cannot remember.'

'How many African soldiers are there in India?'

'I think about a million.'

'You lie!' Thwack!

'I am sorry. I won't lie again. Just over a million and a half.'

'What sort of armaments have you?'

'We have a huge new cannon, which a man can carry and fire without hurting himself.'

'What is the establishment of these?'

'Two to a company. Eight to a battalion. Sixteen to a division. Thirty-two to a corps – parachute corps.'

'How many parachute corps are there?'

'I do not know – two or three, I think.'

'Will you lead us to where you landed?'

'Of course. Why not?'

He led them to Broadway.

On March 26th a Kachin brought the information to Broadway that a large enemy force with two guns had crossed the Kaukkwe river the preceding night, and was moving south to attack the airfield. The floater company was not in wireless contact. Scottie was unfortunately way over east near Sinbo on the Irrawaddy on a wild Jap chase, pursuing a rumour. So Claude Rome sent Major Astell, Burma Rifles, who really belonged to 16 Brigade but happened to be passing through, with half his reconnaissance platoon to find the enemy and report his strength and line of approach.

Major Astell found the enemy in bivouac at dawn the next day slightly south of Broadway. He opened fire with all he had and claimed at least seven dead and more wounded, then withdrew. The floater company was contacted and ambushes laid. At 1600 hours on March 27th Astell's boys shot up a Jap patrol approaching the airfield. Claude Rome discussed with the light plane commander about flying out the planes, but they put it off till next morning because of lack of daylight.

We, in White City, had had priority in the matter of barbed wire, defence stores and ammunition, and Claude was still a bit short, so he was anxious that the Dakotas ordered for that night should still land if possible. But at

2245 hours, just after the Dakotas had taken off from Assam, heavy firing started, with much yelling and cheering, in the area where the floater company was in position. Claude withdrew into the stronghold the .5 m.m.g. A.A. posts which were distributed around the strip. Fighting at the far end of the strip continued very fiercely until just after midnight, when it died down. Wireless contact had been lost.

The Japs then crossed the strip, receiving a number of casualties, and reached the perimeter wire. The attack then flowed all around the perimeter till dawn, the Japs seeking a way in. At dawn three Japs with a light machine gun were killed twenty yards inside the wire. Other bodies were found all round the wire. The Japs, after this determined attack, withdrew, foiled by the strength of the defences and the determination of the defenders. With their usual over-confidence they had attacked with too little, and too late.

Just after first light, about two platoons of the floater company under a subadhar entered the perimeter. The floater company of the 3/9 Gurkha Rifles had fought extremely well, killing about seventy Japs, including the second in command of the battalion, and then fought their way back with admirable control and discipline.

Our casualties, including the floater company and garrison, were about sixty killed, wounded or missing.

At 1000 hours, a company of 3/9 Gurkhas counter-attacked the enemy north of the perimeter, killing about eighteen in a kukri charge, but were then forced to withdraw, losing eight casualties themselves by the heavy sniping from the trees.

82 Column, under Major Gaitley, had now arrived and, at 1600 hours, were ordered to attack. For some unknown reason only two platoons were put into the attack, and as they found the Japs entrenched in slit trenches dug strictly against orders by the light plane force, they did not press home their attack.

That night, the enemy made another strong attack against the stronghold, suffering many casualties whilst inflicting practically none.

In the morning a patrol found about 250 Japs digging in north of the stronghold. They were mortared intermittently throughout the day.

During the day, the Jap infantry gun started shelling, but

was immediately knocked out by our troop of 25-pounders. This information was later given by our parachute friend from the Nigerian Rifles, who then promptly escaped. He said that he had sited the gun himself so that it was opposite our 25 pounders! Whether this was true or not, a lot of what he said was corroborated by the copy of the Jap interrogation report, and he certainly came in grinning from ear to ear, recounting all that he had done.

At midday Capt. Coultart of 82 Column put in a most determined attack on the Japs who were digging in. Flame-throwers were used and the attack was pressed right home with the bayonet. The enemy was dislodged, but owing to the lateness of the hour, and general disorganization, and the gallant death of Coultart himself who was in the lead all the time, our troops withdrew to reorganize. Twenty-two Japs were counted killed. Our own casualties, including Capt. Coultart, were thirty-six killed and wounded.

That night, the enemy contented themselves with prowling around the wire, making odd attempts at sniping and cutting it.

At first light Gurkha patrols reported that the enemy had withdrawn from the positions north of the stronghold, and had all concentrated in an area south of it.

Gaitley's column needed replenishment, ammunition and rations, etc., and Claude Rome gave them permission to withdraw four to five miles where they received their supply drop that night. Many captured Gurkhas and West African troops escaped to the stronghold. A Chinese captain, used by the Japanese as an interpreter, also escaped. He identified the battalion as one from 18 Division, and stated that they had suffered some 200 casualties, and that one company with the wounded had already withdrawn across the Kaukkwe. This was the company which had been severely mauled by the floater company and Capt. Coultart.

That day, one enemy reconnaissance plane was shot down by our anti-aircraft fire, and one of two large enemy aircraft attempting to drop supplies was shot down in flames.

The majority of the supplies fell into our stronghold. During the afternoon two of our light aircraft, unaware of the situation, landed and took off again successfully. They were fired at, but took off under cover of a neutralization shoot on to the enemy position by our 25-pounders and mortars.

An attack by the combined 82 Column and floater company, supported by air attack, had been arranged for March 31st. The enemy was first severely mauled from the air, but there was a bit of a time lag before our attack went in, with the result that when our troops reached the enemy they found only minor opposition; the main body retreating in disorder and leaving much equipment behind. 82 Column, although ordered to pursue, were slow in reorganizing, and the enemy got away. The commander of 82 Column had tried to command his column from behind as taught in military text-books. This is quite hopeless, and always leads to missed opportunities and lack of control. A commander must place himself where he himself can influence the battle at short notice; otherwise he is nothing but a military commentator. The commander himself had no lack of personal bravery, was a parachutist, and was later killed in Malaya in 1948. But he had become too imbued by the erroneous doctrines taught in England at that time, on how to command a battalion from a coal-cellar.

The Kachins, picking off stragglers all the way, reported about 250 remnants of the battalion wearily retreating with their wounded to Mohnyin, many dying en route.

A survey of the destruction caused to the light planes and their stores showed surprisingly little intentional damage – any that had been done was unintelligent, and easily repairable. Much real damage was caused, however, by small arms and mortar fire during the fights around the light plane pens. But in spite of that, only about five aircraft were completely destroyed or irreparable. Petrol and ammunition left outside the block was untouched.

Thus another battalion of the Japs' crack 18 Division had been badly mauled. General Wingate's ideas, most ably put into practice by Colonel Rome and the troops under his command, had proved themselves once again.

During the battle I had received an urgent order from Special Force H.Q., in the absence of General Wingate, to send some columns to the 'rescue' of Claude Rome. This was quite impracticable. It would take from five to seven days to march the distance, during which time these columns would be of benefit either to White City or Broadway. During this period Claude Rome would either have won or lost, and in either case there would be little the columns could do. Broadway was designed to withstand a brigade attack, and was being attacked by only one, though admittedly a most aggressive, battalion. I had, therefore, complete confidence in the capabilities of Claude Rome and the troops under his command to deal with the threat. He kept me in the picture, and I was never anxious. I therefore took no action in the matter, explaining my views.

But this does bring out an almost universal fault in military tactics. If things are going badly, the tendency is to start switching troops to reinforce a possible failure, rather than to regain the initiative by attacking elsewhere. There are of course limits as to how much this latter doctrine can be carried out, depending on the nature of the threat, and the risks you can take. But taking the Burma campaign as a whole, in my humble opinion, and as General Wingate had indicated, it would have been far better, when Imphal and Kohima were threatened, to be less prodigal in sending divisions to reinforce that theatre where we outnumbered the Japs by a at least two to one in combatant battalions, and more than five to one in guns, and to spare at least one division to consolidate our success. The effort for the air supply of a division in Burma would not have greatly exceeded that for the air supply of a division in Imphal.

THE DEATH OF WINGATE

Just after our capture of Mawlu we learnt to our utter dismay that General Orde Charles Wingate had been killed in an air crash in the hills near Silchar on his journey back from Broadway after his visit to White City. His A.D.C. Captain Borrow, two war correspondents, the pilot and crew of a Mitchell bomber were killed with him.

It was February 1942 in Maymyo, the summer capital of Burma. I had just returned from a raid down the Irrawaddy after the fall of Rangoon, in which we had destroyed a number of boats, trains and bridges, supposed to have been already destroyed in our 'scorched earth' policy. I returned to my office at the Bush Warfare School of which I was Commandant, and found a strange man sitting at my desk. I asked, 'Who are you?' 'Wingate. Who are you?' 'Calvert.' Silence. 'Excuse me, but that's my desk.' 'I am sorry.' He moved aside, let me sit down, and then started to talk and ask questions.

He had been sent by General Wavell to take charge of, and coordinate, all irregular and guerrilla activities in Burma.

The Bush Warfare School was part of a mission to the Chinese which had been formed before the war with Japan broke out. It was closely linked with the American Volunteer Group (A.V.G.) of flyers which were also to help China. The object of the mission was to try to raise the standard of efficiency of the Chinese guerrillas from 1 per cent to 2 per cent, thus, perhaps, tying up another quarter of a million Japs in China. Already detachments, which were erroneously called commandos, had entered China. There detachments consisted of a lieutenant-colonel and a number of officers and N.C.O.s. The object of my school was to give

84

them some training in guerrilla work, demolitions, and some idea of the type of country. The words 'Bush Warfare' were a cover name to conceal our true task. Later I was criticized as being 'responsible' for the bad jungle training of the Burma Command, in that I had obviously failed in my job! We purposely avoided the jungle in our training, as the areas in China in which our chaps were to operate were flat paddy land.

Brigadier Wingate told me about himself. I had explained the situation – all the interests already vested in this type of warfare in Burma – all the people who thought that they were experts. He talked and gave me his ideas. I had been trying to learn and teach that type of warfare for the last two years. I had met many people from all the last few wars – Spain, Abyssinia, Palestine, Turkestan, Boer, Irish Rebellion, Dunster Force, China – and had tried to learn what I could. I had listened to Colonel Holland, Major-General Gubbins, General Chauvel, and most of the early Lochailort boys. But I realized that here was someone at least two stages ahead of anything that I had ever heard. He had developed his theories, put them into practice, further developed or redeveloped those theories again, and was still experimenting, theorizing and experimenting again.

He talked as we walked through the woods and the jungle. He wanted to see the countryside. We went down by station wagon with my lady stenographer. Every now and again he would lean back and dictate something about the countryside. I realized that I had been looking at it with unseeing eyes – yet compared with others I thought that I was rather good. We motored all the way down to General Slim's Headquarters, north of Prome. General Slim had recently been put in command of Burma Corps. There had been difficulty over concentrating the two divisions, owing, so it was said, to slowness by China, and certainly through difficulties of communications. General Slim wanted to start an offensive south to retake Rangoon as soon as his corps was concentrated. Unfortunately the Japs seized the initiative, and it became too late.

We had some difficulty getting by a rather poisonous staff officer. Then I introduced Brigadier Wingate to Lieut.-General Slim and left the room. They talked for a long time. I think that we refused lunch as we did not want to impose

85

ourselves on them. On the way back, Wingate told me that he had been most impressed by Slim: 'The best man, bar Wavell, east of Suez.'

We returned. Brigadier Wingate was put on the mat by the Chief of Staff for taking a lady into danger. He had a long discussion with Lieut.-Col. Stevenson, who had good ideas on raising Kachin levies. He put up a paper to the Commander-in-Chief, who was still General Hutton, on what he required – at least two battalions as far as I remember. General Hutton told him that he thought it was quite out of the question to obtain these from inside Burma – with which Wingate agreed – but that he would pass on his views to Delhi.

Chiang Kai-shek arrived in Maymyo to talk with General Alexander, who had now taken over as Commander-in-Chief. Wingate wanted to have a talk with him. So, through our mission, I arranged that he should fly on the same plane to Chungking. This was done.

He left me with a list of instructions and appointed me his deputy. Almost as soon as he had gone, the staff started to go against the arrangements which the Commander-in-Chief had agreed with Wingate. I protested, and was told it was none of my business. I wanted to see the Commander-in-Chief, and was asked by the G.S.O.1., 'Who are you, as a major, to see such an august personage?' So I said that I would put my views on paper, adding that I had been prevented from seeing the Commander-in-Chief in spite of Wingate's instructions, and that I would give him a copy of the letter to show to the Commander-in-Chief. Then he made that classic remark which has become a standing joke amongst us, 'You know, us regulars must stick together.'

When Wingate returned, he at once saw the Commander-in-Chief and got all his staff's decisions revoked.

Wingate told me that Chiang Kai-shek had been most interested, and had said that Wingate spoke like a man after his own heart and he would always give him his support. He also told me how delicately Madam had been sick into a paper bag. She did it so nicely and with such charm, it was like watching a beautiful gesture.

He told how they had heard that they were being chased by Jap fighters, and had sought refuge in very bumpy clouds near the mountains, and how the Generalissimo's and Madam's expressions had not altered the slightest at the knowledge of the new danger. He also noticed all sorts of little unimportant things during his short stay, things which only a poet would notice.

As the Japanese tide crept up Burma, there was no point in his remaining. He had arrived too late to do anything, in any case, and there were no troops available which had not already been committed, except my Bush Warfare School personnel and the few students. So, after a further good long journey around Burma, he left by air some time before Maymyo fell, having been recalled to study the problem from the other side. He spent days writing a paper on what he wanted to do, and what he required to do it with. This he submitted to Wavell. He then waited. He often spoke to me later of those weeks and months of waiting – to be available at a moment's notice – in Maidens Hotel, Delhi. Eventually he was summoned. Every branch questioned him, and asked for elucidation on various points. He was able to answer all of them. Finally he saw General Wavell, who had so long been his champion. Frankly he was given his charter, but regrets that the raw material from which he must fashion his weapon might not be of the best. Perhaps it was a good thing. Wingate some time later said to me, 'God often gives man peculiar instruments with which to pursue his will. David was armed only with a sling.'

This was about May or June 1942. I came out of Burma about that time with the remnants of the Bush Warfare School. I had been ordered by General Alexander to form a force from everyone available, to hold the Gokteik viaduct. Later we were required somewhere else, and soon became the Bush Warfare Battalion comprised of about five officers and seventeen other ranks of my own staff, and the remainder some very good and some very bad British officers and troops from convalescent camps, hospitals, offices, railways, signals, military police, detention barracks, etc.

With this merry throng we had quite a lot of quiet fun, and even fought the Japs a few times, and finally were about the last to leave. We arrived out sick and emaciated.

When Wingate heard that I was alive, he sent for me. I brought a very sick captain, George Dunlop, with me whom I had previous deposited in a completely unstaffed hospital

87

in Ranchi, and who, I found a day or two later, had never been touched. There was a dead airman in the ward when I arrived, and no one had been strong enough to help him die. Dunlop went straight to Delhi hospital.

Wingate told us that he had at last obtained orders to raise a Long Range Penetration Brigade. Would we join him in helping to train it for a return to Burma? We agreed immediately, and vouched for a proportion of the Bush Warfare School to assist. Seeing our condition, he then told us to go on leave and get well. I was nursed to health in Bangalore by my sister, whose husband had escaped from Singapore and was in a similar condition.

In August, I joined 77 Brigade at Patharia. The brigade itself was in the middle of the jungle under full monsoon conditions. Here, stripped to the waist, in the dripping rain, we would sit around an old eighth-century well, part of an old temple, and listen to Wingate explain the jungle lore, the art of jungle fighting and guerrilla fighting. Many were sceptical, none more so than the 3/2 Gurkhas, who thought that they knew what the answer was. They were to pay heavily for it later. I myself was sceptical of many of his points, such as the close-quarter use of machine guns to rake the jungle. How little we knew. I had tried out a few of his ideas on the way out, and they had worked well, so I was probably a greater believer than most.

There were one or two incidents at Patharia that I remember well. Once at Brigade H.Q., all the staff were sitting having tea, when a snake popped into the tent and disappeared under the floor matting. We all put our legs on the table, and continued tea. Wingate suddenly came in, and looked at us in astonishment. I said, 'There is a snake under the matting.' So he sat down, put his feet on the table, and during tea there were long discussions during which he gave us his views on what the story of Adam and Eve and the snake really meant.

Wingate used to keep some buffaloes at Brigade H.Q., and the Animal Transport Officer used to milk them. Wingate rarely drank any other form of milk. One day the buffaloes, one after another, got seedy and began to pine away. Wingate and the Animal Transport Officer immediately leapt to their succour. One died, and the other three were in a very poorly state. Wingate put blankets over them, and flitted them with his Flit gun. He got hold of the Medical Officer, who reluctantly gave them some injections of strychnine – with no effect. They only looked more disconsolate under their unwonted blankets. When Wingate, in desperation, started to give them some of our very small stock of mess Scotch whisky, Carol Cooper-Key and I panicked at the thought and finished the remainder.

In the meantime the local aborigine witch doctor arrived from the village – we were many miles from the nearest road – and started work. First he lit a fire. He then examined them, looking at their eyes, and at their dung. After the fire was hot he heated up some branding irons. He uncovered the buffalo and pushed the redhot iron between its legs. The buffalo leapt to her feet, and I don't blame her. He then branded her first on one flank and then the other, and then on the shoulder. Each time the buffalo leapt about three feet vertically in the air. Finally she gave a pained look at Wingate and started to graze. The same procedure was applied to the other two buffaloes. We never had any more trouble with them.

We never knew what disease they had, and no one spoke the aborigine's language, but we used to pull Wingate's leg about it, especially when anyone got sick. He did not mind.

The 13th King's with Scottie, Gilkes and others became his ardent disciples, with resultant knowledge far above the Gurkhas, who having some knowledge to start with, were far more conservative. He taught us about mules, and made us all, including the British troops and Gurkhas, like them, and made them our willing allies. He taught me how to enjoy riding. I had been so put off by the absurd and vindictive efforts of our riding instructors at the Royal Military Academy that, although I found that I could ride, I had disliked it intensely. Rides with Wingate were exciting, interesting and instructive journeys.

He tried out theories and discarded them. He liked people to tell him if they thought that he had taken the wrong turning in his training. He liked a true critical spirit amongst his officers. He preferred that to the hole-in-the-corner, non-co-operative methods of a certain number of the Gurkha officers. He did his best to get to know the Gurkha. He failed only because he did not have the full co-operation of the his officers whose insubordinate tendencies were continually recharged by certain senior officers in Delhi and the depots, who did their best to put a spoke in the wheel of 'this person who was trying to teach the Indian Army its job'.

Wingate liked his comforts. He liked his whisky, and many a time have some of us become very cheerful with him over a bottle of whisky or rum. But he knew that he liked a party, and so, on the whole, steeled himself to avoid such frivolities. He had not got an athlete's body. He had a weak body, in fact, but he hardened it as he hardened his will and his sympathies, since he felt that he had a mission, and had to prepare himself for it. He saw the Indian Army as a well-meaning, well-intentioned army without much vice in it, but trained basically the wrong way for the country in which they had to fight.

This was not entirely the Indian Army's fault at the time. The first priority had been to strengthen our Middle East forces, and there the best Indian divisions had first been sent. The North-West Frontier, with Russia allied to Germany, had to be prepared for a possible attack. Later, during the German rush to the Caucasus, it was wise to be prepared for a complete breakdown of Russia and to envisage the German threat reaching Samarkand and Tashkent. The next best Indian divisions were sent to Singapore and Burma. Therefore, by 1943, India itself had little left, and very great credit is due to the so-called Colonel Blimps in the depots and training centres of India who kept their faith in the Indian Army during its nadir and raised it eventually from a demoralized, unstable wreck in 1943 to its position at the end of 1944 and 1945, when it probably had the highest morale and offensive spirit of any army in the world.

But General Wingate felt at least in 1943 and 1944 that he could give the army in India an example of how to fight in tropical jungle country. General Stilwell felt very much the same. Wingate also kept himself hard, drove himself and his staff hard, because he knew that you have to be hard, both mentally and physically, to beat such an enemy in such a country.

Wingate has been accused of lack of sympathy. He had the real true sympathy and love for the British, Gurkha and all soldiers under his command. But he knew that true sympathy was not to stop and tend one dying man when by losing command of a battle a lot more would die. He knew that his first duty to his men would be to see that they were well trained beforehand. He knew that the assurance of victory is the greatest gift you can give a soldier. Those who accused him of not paying attention to the medical side, may be surprised to learn that we were the first brigade to have mepacrine in Burma, and that very many medical ideas which later were used throughout the Army were first tried out on Wingate's brigade and in some cases started by him. I do not suppose at that time any commander in Burma of his rank took more trouble and interest in the medical health and hygiene of his troops.

One cannot have it both ways. In one breath people accuse Wingate of not doing enough for his men; in another they say that we had equipment which they had not got. One reason for the latter was that Wingate had asked for and obtained it very often at a time when no one else wanted it. Take, for instance, all the barbed wire around White City: I have heard people say, 'Why could we not obtain all that wire? We never had any.' The answer is, 'It was all there. You never asked for it.'

I agree, however, that Wingate did have such confidence in his own ideas that he was always prepared in theory to sacrifice the individual for the benefit of the community. This Stalinesque conception was softened by his own natural sympathy and vivid imagination when it came to putting theory into practice. However, we who believed in him found strength in this theory and it helped us to persevere many a time, to hold on or continue the attack in spite of reports of many casualties. Due to this attitude we were nearly always the true victors by remaining in possession of the battlefield at the end of the day. This meant that we recovered our wounded, thus raising morale and laying the foundation for further victories.

This is all rather serious. Wingate had his lighter side. In fact there was always an impish humour about everything that he did. When travelling by air, he always considered that he was being done down and not being allowed to take enough luggage. He would therefore invariably place his foot under the weighing machine as his luggage was being weighed. The weighing machines in India used to be the old-fashioned type in those days. He would then glare at the weigher-in from under his topee, while sweat, due to the amount of clothes he had put on, poured down from his nose and chin. I used to laugh helplessly in a corner. My luggage was once overweight, and he gave me a long homily as to how to carry my luggage, finishing up with, 'It is all right as long as we are the only people to do it,' and a hint of a smile.

Just before the 1943 campaign Wingate and I and our batmen Bahadar Singh and Bachi Ram, two rogues that I brought out from Burma, were completing our form-filling procedure at Calcutta airfield, Dum Dum, before flying up to the neighbourhood of Manipur Road, to start the long march over the Chindwin. Some military potentates had come to say 'Goodbye'. I had seen that all the luggage and secret papers were safely packed in the plane; someone closed the door of the plane with a slam as the door was swinging on its hinges in the wind; Wingate was giving a farewell speech and suddenly the plane, driven by an Indian pilot, taxied fast to the end of the runway, and, in spite of a series of red Very pistol flares, took off and sped into the distance with all our luggage and secret papers and maps of the expedition. I was, of course, smothered in a volume of abuse as I dashed to the operations rooms where the R.A.F. eventually sent up a Hudson after our plane to bring it down or bring it back. Fortunately he made it return. Evidently the civil pilot, who had had a very large number of flying hours in a short time and who had had a night out in Calcutta, was a bundle of nerves, and also was in a hurry to get back to Calcutta for a date. When he heard the door slam, he thought that we were all in, and took off. I am afraid that I could not help laughing, which annoyed Wingate until I told him that it had reminded me of the story about Chaliapin, or some such singer, who was singing in *Lohengrin*. He was at the stage when he sings like mad and steps on to the swan and is wafted away offstage, in a fade-out. On this occasion, so I was told, still singing, he felt with his foot for the swan, and not finding it there, he turned to see it sailing off backstage. However, with perfect sang-froid, he stopped singing, looked at his watch, and turning to the conductor said in an audible whisper, 'Excuse, what time is the next swan?'

This story mollified Wingate and helped us through a ghastly trip on which the now completely broken wreck of a pilot landed on one airstrip downwind just as a Dakota was taking off in the opposite direction, and at our destination came in a so low over some bushes that when I inspected the plane I found one or two bushes entangled in the undercarriage. Some officers who had hoped to get a lift back to Calcutta decided to go by train when they saw the pilot's antics.

If I was summoned to Wingate's Headquarters at any time I would always come with my sleeping bag and gear weighing under 40 lb., all ready for travel, because a conversation at dinner or in conference would so often finish up with, 'We will go and see so-and-so straight away. When can you start?' It was pleasant to be able to say, 'Now.'

I remember another air journey with him during which I had been reading a book on Wellington, and found the following passage, which I read to him:

The Government was contemplating the dispatch of an expedition to Burma, with a view to taking Rangoon, and a question arose as to who would be the fittest general to be sent in command of the expedition. The Cabinet sent for the Duke of Wellington, and asked his advice. He instantly replied, 'Send Lord Combermere.'

'But we have always understood that your Grace thought Lord Combermere a fool.'

'So he is a fool, and a damned fool; but he can take Rangoon.'

This hugely delighted Orde, and he insisted that I should remind him of it, so that he could bring it out at a conference in Delhi. He delighted in pulling people's legs and pricking pomposity if he ever had the chance.

He had the worst luck before this particular campaign in being struck down with typhoid a few months beforehand. However, even that did not deter him, although there were those who hoped it would. His amazing will power, which he had consciously trained by abnegation and by setting himself tasks to do, overcame this illness, and it had hardly left him before he was chasing us again into a hard training exercise. I finished up in hospital after that with a bout of jaundice, so I missed his summing-up, but I am told that it electrified the audience of officers, many of whom had never seen him

93

before, and thought that what we had told them was exaggerated.

Now he was dead. We were still numb from the shock. We could not yet understand or appreciate the consequences. It was like going smoothly along in an aeroplane when the navigator comes in and says, 'The pilot has died of heart failure. There is no co-pilot and none of us knows what to do.' You may realize from this a little of what we felt. So much was locked away in him. He used to do something, in order to do something, in order to do something, and so on. He was an opportunist, and our operation was not meant to be an end in itself, but as a means to an end, as his 'Forecast of Events' already quoted shows. He was an artist at war.

Well, I will not go on. We will see what happened.

Some of his enemies did not leave him alone even after his death. There was a letter from the War Office proving that Wingate had only been a Major-General so long, and from that time they must take away the period that he had typhoid, which left an insufficient period for him to call himself a temporary Major-General, therefore it would be right to call him 'Brigadier', and his wife to get only a brigadier's pension. Auchinleck, I am glad to say, when I sent the letter to him, flung the thing back to the War Office with the appropriate remarks attached, as to what they could do with it.

PART TWO

CHAPTER ONE

THE SITUATION REVIEWED

Soon now, after our initial success, we were coming to a great change in our plan of operations. The enemy and outside events were at work deflecting us from our object. It is appropriate, therefore, at this juncture to review the situation as at April 3rd, 1944.

77 Indian Infantry Brigade

77 Brigade had cleared the railway from Kadu to Pinwe, and all the country east of that line to the Irrawaddy was clear of the enemy. Our airfield and stronghold at Broadway had withstood attack and proved itself.

A very strong block had been installed across the main road and rail communication to 18 Division facing General Stilwell, the only leakage being through the Bhamo-Myitkyina road.

Two Jap battalions of 18 Division, and two Railway Engineer Companies, had been decisively defeated, while much information had been gained from the sack of Mawlu.

'Morris Force', which was the name now given to the forces operating east of the Irrawaddy under the command of Lieut.-Col. (later Brigadier) Morris, who had been commanding 3/4 Gurkhas had cut the road south of Bhamo. The 3/4 Gurkhas were part of 111 Brigade which had landed at Chowringhee, the other side of the Irrawaddy, to join the remainder of Lentaigne's brigade, and so had been given orders to operate against the Bhamo road and join up with Lieut.-Col. Herring, commander Dah Force.

Lieut.-Col. Herring had crossed the Irrawaddy after landing at Broadway, and after one or two skirmishes, was temporarily on the run in the high Kachin hills, north-east of Bhamo, where it was friendly country and easy to hide.

I have purposely not discussed the operations of the other brigades of the force, as I am not well acquainted with the details, and the operations of 16 Brigade, particularly, have been admirably recounted by the brigade commander, Bernard Fergusson, in his classic *Wild Green Earth*. It is, however, obviously necessary to mention their effect on operations as otherwise it would appear that 77 Brigade operations were an isolated whole, whereas in fact we were carrying out part of an integrated plan in which all brigades took part. We were fortunate in having a possibly more colourful role, but I will try here to show how the operation of all the brigades married up and how we all helped each other.

Bernard Fergusson has recounted his epic march from Ledo, via Lonkin to Indaw, which he attacked on arrival. There are two points that I would like to stress. First, on his way, he passed through what always seemed to me a most captivating area, a part of the map which was completely white with the word 'Unsurveyed' written across it. He had to report his location daily, and he took the wonderful opportunity of reporting his location as '3 miles south of the second "U" in unsurveyed'.

I think that the real explanation of that blank white triangle on the map is that there is a divergence due to the curvature of the earth or the projection, or some such surveyor's wizardry, in the survey of India and the survey of Burma, with the result that the two maps produced do not fit together. So the cartographers, in their wisdom, left a blank area where any unwanted contour lines, rivers or ranges which appeared to have no future could be disposed of without rancour.

One of the things which always intrigued Orde was how the bold sure contour lines of Burma in the maps which were given to us lapsed into a vague wispy willow pattern on entering China.

To revert to 16 Brigade.

In his book Bernard blames himself for the failure of the attack on Indaw. I think that in this case General Wingate was really to blame, in that as soon as Bernard had arrived in the vicinity he hustled him into the attack. His troops had carried out one of the most epic marches in history, through

96

1. *Major-General Orde Wingate, with Lt.-Col. Gatey, U.S.A.A.F., awaiting reports of glider landings.*

2. *Broadway night, 6/7 March.* Left to right – *Col. Alison, U.S.A.A.F.; the author; John Borrow; Wingate; Lt.-Col. Walter Scott; Major Francis Stuart.*

3. *Major-General Orde Charles Wingate, D.S.O. and two bars.*

an appalling tangled, jumbled, pathless mass of inaccurately surveyed, high, jungle-covered slippery hills. Near the end they had put on a spurt when, after I had reported that owing to our supply of consolidation stores being dropped in the mountains instead of White City, we were in a precarious position until more supplies could be dropped, General Wingate, unknown to me, had signalled all Bernard's columns to come to my aid. This order was cancelled shortly after, but not before most of his columns had made a killing forced march in the direction of White City.

Bernard's columns had attacked Indaw. They had attacked as clutching fingers from all sides and not as a fist. One or two fingers got into trouble from ambush or lack of water, and the attack failed. This attack was redeemed by two features. First the 2nd Leicester Regiment under Lieut.-Col. Wilkinson advanced south on to Indaw with their right flank on Indaw Lake. They had nearly reached Indaw when they were attacked. The attack lasted, with ever-increasing numbers of the enemy, for three days during which the Japs were always trying to turn his flank. With accurate fire, and the textbook-like use of Cochran's Mustangs, Wilkinson inflicted very heavy casualties on the enemy, before he decided to make what was a masterly withdrawal. This battle helped us to a great extent in the block, as can be realized, for Wilkinson was engaging the enemy which might otherwise have been attacking us.

The second feature, and possibly more important in its results, was that one of Bernard's R.A.F. officers, either carrying out a reconnaissance or by chance, found a very large ammunition and stores area north of Indaw whose position he completely plotted. Later, in a light plane, he led a force of bombers to this huge arsenal, showing them the place himself, and left them to destroy it, which they returned again and again to do. In their interrogation after the war, the Japanese High Command stressed that this dump was the reserve ammunition for the division attacking Kohima, and its destruction had 'a very great effect on the fortunes of the battle of Kohima, a very great effect indeed'.

So the attack on Indaw had borne these two most fruitful results. Bernard had by now established a stronghold – called Aberdeen – at Mankhton, the permanent garrison being provided by the 6th Nigerian Rifles who had landed at Broadway, and had got into trouble north of Mohnyin. His brigade columns were returning by roster to Aberdeen for rest and refit while others forayed around the Jap communications spreading west from Indaw. Later 16 Brigade overran Indaw airfield but found it unsuitable for development.

14 British Infantry Brigade

It had been General Wingate's original intention to form six brigades so that there would always be two brigades operating, two just coming out and two just coming in, the maximum period of maximum efficiency on dried rations and hard living being judged as between two and three months. In this way two fit brigades would always be operating and there would be no close season. However, these theories seldom work out in practice in war, as the Navy and the R.A.F. know, and it is usual for any unit which is at all capable of fighting, especially during the turning-point battles of the war, to be thrown into the fray.

14 Brigade at first had an unlucky time. I am not certain whether they were put in before or after Wingate's death. As Wingate had said in his forecast, he had envisaged them being put in at Pakkoku in the Kabaw valley due south of Imphal. One of the great snags of airborne and air-supplied brigades of this nature is that they are almost too mobile, with the result that unless the commander keeps his eye very much on the ball, their plans are liable to be changed at very short notice at each twist of the general situation. 14 Brigade, as far as I can gather, were first put in to operate against the Jap line of communication from the railway to the Chindwin to assist our defeat of the Jap invasion of India. They had not been on that very long before they were switched again and then again. They marched and countermarched, and who can blame them if at the end they did not march as hard and with as great enthusiasm as when they had started. It is so easy to switch columns or brigades about on the map, but I suggest that a cardinal rule in this type of warfare is not to change one's mind in less than a fortnight at a time. Poor 14 Brigade, having marched all over the place with little chance to fight, were then criticized by the pundits who were against L.R.P. in this manner: 'Look at 14 Brigade. They hardly did any fighting.' Geoffrey Lockett,

who was part of our quadrumvirate in 3 Column in 1943 (Bobbie Thompson, Taffy Griffiths, Geoffrey Lockett and myself), was a column commander in that brigade, and he certainly fought, as will be related.

111 Indian Infantry Brigade

This brigade had been formed while 77 Brigade was operating in 1943, under command of Brigadier Lentaigne, who was later to succeed Wingate. Joe Lentaigne had commanded a battalion of Gurkhas in Burma in 1942, and had had a good deal of experience of the Jap and the country. He was a lantern-jawed (I think that is the correct phrase), long, lanky Irishman with a gleam in his eye, tempered by years of service, including a period as instructor at the Staff College where he had taught people how to do the 'right' things. He was enthusiastic, and had unorthodox ideas and was not ashamed of them. But if someone trotted out the catch phrases, 'Must not make detachments for the main battle' or other such Staff College clichés, although he knew that in our case we were trying to show a novel method of warfare where you get inside the enemy on his nodal point of communications and fight outwards, he could not help being influenced by orthodoxy in spite of himself. We always found our ideas so much better understood by the R.A.F and U.S.A.A.F., whose job it is to look 'over the other side of the hill' and destroy communications.

Lentaigne's brigade had been given an unenviable job, for which he blamed me originally, although only in a good-humoured way. While my brigade had had the plum job, he had been told to land at Chowringhee with his whole brigade, and then cross the Irrawaddy. This is a tremendous operation in itself as I well know, having crossed with only a column the year previously. The river is at least 1000 yards wide, with unpredictable sandbanks, and little cover on the banks. Even though boats were going to be landed on the sandy spits by glider, to start a campaign with an operation of this nature would be enough to put anyone off. However, Joe went ahead with it. After he had landed by glider (single tow after the experience of Broadway) and made his Dakota strip – without, I think, any accidents at all – he managed to get down one battalion before the Japs interfered. He then got one column and his Brigade H.Q. over the river before the Japs interfered again. His other two battalions were landed at Broadway, while he lost the three columns to Lieut.-Col. Morris who had been sent, as has been related, to reinforce the Kachin rising in the Bhamo area.

In spite of these initial great difficulties and disappointments his columns had ranged far and wide, ambushing enemy transport and raiding camps and dumps in the Wuntho area right over to the Pinlebu-Pinbon road, which we now know was one of the Jap routes of supply to the Kohima battle. They were operating on the more orthodox L.R.P. principles of raiding and harassing rather than holding. Again, by their depredations well south of the block, and especially one most successful ambush of a long convoy of enemy transport, they had delayed the main build-up against the block and depleted its strength. As I have said, I cannot myself do full justice to the operations of this brigade, but I would like to stress that we were all one, and all trying to do our duty in our separate roles.

23 British Infantry Brigade

This brigade was taken away from Special Force by Slim as it was the only formation at that time available in India trained to fight away from the roads, and was now required in the Kohima area. Here, operating on the left wing of an encircling movement, and being moderately visible to the staff, formations and troops of 14th Army, it gained deserved renown.

Bladet

This was an experimental raiding unit formed under command of my sergeant-major in 1943, now Major Blain. He had done very fine work in my column, and was a well-known character in the Commandos. Bladet had carried out some raids on the following lines:

A glider full of specially trained troops would land. They would then carry out a demolition or a raid. Then they would signal that they were ready, and erect the snatching gear. The next night the Dakota would return and snatch up the glider and take them safely home.

They were operating still further to the south of 111 Brigade, and brought off some very fine coups. They also specialized in flame-throwing, and were all parachutists. We met them again later.

General Stilwell's forces

General Stilwell's forces had ceased all offensive operations while they awaited the outcome of the battles around Kohima. If 4th Corps failed to hold the Japanese, the railhead at Dimapur would be taken, and Stilwell's only rail line of communication would be cut.

The Chinese forces on the Salween had been stationary for almost a year. They had learnt their lesson when they came to our assistance in Burma in 1942, where they had lost very much equipment and had had some of their best divisions decimated. They were not going to move until they were certain of some chance of success.

All this meant that the Japanese could afford to turn their attention onto the Chindits.

14th Army

The Japanese had attacked Imphal and Kohima and the intervening road communications with three divisions. These divisions had three lines of communications: through Kalewa and north, through Pinlebu and west, and through Banmauk and west. We had cut the two northern ones, but the battle was some distance away, and there was still plenty of sap left in the branch to be used up before the effect was felt at the extreme end.

Against these three divisions we mustered 17 Indian (Light) Division, 20 Indian Division, 23 Indian Division, 50 Parachute Brigade and part of 5 Indian Division which was arriving from Arakan. This force was reinforced, as soon as the L. of C. permitted, by 3 Commando Brigade and 7 Indian Division, also from Arakan, and a 2 British Division from Bombay, and with four more brigades (23 LRP, 268th, 35th, Lushai).

This was the great 'Invasion of India,' and it was the Japanese last throw in the hope that India would arise against the British. One Indian 'National' brigade, trained by the Japs, were in the forefront to start this revolt. It was, in actual fact, mainly a 'penetration' invasion and, unless some important town like Kohima or Imphal could be taken, the Japs could not press farther on as their communications were precarious.

While it lasted it caused a 'flap' both in India and in Great Britain, and was of course given first priority. However, led by stolid 2 Division, after a brilliant defence of the town by a scratch force of British and Indians, 14th Army broke the Japs at Kohima, and started a most magnificent campaign which ended, in the virtual conquest of Burma in 1944, a year before the planners had anticipated.

The Japs, in their conceit, had attacked with too few, and held on too long, as they had done twice in a small way at Broadway and White City. This conceit was justified then, as, until that time, except in the Pacific, the same number of Japs with the same determination had proved successful against us far too often, and the whole Jap Kohima operation does credit to the Japs' determination and courage if nothing else.

However, we at the time, in our parochial way, thought the Chindits had started the invasion of Burma, and decried all the attention the Press paid to Kohima. We wanted reinforcements to hold what we had taken and then we would go on and conquer more. That was how we felt. I had the honour to show my report containing these sentiments to General Slim shortly after we came out, and before his victorious advance. Being the great man he is, he said that he agreed with me up to a point and sympathized with our point of view, but from where we were, we could not see the whole picture. Personally I do not think that he was informed by his intelligence staff of the full nature of our successes, as I feel that his intelligence staff, for some reason best known to themselves, frankly did not believe us; they thought the whole thing too incredible to be true, and in any case they had previously predicted that it would be doomed to failure and therefore wrote it down as much as possible.

Bernard Fergusson had visited White City during this quiet period and it was good to see him again. I flew over to Aberdeen twice in anticipation of the conference, but twice it was postponed, bad thunderstorms in Assam having prevented General Lentaigne from attending. I had also flown over to visit Claude Rome at Broadway and found them all in great heart for their victory over the Jap. At Aberdeen I was received with old-world courtesy by Bernard who, as the Squire of the Manor, showed me around his territory and his headquarters. He had a difficult area to defend. The airstrip was a flat bit of paddy land between high hills ending abruptly in another hill. There was no chance for a plane to overshoot the mark: once the pilot had decided to land the plane, it had to land or hit the hill. No two-turn Charlies could operate here. In spite of this, only one plane had crashed, without casualties; and since it was being attacked by a Zero at the time, the pilot can hardly be blamed.

Aberdeen had not been installed for long, but had already been shot up a few times by Zeros, of which a number had been shot down. There were no special features which could be made into a stronghold, and Bernard was worried about the defence. Fortunately, White City turned out to be a sufficient magnet for the Japanese. Aberdeen never suffered ground attack. This was also due to the positive activities of patrols and columns which dominated the area around. White City, however, was the real insult to His Imperial Majesty, and fortunately they were to attack that.

Before the brigade commanders' conference which was now to be held at Aberdeen, I had sent Lieut.-Col. Skone with his battalion, less some heavy weapons and mules, to join Hugh Christie near Kadu and demonstrate around Mohnyin. I still had in my mind the idea of clearing up the railway north from White City. I did not like remaining passive and losing the initiative, so Skone and his thousand were prowling around Mohnyin as the conference started. I had anticipated that the West Africans would take over White City and that I could join Skone with the rest of the brigade and go north up the railway with all flags flying.

At last, on April 3rd, the Aberdeen Conference opened. Its object was, now that there was obviously a turning-point one way or another in our affairs, to test the opinion of all brigade commanders who had been operating in the field, and perhaps to evolve an agreed course of action which Joe Lentaigne could put up to General Slim.

Besides that, it was an excellent opportunity for him to hear our points of view and for us to 'get into his mind' – essential if a commander is efficiently to command formations below him from a distance and without frequent contact.

Those who attended the conference were: Major-General Lentaigne, G.O.C. Special Force; Brigadier Fergusson, Commander 16 Brigade; Brigadier Brodie, Commander 14 Brigade; Brigadier Gilmour, Commander 3 West African Brigade; Brigadier Calvert, Commander 77 Brigade; Lieut.-

Col. Fleming; and Sqn. Ldr. Thompson, representing all Air Forces concerned.

It was a memorable meeting for all of us. Bernard played the part of host with his usual consummate skill. We heard from Joe of the difficulties with which he had been faced first as Commander III Brigade, and then the problems of taking over command of Special Force with very little to guide him. Although General Wingate and he had always got along very well together, he had not been so much in his mind or confidence as the Chief of Staff Brigadier Tulloch or myself. Wingate liked to test his ideas on some hard metal he knew and would try them out on us, knowing that we would be prepared to disagree.

We sat in a beautifully clean Burmese house on the mats provided, a place where we were also to eat and sleep. General Lentaigne first gave us the situation on the Kohima front, of which we knew little or nothing. He then discussed various alternative plans in order to hear our views.

I was a very keen advocate of holding White City with a garrison brigade of West Africans, with at least another brigade in the vicinity, and driving north to meet Stilwell with the remainder of the force to open up the railway route before the rains started on May 15th. General Lentaigne told us about the very strong pressure brought to bear on him to move our force on to the Chindwin and thus cut the Japs off in the Imphal-Kohima area. This, no doubt, we could have done. I felt very reluctant to give up White City and Broadway so soon after they had been strongly installed with such loss. I pointed out that our object, as laid down at Quebec, was to help Stilwell to take Mogaung and Myitkyina in order to assist the hump airlift traffic to China.

Bernard, as far as I remember, wanted to have another crack at Indaw, and then fly a division to hold it. I think that I said that I would certainly wholeheartedly co-operate in this. General Lentaigne felt that, as the Indaw airfield was not all-weather, he saw little point in this, since the monsoon was due in six weeks' time. His staff were working out the airlift necessary to make either Broadway or Indaw all-weather in the monsoon by the use of pierced steel planking (P.S.P), but he thought that the number of planes required would be prohibitive.

I then suggested that perhaps my brigade could cut across the Irrawaddy and join with my forces (they were still under my command) with the Kachins, but I was told that that was out of the question.

Others spoke, but I regret to say that I mostly remember what I myself said or what General Lentaigne had said. That is usually the way. However, certainly for me, it was a most instructive airing of views, and getting 'into the picture'.

Joe had not come to lay down a plan. It was too early for that. He had come to find out the form and obtain suggestions; then with his own and General Slim's staffs, he would work out a plan to submit to General Slim. But I want to emphasize this strong pull towards the Chindwin in one way, while there was also the adamant insistence by General Stilwell that we must stick to the Quebec plan and concentrate on the capture of Mogaung and Myitkyina.

I was a bit elated by my brigade's successes and was possibly too optimistic in view of what was brewing up to the south of us.

After the discussion we were served with marvellous curry and rice, Burmese style, which to me, after weeks on K rations with only a little extra, was a memorable meal indeed. After dinner when the places had been removed we talked and drank rum, and I was continually amused by Peter Fleming's cryptic and acid summary of the situation. We lay back on our blankets and slept.

Next morning I, for one, wanted a slight recapitulation which General Lentaigne gave. We then departed. General Lentaigne came and dropped in at White City. Peter Fleming also came to stay with us for a while.

I sent a message to Claude Rome, stating that the West African Brigade was going to take over the block by degrees, that I was starting a limited offensive against Mohnyin under command of Huber Skone with 1,000 men, and that I myself, with the rest of the brigade, hoped to join him after the take-over. I warned him that Katha and Indaw were not now threatened by other brigades, and that a possible thrust on Broadway might develop from there. I asked him if Scottie's 81 Column could move secretly north-west and cut the communications north of Hopin to assist our pressure on Mohnyin.

Next day I heard that Hugh Christie's column had had a brush with an enemy company south of Kadu and had inflicted casualties, receiving three wounded themselves, including one officer. To the south on the 4th, my patrols made first contact near Sepein with the Japanese 24 Independent Mixed Brigade.

During the quiet period Bobbie Thompson had chosen a site for a Dakota strip in the paddy a few hundred yards west of the block. First a glider strip about 400 yards long was constructed. About eight gliders landed successfully that night with the bulldozers, jeeps and other equipment in them. Then just as the last glider was running down the strip to turn smartly into its place at the end as we had hoped to do at Broadway, a Dakota landed! It managed to stop within the 400 yards, and twenty Black Watch came out expecting to be in Aberdeen. The Dakota pilot had followed another plane, not realizing that there might be other traffic, and had landed on a lit runway thinking it was his destination. One of his wings which had scraped a glider was a bit torn, but otherwise the plane was perfectly serviceable. The pilot, a young chap called Harris, was very worried about what his squadron leader would say. We sent over a signal saying that he was safe. Then, after lengthening the runway a bit, and felling a lone tree, and mending the part of his wing with the R.A.M.C. elastoplast, and cutting off another bit, he took off next morning and got what was coming to him. It certainly showed the amazing versatility of that wonderful plane, the Dakota.

The American glider pilots went on a souvenir hunt, and were quite surprised when they were fired on by some Japs. They were a good lot, and it was pleasant seeing new faces around the fire of an evening.

That day my patrols to the south reported much troop movement, some of which they fired on. When Skone had gone north I had brought Shuttleworth, less his reconnaissance platoon, to augment the deflated White City garrison. David Monteith was now on his way back from the Irrawaddy to rejoin Shuttleworth's column, having handed over the Irrawaddy to the King's.

CHAPTER TWO

ATTACK ON WHITE CITY

Our embryonic plans discussed at the Aberdeen Conference were still-born. Ever since the taking of Mawlu and
the failure to take Indaw, the offensive tempo of the force
had slowed down. This was partially due to the convulsions
after Wingate's death, partially due to the repeated post-
ponements of the Aberdeen Conference owing to a period
of thunderstorms and floods in the Assam valley, and possibly
mainly due to our own pause for stock-taking and making
new plans.

After the failure by the 3rd Battalion, 114th Regiment, to
dislodge us, it became apparent to the Japanese High Command that they were faced with something far more formidable than they had first imagined. Incessant raids on their
communications to the Chindwin, coupled with the complete destruction of their reserve dump at Indaw, only made
them more certain that they must blast out this block once
and for all. They did not change their plans for the attack on
Imphal and Kohima which were already launched. But they
gathered together a force which they considered big enough
to destroy us.

They had long feared a seaborne attack in the south of
Burma, and stationed troops at Bassein and Moulmein in
anticipation. Now that we had shown our hand by our airborne invasion (we now had nearly 20,000 troops in their
guts), the enemy appreciated that this was our major stroke,
and that we could not do this and invade by sea. If we were
going to invade by sea, we would have to use our airborne
forces to assist. So the Japs felt that without calling upon
new formations they could risk removing a proportion of
their anti-sea-invasion forces to form a force to eradicate us.
They therefore formed the Také Force or 24 Independent Mixed Brigade consisting of two battalions from

Bassein, two from Moulmein and two from Siam, supported by a battery of 77 mm. guns, a battery of 105 mm. guns, heavy mortar and ancillary troops.

At our first patrol encounter we captured a 15th Army order of the day dated March 20th from General Mutaguchi: 'Enemy moving large forces by air to rear of 18 Division. We will use large counter-attack force. Duty Army Group troops to annihilate enemy. Attack by night and use surprise.'

Later the Burma Area Army Commander issued an order of the day, which was also captured, stating, after a certain amount of rigmarole, that they were going to blast us out of our positions by a mass of artillery.

Two new divisions were entering or had just entered Burma as reserves for the Indian invasion. These were 2 and 53 Jap Divisions. Eventually formations from these two divisions had also to be drawn upon to fight against us, and our presence also delayed their entering the Imphal battle.

The forces under my command as this threat grew were not all ideally situated, as I had sent 1,000 men to menace Mohnyin. According to my policy of not rushing some column in one direction and then recalling them before they had had time to do anything, I purposely left Skone where he was.

My forces not including those at Broadway were situated at that time as follows:

White City Garrison
   Detachment Brigade H.Q.
   1st Battalion, South Staffords.
   20 (Shuttleworth) Column Lancashire Fusiliers less Monteith's detachment.
   Lancashire Fusilier machine guns and mortars.
   Two platoons of 17 Column, 14 Brigade (who were passing by and which I had quickly whipped into the block).
   Mortars and machine guns of 36 (Shaw) Column, 3/6 Gurkhas.

Striking Force under Lieut.-Col. Skone nearing Kadu.
   Brigade H.Q. and Defence Company less detachment.

3/6 Gurkha less some machine guns and mortars.
50 (Christie) Column, Lancashire Fusiliers, less machine guns and mortars.

Floater Battalion near Auktaw temporarily under command
2 Leicesters (Lieut.-Col. Wilkinson).
Reconnaissance Platoon 20 Column (Bell) watching
Pinwe area.

Monteith's detachment at Ponhon.

A part of the risk I was taking was mitigated by the fact
that we were still getting the Japanese situation reports daily
over the phone, and I had proved by tests that they were
reliable. They had said that they were going to raid Musgrave Wood's light plane strip at 1100 hours on a certain
day, and they did so on time. Unfortunately Skone could not
get there in time to intercept them. Musgrave Wood was
safely hidden away and therefore the Japs found that the
cupboard was bare.

On the afternoon of the 4th, Ron Degg reported that one
of his patrols was in trouble at Spein. They deserved to be.
They had confidently walked across the open paddy to
Sepein, had been fired upon and pinned down. We took a
machine gun out in a jeep and, with covering fire from that
and a platoon, extricated them without loss. The enemy
showed himself to be raw; no 18 Division unit would have
allowed our men to get away with it. The patrol was lucky.
Also we found that this new enemy bivouacked in villages,
which all Japanese in Burma had learnt was a most unwise
thing to do – they were liable to be visited by the R.A.F. and
U.S.A.A.F. I sensed a new unit in Burma, and so it turned
out to be – a unit from Siam. Peter Fleming not only accompanied us on this outing, but was the main source of our
offensive spirit.

On April 5th our patrols reported Japanese transport between Indaw and Sepein, and stated that our mines had
damaged some of their vehicles. I requested aerial reconnaissance and strafing, but at this time Cochran's planes
were bogged down in a flood in their fair-weather strips in
Assam. Further reports indicated at least two battalions at
Sepein.

I wanted to land some guns that night. Peter Fleming asked if he might take a jeep with a mortar in it to Mawlu, and harass the Japs who were in range. He did so to great effect that evening. Also we heard on the telephone that the Japs were not going to attack our airstrip that night but were going to make an armed reconnaissance.

With some trepidation I put a platoon on each likely approach and told Assam that I could receive the planes. It was a risk with two Jap battalions so close at hand, but fortunately they were raw and now harassed by Fleming and his mortar. That night twenty-five Dakotas landed with six Bofors anti-aircraft guns, and four 25-pounders and their crews, and one company of the 6th Nigerian Rifles. Thanks to the excellent discipline and hard work of the crews and the Nigerians of the West African Brigade, all guns were hauled into the block and were being dug into position by the following morning.

At a time when most of the planes were on the ground, I heard firing quite close. The Gurkha subahdar in command of the platoon had allowed the inexperienced Jap patrol to walk within a few yards of them, and then shot and killed one officer and four men. The officer's pack had some explosive in it presumably meant for a plane. Identifications showed that these men were from 2 Division from Malaya. One even had an itinerary on a map with dates!

From diaries captured later we now know that the Japs had three battalions at Sepein, and the mortification expressed in their diaries at all these planes coming in low over their heads and landing made most amusing reading. They also showed that Peter Fleming's efforts with the mortar caused consternation and casualties. I had paced up and down all that night outside the block on the airstrip with my heart in my mouth. How I blessed the efficient gunners who could put their guns together from out of a Dakota so quickly and with such little bother and confusion. That was their first landing in Burma, and it was a very good start.

On hearing the firing, a responsible pilot asked me whether they were being attacked. All seemed confusion in the darkness with twenty-five planes unloading and stores strewn everywhere. I had to do the 'confident Commander' act, and said, 'Nonsense, that goes on every night. There is no need to worry.' I went away wondering what sort of rocket I would get from Joe Lentaigne if twenty-five of Air Vice-Marshal Williams's Dakotas were destroyed on the ground.

On the 6th, I asked the Leicesters to take action on the Indaw road, which they did to some effect, but it did not stop the build-up. I asked for bombing and strafing of the road, but our planes in Assam were still bogged down.

David Monteith arrived on the road near Pinwe, but was not very much in the picture. As he arrived, he heard a lorry, and with the quickness of action one would expect of him, he led his troops to shoot at, and grenade it, and killed all occupants without loss. This proved, from diaries, to be a Jap liaison group between Sepein and Indaw.

On the afternoon of the 6th, we saw a long column approaching us over the paddy from the west. After identification I put on my red hat and, with my mounted bodyguard, rode over to welcome it. It was the remainder of the 6th Nigerian Rifles who had landed at Aberdeen the previous night and had marched flat out to White City. I saluted them and welcomed them, and they took over the sector facing south.

I was debating whether I would cancel the next lift of Dakotas which were scheduled to land that night at White City. I had just told my Orders Group that I would cancel the Dakotas, when the first shell whistled over White City, causing us all to sit up.

The bombardment, which started with a few airburst ranging shots, soon settled down to a heavy pounding of the 1,000-by-800 yard block. We heard some very loud explosions which I thought at first must be one of our mortar-bomb dumps going up. It turned out that the Japs had a 6-inch mortar; it became the bane of our existence. Many of the shells skimming over the trees in low trajectory were probably from some A.A. guns that had been brought up. Later they were used against our dive-bombers. While the numerous folds in the ground gave much cover to all, except from that mortar, and the very deep digging and overhead cover gave adequate protection against everything except a direct hit on a loophole, those on the forward slopes facing south and on O.P. Hill took a heavy pasting. These positions had been occupied that day by the 6th Nigerian Rifles. It was their baptism of fire and a heavy one. Owing, as I said in my report, to their battalion commander's and officer's example of visiting each post during the shelling, and to the West Africans' innate warlike nature, they were not unduly shaken and gave a good account of themselves that night. The block was also bombed by Jap bombers using 250- to 500-lb bombs. Fortunately, in that crowded area, none of the bombs landed on any of our bunkers, although some of the craters played havoc with our wire defences. After the bombing we were machine-gunned rather feebly from the air. Our Bofors guns opened up and claimed at least two hits, but they had had little time to get themselves organized.

Our 25-pounders, which were not yet fully dug in, answered some of the fire, but it was difficult to calculate the position of the Jap batteries, even from the good observation from O.P. Hill. During the quiet period I had ordered that a very strong camouflage observation post should be erected on O.P. Hill. I ordered that camouflage nets which we had in our possession should be first put over the area before any of the bushes or lantana scrub be cut down. However, during the time I was away the Sapper officer thought that he knew better, and finally there was erected a monstrous sand-bag two-storey eyesore on top of O.P. Hill, the bottom storey below ground level. It was very strong as far as sandbagging allowed, and gave very good all-round observation, but its prominence made it an obvious place to shell, and two out of three of our gunner officers were killed there.

The shelling continued from 5 p.m. to 6 p.m. The Japs then gave us an hour at dusk to mend the wire and prepare for their attack, and have our hot tea and food. The shelling had included Mawlu, which, probably because of Peter's and others' jeep forays and the inexperience of their troops, they thought was occupied by us. The hour's grace included their attack on Mawlu. As night fell, with the usual wild cries the attack started. It came from the east on the sector held by Shuttleworth's Lancashire Fusiliers and on to the South Staffords at the northern end, and was also directed against O.P. Hill, held by Ian MacPherson.

Our first barrage of mortar shells must have caused very many casualties; then, on reaching the extensive wire, the attackers were lit up by our 2-inch mortar star shells, and mown down by Vickers machine guns, Bren guns, rifle fire and Mills grenades. Their rear files, in the meantime, were pumping their noisy but comparatively harmless grenades into the block. After an hour or two they had had enough and withdrew. Ian MacPherson asked for more grenades, which were sent up to him, and Shuttleworth and Degg said that all was well. One mortar was firing well away from its target, so, while everyone else stopped, we slowly got it firing in its proper place.

Francis Stuart and myself had been lying in the same dug-out keeping in touch with all sectors by telephone. At the same time our supply-dropping fires had been kept alight on the western ridge, and supply drop planes zoomed over us all night, adding to the noise, especially when some bad consignments of mortar shells free-dropped and exploded on hitting the ground. We later sent a stiff note to our rear headquarters in Assam about this. At about midnight the shelling started again and we all scuttled back into our holes. The Japs tried another attack, but with equal havoc to themselves, especially from our curtain of 3-inch mortar shells, of which we fired about 500 that night.

At dawn we surveyed the scene. Our casualties from the bombing, shelling and attack were two dead and six wounded. Light planes landed on our light plane strip, which was concealed from nearly all directions, on one side by the block and Pagoda Hill, and on the other side by the railway embankment. The faithful light plane force evacuated our wounded. We found very many Jap dead and dying on the wire and beyond. Several unexploded Bangalore torpedoes were picked up. These are usually manned by three suicide men stripped of all their clothing, who hurl themselves with the torpedoes on to the wire. This attack and its failure gave us confidence to withstand further attacks as long as no new factor appeared. During the day, enemy tanks were sighted in Mawlu, which made us improve our anti-tank defences. Identifications showed that we had been attacked by 1st and 2nd Battalion from 4th Independent Regiment.

The next night the bombardment started at about 5.30 and continued until dusk, when the Japanese put in an identical attack on O.P. Hill and the eastern sector. Later they also attacked from the north, and this attack continued until dawn. Major Shaw, who was commanding the floater company, was ordered to put in an attack in their rear, but was himself inextricably involved in a life-and-death struggle in that very place. We put in a strong counter-attack to relieve him. The West Africans took one prisoner in this attack, besides killing a number of Japs. Shaw's company was extricated, having done very well and inflicted on an inferior trained but much more numerous enemy many more casualties that it had received. Capt. Gordon, M.C., R.E., who was commanding the commando platoon, excelled himself in this action and repeatedly charged or repulsed enemy attacks. However, I decided that a floater company in such a maelstrom as this could not exist, and withdrew them into the block. The Leicesters were asked to step up their activities against the Jap communications, and they did carry out a few successful ambushes.

And so this long-drawn-out battle went on from April 6th to 11th, when I departed to make a counter-attack, and again on until April 17th. The sequence of attack was the same practically every night and only varied in intensity. The Jap would start shelling at about 5 p.m., continuing until dusk. He would then attack, just after last light, the east and south-east perimeter through the jungle. He would be met with a curtain of up to 500 mortar shells on his forming-up areas. What was left would then run into our booby traps and minefields, which were regularly re-erected each day. He would then meet our outer wire where he would be lit up by 2-inch mortar flares and greeted with the continuous fire of up to thirteen Vickers machine guns, coupled with a very large amount of small arms fire and grenades. He would pump discharger grenades into the block while his 6-inch mortar (the coal scuttle, as it was called) would also crump us. Having done his best, and all his 'suicide' Bangalore torpedo parties having been wiped out, fighting would die down. Sometimes he would make a further attempt at midnight. Then between about 2 and 4 a.m. the bombardment would open up again, during which he recovered many of his wounded and dead, and withdrew. At dawn, we would collect documents off the dead if they were not in too dangerous a position amongst our traps, re-erect our traps, evacuate our wounded, repair bunkers, sleep and direct the ever-willing Mustangs on to his positions. As we used to say, 'the forces of evil would operate in the dark, but at dawn, like the creatures of a nightmare, they would vanish away'.

114

It may be wondered why they never attacked or kept up their pressure by daylight. They did try to in the first few days by occupying that hill to the north of the block. Our Air Force and our mortars literally killed them all off. The Mustangs came again and again. Later, when our patrols visited the area, we found a pathetic message from the commander, never delivered, beseeching to be relieved from this position as he had only one-third of his company unwounded, and he expected the remainder to be destroyed soon by the incessant bombing and mortaring. He was never relieved, and only after he and most of his men died did the others leave without orders.

During the day the enemy remained quiescent and we could wander at will in the paddy and for about 300 to 400 yards into the jungle. Sometimes he would leave a very heavily camouflaged observer hidden in the bushes or amongst the leaves. A West African, who had wandered a little distance from where he had been washing in the stream suddenly tripped over a bunch of leaves, which got up and ran away, to the amazement of the African.

Tanks were tried on us one evening. Under cover of a very heavy bombardment of the 6-inch mortar, two tanks appeared, unfortunately not seen by our anti-tank gunners who were forward in a very strong position on the railway line.

Next evening these two tanks again attacked in daylight, supported by artillery and heavy mortar fire, but were driven off by our 2-pounders and .5-inch American m.m.gs. One hit was scored on the track of one of the tanks by our 2-pounders. Later at dusk it was towed away by the other. On another occasion they used their remaining tank at night to try and evacuate wounded, but it got bogged down in the darkness and only just got away by dawn. After that we heard no more of them. They were light tanks, and may possibly have been captured during 1942.

The bombardments were getting more intense, or so it appeared, each day. Often through sleeplessness or strain I would lie in my hole giving way to uncontrollable fits of shivering. The good Francis would often come in with a bottle of rum and talk and cheer me up. I hated lying in a hole being bombarded, as most people do. I used to prefer to get out every now and again. One night I went up to the Lancashire Fusilier front, telling everybody in a loud voice which I hoped that they recognized, that I was coming. I heard a lot of shouting and found that an excellent sergeant was playing a sort of 'Are you there, Moriarty?' game with the Japs. The Japs would shout out, 'You dirty hairy bastards' – at which one or two of our men would throw grenades. Then the sergeant or one of our men would shout, 'You bloody yellow bastards', or words to that effect, and there would be a shower of grenades back. I joined in for a while and then went away. Later, the sergeant who had been the life and soul of the defence in that sector was killed.

The 6-inch mortar or coal scuttle was what we hated more than anything; it was big enough to go through most of our overhead cover unless the position was dug deep into the hillside. It would often operate during the day. You would hear 'thump' in the distance, the conversation would gradually cease, then thirty-two seconds later, whirr, whirr, whirr and crash! and then the humming away of the metal as it flew through the air, and the conversation would start again. I was nearly caught when I was visiting Pagoda Hill and was passing the airstrip. I had not heard the thump, but suddenly heard the whirr and there was an almighty explosion near me. I got up unhurt except for a cricked neck. I like to think that it was the blast which cricked my neck, but I think that I threw myself on the ground at such speed that my head had not time to follow suit and got left behind.

One morning a groom greeted me with the news that one of our mares had foaled, and that both were doing well. She had foaled during a bombardment. The foal used to attend our morning conferences and became very tame, and a great mascot. Later the Lancashire Fusiliers got her flown out to their depot in England. Quite a number of our animals were killed, but they were pretty well dug in and sandbagged up, and the majority survived. The only real threat was the 6-inch mortar and bombing, as no field gun can do anything against strongly dug-in, covered-in positions, except make a lot of noise.

The Intelligence in India did not believe our story about the 6-inch mortar, so I sacrificed the sending out of two wounded men and put a dud projectile in the light plane, and it was then flown on out by Dakota. It was a fearsome-looking thing, about 5 feet 5 inches high and 6 inches in diameter. Fortunately it did not disintegrate well, so that its killing power was chancy, and large pieces hurtled through the air with sufficient force to cut down a 6-to 9-inch tree, but there were few of them. However, it was an ideal weapon in the jungle, and in hilly country, and far and away better than the rather useless field guns.

Our gunners did their best at counter-battery work, and, later, we found at least one wrecked gun, but whether this was done by artillery or bombing I do not know.

One evening, during a battle one of the A.A. gunners (many of whose guns, in order to obtain a good field of fire, were sited on the perimeter, and whose crews helped to man the western perimeter), thought that he was being attacked. He flung a four-second grenade. This hit the parapet and rolled back in the hole he shared with another young gunner. He promptly put his heavy pack on it and sat on it. It went off but he and his chum were unharmed. He later got the B.E.M. for his quick and courageous action.

Earlier I had wanted David Monteith and his party to rejoin his column in the block. I sent out a patrol under command of an officer to bring him in. Later that night the young officer came back very shaken and said that he could not get through. I said 'What are your casualties?' He said 'None.' So I sent him out again, and told him not to come back without Monteith. He brought him in. He later thanked me, and from then on never looked back. I had learnt that method from an old and experienced officer in 1940 in Norway. I had been doing some of the demolition seventy miles south of Aandalsnes, protected by a platoon of marines. Suddenly two lorry loads of Germans arrived. Some of the marines departed while I hurried on with the demolition. A very young subaltern of the marines, named Stroud, who had come to visit the platoon managed to keep the Germans at bay. I sent a message to my C.R.E. Lieut. Parker – a marvellous elfin-looking chap who carried a rifle to shoot down dive-bombers and was always having a crack at them while we took cover – saying that we could hold out no longer. After about two hours I got a message back: 'What are your casualties?' On finding that they were negligible I felt such a fool that we completed the task before withdrawing. I had learnt my lesson.

Supply dropping used to be carried out every night to replenish our stock of ammunition, especially for our most lethal weapons, the mortars and machine guns. Once I was told that our H.Q. in India were sending food instead of ammunition, stating that we must be out of stock. I sent back, 'We can live without food, but not without ammunition. Please send ammunition.' Actually during this time we did not eat our full rations and lived much on our own reserves.

Men do not eat much during continuous action and during periods of strain. Staff officers should remember this, and should cut down the food and increase the ammunition. One never needs maximum quantities of both at the same time. As soon as the action is finished and reaction sets in – that is the time for increased rations. It is absurd to have standard daily quantities of rations for troops in the line.

Reliefs of the eastern perimeter were arranged in succession, as our only danger appeared to be from fatigue. It was encouraging that platoons hated to leave their positions, having become proud of their defence of them.

On April 11th after five days and nights of attack, I received orders from General Lentaigne to form a counter-attack force outside the block, and to attack the enemy. I had not recalled Skone in view of my principle, from the point of view of morale, of letting an action develop before recalling a force. I had hoped that, with this independent command, Skone would have a chance of an action on his own, which was probably what he wanted, instead of having to listen always to me, twelve years his junior.

However, he could hear sound of battle plainly, twenty miles away, and thought that his first duty was with the brigade.

The striking force had left the block early on April 4th. They spent the first night at Mawhun and had advanced on the night of 5/6th a mile or two distant from their objective, when they heard the sound of the attack on White City. On the 7th Skone decided to return. On the way he ran into a small party of enemy, which he overcame. At the same time, as he had failed to place covering troops to block either flank of an indeterminate road that they were crossing in the dark, two Jap lorries ran into the centre of the column and caused some mules to stampede. The lorries were stopped and all occupants killed. About seventy of the Gurkhas had fled; many later reached White City where they told lurid tales about attack by tanks, and also the old, old story which every officer must have heard on every front since the world began: 'We are the only survivors.' I was not particularly worried by this, having heard the phrase so often before, especially during the retreat in 1942. Later I contacted Skone, and after hearing his story, agreed that he should come back to an area west of the block. Their few casualties were evacuated by light plane from Musgrave Wood's strip at Naman.

Francis Stuart flew over to liaison with them and to put them in the picture, and to arrange a rendezvous which was to be in the vicinity of Malu (not to be confused with Mawlu), a few miles west of the block. I heard later that one of the lorries had struck a mule, and that another mule, carrying the flame-thrower fuel, had been set alight and dashed down through the column, causing a certain amount of panic in the dark. Skone himself personally stopped the rout by standing with his arms outstretched in the path. This affray, although it had a successful sequel in the destruction of the lorries and occupants, did, for a while, play on the nerves of the columns, who remained jumpy for some days afterwards. Further, at the beginning of this period, Hugh Christie, who was with Skone, had sent back several sick men, the less sick escorting the more sick; he had not realized the new situation at White City. These men were not seen again; they were killed or taken prisoner.

So, on April 12th, after another night battle in the block, while Francis took Tactical Brigade H.Q. with Ian Macpherson and his men over the western paddy to the rendezvous, I flew out, reconnoitring the country for my attack en route, having handed over the block to Brigadier Gillmour, Commander West African Brigade. He was ably advised and assisted by (now) Lieut.-Col. Degg, Commanding South Staffords, who had been foundation member of the block, and who, with his late colonel, had done so much to evolve and perfect the defences and fireplan of White City.

I was thankful to get into an active role again. In more ways than one, White City was an unpleasant place to be in. Besides dead mules and the odd dead bullock which we had vainly tried to dispose of by various means, by now there were upwards of a thousand dead Japs in various stages of decomposition on our wire. We had tried flame-throwers. We had a lot of quicklime dropped to us, but we could never get rid of that sickly smell of flesh rotting in the hot sun, nor the sight of variously decomposing bodies. Flies were everywhere, and our water supply – our effort at well-digging having borne no fruit, or rather, water – was tainted by the corpse-ridden ground. Our own men had been buried in a graveyard consecrated by our padres.

My pilot told me as we flew, 'We can always find White City easily now. We navigate by smell.'

CHAPTER THREE

THE COUNTER-ATTACK

After their famous march and subsequent actions, 16 Brigade were due for relief, and were about to be flown out. One of their battalions, which had had the misfortune during the attack on Indaw to go waterless for two days, had been reorganized and reformed under Major Astell, who was now made lieutenant-colonel. He was the officer who had started the battle of Broadway. He was a pugnacious ball of fire, and was just what this battalion wanted. They were to fight their last action under my command before they were flown out.

After landing I met them and told them the position. I told them that I was very proud to have them under command, and that they were not going to cease being under my command until the Japanese in this area had been defeated. Then they could go home.

They were a good lot, these chaps, but they had been formed as a Divisional Reconnaissance regiment in tanks and armoured cars, and they had at first taken hardly to being used as infantry. On the whole they were Cornishmen, and they had grown enormous patriarchal red beards during their long trek. General Wingate had ordered that beards could be worn. On the first campaign I grew a black bushy thing, with a list to the left. This time I was cleanshaven. Beards very definitely have their uses. If a man feels that he is tough, and looks tough, he will very often act tough. One particular person whom I had never seen without a fearsome red Navy Cut beard was terrific in action. Later, when I saw him with his rather weak chin and weak mouth, all his self-confidence had gone. In my brigade I amended General Wingate's order and said that only aggressive beards would be worn. I followed the Navy's example; men had either to have a beard or not a beard. They could not be unshaven, or have a wispy thing floating about their faces. The result was that what beards we had we were proud to have. There were Van Dycks, Navy Cut, Spanish Conquistador, Capt. Kettles, Assyrian type, Henry VIII, Long John Silver, etc., and one or two Pard type, but there were no Moses, Abrahams, Isaacs, Greek Orthodox, Rasputin, Father Christmas and the oldest club-member types – these latter were sometimes cultivated by the Recce Battalion. One tended to feel all the weariness of the wandering Jew or the lost Tribe of Israel when seated amongst some of them, except that their beards tended to be red. They had some very fine Navy Cut type as well, but length appeared to be the criterion rather than aggressiveness. Still, as they showed later, 'There is many a good heart that beats sound beneath a shaggy beard.'

The first to welcome me were the 7th Nigerian Rifles commanded by Lieut.-Col. Peter Vaughan, ex-Worcester Regiment, ex-Irish Guardsman, ex-motor-car racer; Capt. Rogers actually met the plane on the ground.

Peter had tremendous pride in his Nigerians, and nursed them like a father. He was ably assisted by his second in command, Major Carfrae, who knew the language well. His company commanders were mostly men who were either born, or who had worked most of their lives, in Africa. His youthful platoon commanders had come out recently from England. Below that he had a mixed collection of British N.C.O.s. The patriarch of the battalion, aged at least fifty-six, was an old West African with more than thirty years' service to his credit, whom Peter had insisted on bringing as he reckoned his mere presence was worth at least a platoon, even if his pack had to be carried for him. He was a very old soldier and knew the fathers and grandfathers of half of the men. So if any of them did badly it would not end in the battalion, but the disapprobation would follow them for the rest of their lives and their descendants after them.

I assembled them all, and gave them a welcome and an outline of what the position was, and told them what we were going to do. In order to reach us in time for the battle, the 7th Nigerians had marched off from Aberdeen without their mortars and machine guns, and without some of their officers. These landed later on.

With the arrival that night of Lieut.-Col. Skone, I had quite a formidable force under command:

Tactical Brigade H.Q., with R.A.F. detachment, and with the complete defence company.

3rd/6th Gurkhas less some support weapons.

Reconnaissance Regiment, about 450 strong.

7th Nigerian Rifles, less support weapons.

50 (Christie) Column L.F., with their mortars and machine guns.

Artillery O.P. with wireless set.

The total was about 2,400 men.

I had appreciated that Sepein was a nodal point in the enemy's organization for his attack. Sepein was a roadhead and road junction. His anti-aircraft guns were in this area. It was visible from O.P. Hill so that, with the aid of our gunner officer and wireless set, we could be supported by fire from our own 25-pounders in the block.

I therefore decided to attack Sepein from the west, take it and hold it, and exploit further east from there later on. The Japs were also to the north-east of Sepein as far as Nathkok-yin, where their hospital was situated. By air I had reconnoitred Thayaung as a good base for an attack. It was the meeting-place of innumerable streams, most of which were dry, whose banks would give good cover from fire. There was a possible light plane strip at hand, and it could be approached under cover from observation. I could carry out no further reconnaissance as all ranks were tired, and I had orders to apply pressure as soon as possible. I decided therefore to attack next morning without further reconnaissance. 50 (Christie) Column seized Thayaung that evening, and the remainder of the brigade moved in. We surrounded the village so that no one could escape and give the show away. We also seized the villages of Sinkho and Ponhon during the night, killing – unfortunately, as he might have been of some use – the only Japanese in Ponhon; he was probably there for illicit purposes. We also seized a large quantity of rice and a convoy of bullock carts which had been collecting supplies for the Japs.

The plan I gave out that evening was:

   3rd/6th Gurkhas to attack and take Sepein at dawn.
   Artillery support from the White City could be obtained by the artillery Forward Observation Officer who would accompany them. He would make all necessary arrangements at once.

50 Column to cross railway at dawn and attack lorry park at junction of the road and Nathayan Chaung.

Reconnaissance Regiment to move forward between 50 Column and 3rd/6th Gurkhas maintaining touch and searching for the gun positions believed south of Sepein.

Nigerian Regiment in reserve at Thayaung. One company would relieve Reconnaissance Regiment at Ponhon as they moved forward.

Intercommunications would be radio-telegraphy to Brigade H.Q at Thayaung, and by galloper.

Medical evacuation would be from light plane strip at Thayaung.

I should explain that Sepein was the main headquarters, roadhead, and administrative area of the forces attacking White City. By destroying these I hoped to hamstring the enemy forces. My intention was first to capture Sepein, then establish it as our base for a further attack on the main enemy concentrations attacking the block. This gave little or no time for battalions to reconnoitre, but I thought that that was justifiable at the time as I was hoping to achieve surprise.

That night we again heard the usual noise of the attack on the block, with the familiar thump-crash of the 6-inch mortar. It all sounded very frightening from without. Bernard used to hear it from Aberdeen, and said that it sounded worse than the noise of Tobruk.

The Gurkhas' attack started well. Without a preliminary bombardment they overran some Jap positions, killing the Japs. Then 100 shells were rapidly put into Sepein and later I heard that Sepein village had been taken.

The Lancashire Fusiliers also reached their objective, only to find a well-camouflaged lorry park empty. One of the Reconnaissance Regiment's columns kept well alongside the Gurkhas and helped them on the flank. The other, which had started from Sinkho, lost itself and left a gap on the left of the Lancashire Fusiliers. I ordered a right wheel based on Sepein. The Gurkhas informed me that the Japanese main position was beyond Sepein in the lantana scrub. They were mortared. After a further bombardment of 100 rounds from our 25-pounders in the block, the Gurkhas attacked again but could make little headway against strongly dug-in Japs in thick lantana scrub. This is terrible stuff in which the defender can lie still in the scrub and wait till the unsuspecting attacker is very close to him before he shoots him. We later worked out a method of 'a creeping barrage' of grenades to clear such areas. Troops advanced crawling in line, throwing grenades to their front, to clear the area before their next advance.

The Reconnaissance column then attacked from the south. They made some headway but were also halted. The Mustangs I had called for now bombed the enemy positions. But unfortunately I had left myself no fresh troops, and those engaged were now tired and disheartened. When I had heard early in the day that our objective, Sepein, had been taken, I had sent my reserve of one column of the Nigerians to attack Mawlu. Under Lieut.-Col. Vaughan they advanced with vigour, killing many Japs on the western outskirts, taking them by surprise. They eventually captured the railway station and so dominated the area that they could evacuate their wounded along the railway line straight to White City. We now held the railway line from White City to point BM 457.

Wireless communication had been bad throughout, thus making the whole conduct of the battle lethargic. I should have brought out telephone line. Some of my gallopers had jibbed at delivering messages when there were some 'overs' coming past. Eventually I galloped around the whole front, except Mawlu, and learnt first-hand what the position was. I had sat stationary on my bottom too long. The Lancashire Fusiliers, in pressing on, had overrun a regimental artillery headquarters complete with telephone exchange and other equipment and caused some casualties. They picked up a most valuable diary which showed the whole artillery layout of Burma. This was sent back, but I believe it was stolen as souvenir by some aircrew, who did not realize its value.

After I had been around the front I saw that we could not hold our present rather extenuated line without the positive capture of Sepein. Three attacks on it had failed, and the troops were disheartened. I had no further cards up my sleeve. I made the decision to withdraw on to our base at Thayaung.

At 1530 hours, I gave orders to break contact in succession

from the right and withdraw to Ponhon and Thayaung, taking up our original positions, the withdrawal to start with Lancashire Fusiliers. They were counter-attacked strongly, but by next morning all the columns were complete at their rendezvous. After covering the withdrawal by mortaring the Japs, the Gurkhas withdrew safely by dusk, and the West Africans just after dusk.

Our casualties were sixteen killed, thirty-five wounded. We had counted fifty dead, mostly during the initial surprise in each phase of the attack. It had been an inconclusive and unsatisfactory attack. The administrative arrangements had worked very well; light planes bringing in ammunition and taking out wounded as they occurred. The reasons for the inclusiveness were due to mistakes, mostly of my own.

(a) I launched my reserve too soon.

(b) It is extremely difficult to choose a cut-and-dried objective in the jungle. I had chosen Sepein, hoping to make it my base for a further attack. The real strongpoint turned out to be just beyond Sepein. A reconnaissance during the night would have paid good dividends, but we had had little time.

(c) W/T intercommunication had worked excellently, but Brigade had not sufficient sets, and we were not well trained in its use. Line communication would have been invaluable. There was a pause of two hours during the day, when I might have put the Reconnaissance Regiment into the attack, combined with the Gurkhas. 25-pounders fire had been accurate but had little effect on troops well dug in. We were not experienced in making full use of them. We had at least applied some pressure and hoped that it might relieve the block. But after quite an intense bombing and strafing by six bombers and sixteen Zeros and another heavy bombardment, the Japs attacked the block again, hoping to take advantage of the weakness of the garrison.

I had found that the Gurkhas had lacked their usual fire, and that all except the Nigerians lacked energy and offensive spirit. I therefore decided on a new plan. I would leave Christie's column with the Royal Artillery F.O.O. in the Ponhon area to harass the guns and communications, while we would move south and block all road and tracks used by the Japs. I asked the Leicesters, who had been operationally placed under my command, to block the Auktaw route.

With a supply drop en route, the striking force, less Christie's column, moved to the line of the Tonlon Chaung just north of Tonlon. The road had been used by motor transport and the railway – not yet in use because of our demolitions – by marching troops. We blocked the valley with the 3rd/6th Gurkhas on the railway, the Reconnaissance Regiment on all tracks between the railway and road, and the Nigerians on the road as far as Nahpi where Capt. Bell still had his headquarters. He and his troops showed us over the area.

On the night 16/17th the Nigerians ambushed one lorry, others getting away owing to the disobedience of a Nigerian soldier who opened fire too soon. He was punished on the spot.

I felt that now I could squeeze the enemy by throttling his communications until he was weakened enough for us to beat him, or until he turned from White City and attacked us. In the meantime we could get some rest, and have time on this occasion for detailed reconnaissance of the enemy's position.

But the block had again been attacked heavily. On the morning of the 17th I received a message from Brigadier Gillmour that his garrison were getting very weary of constant attacks. The enemy had broken through the wire the previous night but had been ejected. Unless I could attack hard soon and remove the enemy, he could not guarantee to hold out.

At this appeal I decided to move north and attack the enemy from the rear, cost what it might. My own officers in the block told me later that they knew nothing of this signal, and that they thought that it was a bit exaggerated. Before I describe this attack, which was one of the hardest bits of fighting that we ever encountered, I will bring affairs in the block up to date.

Since we had left, the shelling had increased in volume and continued for periods in the day. The coal scuttle was especially active, and one unlucky shot landed on Paddy Ryan's dug-out, wounding him badly and necessitating his evacuation. Our gunners were doing their best in retaliation, but also suffered casualties.

The 12th Nigerians under Lieut.-Col. Pat Hughes had taken over O.P. Hill from Ian MacPherson whose fine defence of it had been a great factor in the resistance of White

City. Ian, with his boys, was now with me. The bombing which we had seen was quickly followed by an increase in shelling and a strong attack on O.P. Hill and the eastern sector. The Japanese at last penetrated the wire at O.P. Hill by means of Bangalore torpedoes, and, after a fierce fight, succeeded in holding a bridgehead. Next morning a company of the Nigerians counter-attacked strongly and not only drove them out, but pursued the remnants some distance down the other side, casualties on both sides being caused by booby traps. One Nigerian, who had seen a Jap face peer at him over his parapet, had seized by the rope handle a grenade box full of grenades, and had flattened the Jap's head into the ground. Next morning he attacked with the grenade box as his only weapon, laying about him with great effect. The Nigerians were elated with their charge, and many who had done deadly work with their machetes carried their enemy's heads as souvenirs to their dug-outs.

That was the position when I received the appeal, which I thought was a request to attack at all costs.

In my previous attack, I decided that I had dispersed my strength too widely, with the result that I had not sufficient thrust available to take advantage of initial gain. Also, although the administration and evacuation of casualties could not have worked better, the fact that I myself had been some distance from the battlefield had meant delay, during which the Japs had time to recover. So this time I decided that we would advance with the Reconnaissance Regiment as a strong heavy arrowhead which would go through, and overcome as much opposition as possible. As soon as the advance inevitably slowed up, I would swiftly swing the 3rd/6th Gurkhas on to one or the other flank in an enveloping movement. For this, Tactical Brigade H.Q., with the defence company under Ian MacPherson, would be just behind the Reconnaissance Regiment.

This defence company I used to call my 'Old Guard'. It was not composed of the throw-outs of the battalions, but a *corps d'élite* formed and trained under a first-class officer with wide active-service experience – young Ian. With the active support and encouragement of Lieut.-Col. Skone, without which this would not have been possible, MacPherson had fashioned a very fine unit with wonderful morale. His second in command was a young Indian Army officer

4. *Glider on single tow by D.C.3 Dakota over the 8,000 foot high Assam Hills.*

5. *Wingate, with his Chief-of-Staff, Brigadier Dereck Tulloch, D.S.O., M.C.*

6. *A glider from 1st Air Commando U.S.A.F., in the trees at Broadway arouses the curiosity of some water buffaloes.*

named Rooke, from the Sikhs. If I wanted something done very quickly, I had this wonderful weapon close at hand which I could put into the attack at a moment's notice. Mac-Pherson's defence of O.P. Hill and the initial charge at the installation of the block in which part of his company were involved under Freddie Shaw, had earned them the admiration of the brigade. I left Peter Vaughan to set an ambush on the road; his other column was to form a safe base where we could leave our heavy packs, blankets and sick. We all carried as much in the way of grenades and ammunition as we could, because I had said that we would not return until we had defeated the Japs. Peter Vaughan was disappointed at being left out, as he was anxious to show what he and his men could do.

And so, led by the pugnacious George Astell, the Reconnaissance Regiment, now in great form, ploughed through the jungle north into the enemy's vitals, closely followed by Brigade H.Q., and with the 3rd/6th Gurkhas in an unwonted position behind. I had mapped our route so that we were likely to bump into and overrun as many Japs as possible, with the final determination to squash the Japs against White City from south and east during their periodic attacks.

The first paragraph of my report of the operation of 77 Brigade to General Lentaigne which I wrote immediately after reaching India, and on which the whole account is based, reads:

In operations behind the enemy's lines morale, which means willingness to fight and attack the enemy, is of even greater importance than when operating in a more normal manner with fixed lines of communication. In this fighting the man is entirely dependent on the officer for his livelihood and safety and if he strays or gets left he has little chance of succour. It is therefore essential to enter operations with the highest morale and confidence in the leadership of immediate superiors. The following points were therefore stressed in training and in final talks with all ranks.

(i) Every officer and N.C.O. must account for every man of his command alive or dead.

(ii) If in doubt attack the enemy.

(iii) If any enemy is inadvertently seen no man will be wrong who shoots him.

(iv) We are only cautious and move warily as a tiger is cautious when he is stalking his prey. At other times we must be the king of the jungle and behave as such, never taking more precautions than are necessary.

(v) To gain much you must risk much.

Before we started I had ordered Hugh Christie to put in a harassing attack on Sepein and to try and scupper the Jap guns in that area. Evidently he did not receive this message until too late. He had had a few minor engagements with the Japs and, after one supply drop, had been very incensed to find a Jap reading his letters from home! That Jap and others around were killed.

Our objective was the Japs attacking the block. I hoped to advance and attack them in the rear and squeeze them against the block, not ceasing until they were destroyed or scattered. White City garrison would join in by a counter-attack from the block. The objective was the enemy wherever he should be.

My orders for the advance were given out at 9 a.m. on April 17th, and at 12 noon we had started. The excellent navigation and leadership of George Astell enabled us to move fast. We crossed the Nanthayan Chaung and a good track from Sepein to Nathkokyin, on which there were many recent tyre marks. At the Mawlu Chaung the Reconnaissance Regiment came upon a number of Japs washing and bathing. The British troops, who had been told not to fire unless it was necessary, immediately charged with their bayonets, inflicting heavy casualities. Farther back in the column I heard a commotion and was shortly afterwards astonished to see a stark naked Jap running gingerly through the jungle chased by a heavily bearded and accoutred Devonshire man trying to prod him with his bayonet. It was an astonishing sight and reminded me of the pictures of faun and satyr.

Soon after we moved on again, and then there was another halt when a few shots were fired. The Reconnaissance Regiment had encountered some wandering Japs who had run off leaving a few casualties. During the pause I was at a bend of the Mawlu Chaung, and decided to walk across the bend of the stream and see if I could find out what the commotion was about. As I reached the stream again I saw, about seventy yards away, a naked man with his back to me unconcernedly drying himself. He was probably an officer bathing apart from his men. I lay down and levelled my sights on to his back and took first pressure, and then put my rifle down again and went back to rejoin the column. I had felt squeamish about shooting a naked man in the back during his ablutions. I am glad I didn't.

We had one or two more little actions, all in our favour without loss, as we drove up amongst the Jap base area. We reached the next stream, the Nansiaung Chaung, by dusk and I closed in the long tail to bivouac quietly on the northern bank. We were now just over a mile south-east of the block and in an ideal position to attack the Japs in the rear if they attacked the block in the usual way. That night and the next morning we lit no fires, and it was one of the few periods when Brigade H.Q., at any rate, did not have warm tea night and morning.

We had had a very successful day, killing one hundred or more Japs without loss. The force was known as the Long Range Penetration Force, and we had certainly penetrated. But we were disappointed to hear only desultory firing in the direction of the block that night as this meant that there would be no attack, and that we were unlikely to catch the Japs on the rebound. However, we still heard the 'coal scuttle' making a nuisance of itself, and doling out death in the night.

My plan for the 18th was to move north to the Mawlu Chaung before first light, which would bring us to the area of the Jap forming-up place for his attack. There I hoped to surprise him at dawn. We could not make wireless contact that night, but I had arranged with Brigadier Gilmour that if we were attacking the Japs against the block, he would assist us with a counter-attack from the block itself. We did, however, make contact with our rear base in Assam, and I asked for the maximum amount of air effort at 1 p.m., a time which I calculated would be the crisis of the action.

In every action in offence, after initial successes, there is always a critical period when the commander hears bad news, and it is during this period that he must steel his heart and have the courage of his convictions. If, at that time, he can call on some extra strength which can influence the battle in his favour, he can very often break through that difficult period to final victory.

Next morning the Reconnaissance Regiment again went

ahead with élan and vigour. At dawn they surprised some Japs in bivouac, and went into them hard and successfully. They continued to attack until they reached strong opposition at the Mawlu Chaung. They had driven a great wedge right into the Japs' vital area. A party of Japs running up a wide path in threes were mown down by one of our machine guns. A little farther back I suddenly heard, on our left flank, the noise of a battery-charging engine. I sent Ian MacPherson straight at it and he overran and killed the Jap signallers while they still had the earphones on their ears.

The fighting ahead became more intense and casualties started to come back. I heard a mortar firing from nearby at them, and again Ian scuppered it. He found that it was a captured British 3-inch mortar.

I now put my enveloping plan into action. I ordered Colonel Skone to put in a company attack on the left flank. They made some progress but were soon stopped by heavy fire. A further company swung out on their flank, made some more progress but was again halted by strong Jap opposition situated in our old bugbear, lantana scrub. Since their march to the north, the Gurkhas had not been themselves, possibly owing to weariness and to my asking too much of them. This day again they were not at the top of their form. The Reconnaissance Regiment were still pushing slowly ahead against stiff opposition and had now managed to get a bridgehead across the Mawlu Chaung, which here was quite a formidable obstacle, not wide, but with twenty to thirty foot banks. We now had about 2,000 or 3,000 Japs pressed between us and White City half a mile distant. There was little that they could do but fight where they stood.

I paid a visit to the near side of the chaung. Our casualties were now becoming heavy but the men were still cheerful. I talked to a machine-gunner on the edge of the chaung; he said he had rarely had such good shooting as that day, and as he spoke he opened up on some Japs who came running across an open stretch 100 yards away, and brought a few down.

With the aid of a compass I got the direction of the main enemy position and let Colonel Skone know so that he could bring his mortars to bear, which he did. The danger always was of hitting our own troops in the tangled fighting in the jungle, and the Reconnaissance Regiment think that one shot of ours did land amongst them.

There was a delay in our advance owing to the difficulty of carrying our casualties. I had made the cardinal error of not seeing that sufficient stretchers and stretcher-bearers were available. Two platoons of Nigerians would have made all the difference. We had been stationary far too long, and were losing the initiative. We now had about fifteen killed and thirty wounded. Brigade H.Q. was close behind the Reconnaissance Regiment with the Gurkhas behind and to the left flank.

Fighting was becoming intense and we had at least twenty stretcher cases. While stretchers for them were being made out of bamboo and groundsheets I ordered a flank attack on our right flank by the remaining company of Gurkhas. Skone demurred as it was our last reserve, but I told him to withdraw into reserve his left-most company at the same time. Ian MacPherson had already been out on the right flank and come back to tell me that he had scuppered another lot of Japs and that he reckoned he had shot seven himself. It was his big day.

All of one Reconnaissance column was now across the chaung fighting hard and our 3-inch mortars were well in action. We held on our left, and now the Gurkhas were having quite a lot of success on our right, driving the Japs back on to the chaung. It was nearly 1 p.m., and the Mustangs were due.

We could hear, close at hand, the counter-attack by the Nigerians from the block. Brigade H.Q. was in an exposed position in flat jungle, but my signal officer, Capt. Park, had erected his set within fifty yards of the nearest Jap, and we were in touch with White City.

Suddenly the Japs, who had been infiltrating towards us, counter-attacked strongly. The Gurkhas on the right flank were caught in heavy enfilade machine-gun fire and started to run back for cover. This made some others start to run, including some of the Chinese protecting Brigade H.Q., but this near panic was soon stopped by the officers. The Japs then brought most heavy and continuous machine-gun fire on to Brigade H.Q. and the regimental aid post. We lay there flattened to the ground while three machines guns raked the jungle a foot above our heads. I saw the wireless mules studded with bullet holes, little jets of blood in a line, and watched them slowly collapse and die. The nearest machine gun was not more than fifty yards away in thick jungle. I think that it was the most unpleasant period that I have experienced in war. One of the signallers beside me, facing the other way, was shot by a ricochet up the rectum, the bullet entering his guts. He died almost immediately. It had been difficult to find where he was wounded. Major R. E. Strong, R.E., the operational research officer, was lying alongside me. He turned to me calmly and said, 'You know that was a three-minute burst of fire. We have no records of anything as long as that. I wonder what sort of belt they are using.' His devotion to his job helped bring me to my senses. All I had been thinking about was the lack of future.

We then heard the welcome sound of very many Mustangs. Cochran had really shoved out the boat for us. I rolled over to Mungo Park, and found that he was lying with the earphones on talking to White City. He told me that he felt safer with the earphones on, as then he could not hear the machine guns. These, fortunately, had slackened off a bit. I talked to White City, telling them that we were in a jam, and that we wanted maximum air support in an area where we would shortly put down white smoke. I asked that the Mustangs should use everything they had got, but that they must be accurate with the bombs as we were very close to the Japs. I also asked that the strafing should be as vertical as possible on to that spot, and not a general spraying of the jungle. Mungo Park later told me that I spoke very loudly and that each time I spoke the Japs fired in the direction of my voice. Fortunately they were firing two to three feet above the ground while we were pressed as close to the ground as possible. I think there is always a tendency to fire high in the jungle.

I then got up and doubled back to stolid Skone to tell him to put down the mortar smoke. We had the exact Jap positions pretty well taped by now, corrections to our fire being given by the Reconnaissance Regiment who were very intimately concerned that the fire should be correct. As I ran, some of the Gurkhas and Chinese of Brigade H.Q. started to run, and I had to shout to them to stop, and then walk myself the rest of the way. The eyes of the troops are always on the commander. Fortunately L/Cpl. Young, who was always with me, could abuse them in a particularly venomous way which made them pause in their tracks. They were all pretty raw, and this must have been an alarming experience for them.

Down went the smoke. Down went the Mustangs. The whole earth quaked under our stomachs as we shut our ears to the roar of the bombs. They landed plumb right. The Reconnaissance Regiment was jubilant, and later stated that the nearest 500-pounder was within fifty yards of them, and on the Japs. After that came the strafing, which again was accurate, but unpleasantly close. We later learnt that the Japs were just forming up for a charge after their preliminary machine-gun fire, and the bombs in that flat jungle killed very many indeed.

I consulted with Skone and Astell. We had now over forty stretcher cases, apart from sixty or more walking wounded. We debated as to whether we could go on to White City, now only half a mile distant but through unknown opposition, or return the seven miles to Peter Vaughan's.

At that moment the Reconnaissance reported that the Japs were still able to machine-gun accurately down the chaung separating the two columns.

It would mean a further attack to deal with these if we were to go on. I made the decision to retire. This decision was probably influenced by my own harrowing experience. Astell shouted to the column the other side of the chaung, asking which way they preferred to go. They preferred to find their own way back rather than recross that chaung where so many had died.

I left Skone to form a rearguard. The order of march would be the same as before. As we were leaving I asked Francis, 'Where is Ian?' He said, 'He is dead.' I said, 'He can't be.' He said, 'I saw him shot through the forehead.' I said that I was going back to see. I could not leave anyone like that without knowing for certain. I started to go back into the fight. Quite a lot of fire was still taking place. As I went into the jungle alone I must have had a crazy look about me, for Francis rushed up and told me I must not go on, my duty was with my brigade. I said, 'I don't believe Ian is dead.' Francis heaved out his revolver, stuck it in my stomach and said, 'I'll shoot you if you don't go back. I was with him when he was killed.' With a heavy heart I retraced my steps.

Ian had had a wonderful day to end his career. He, with his company, must have accounted for forty to fifty Japs that day.

He was a slim, fey, quiet, almost lonely chap, who lived for his Gurkhas and for soldiering. He would have been well decorated in 1942 if all his company officers had not been killed. His company commander told me that Ian was his best officer; Ian had scuppered a Jap machine gun by himself running across open paddy to do it. Later in 1942, Ian, cut off as all our particular force was, chose to return through the Jap H.Q. near Shwegyn, causing havoc as he did so. His N.C.O.s and men loved him, and his subahdar was desolate for days after. One of the bravest and most carefree soldiers I had ever met had been killed, but he must have taken at least a dozen Japs with him.

The way back was far from easy going. Everyone was a bit shaken. Having probably the best experience of navigation in the jungle, I decided to lead. We slowly retraced our steps to the previous night's bivouac, which was our near rendezvous if anyone got lost. We had to move slowly to protect the stretcher-bearers. We picked up one or two men there, and rested for a while to allow the column to close up. It was with the greatest regret and entirely against my principles that we had left some wounded behind in the chaung, but attempts to succour them had resulted in further casualties. As Francis and I were leaving the battle, a sergeant came staggering out from near the chaung with a wounded man over his shoulder. He was the last man out, and it was a fine effort.

I led the way slowly back, but however slowly I went, gaps could not help appearing as behind us; escorted and carried by the Reconnaissance Regiment, were the forty or more stretcher cases, and sixty or more other wounded. At one place where we had to cross the open, near Nathkokyin, I gingerly crossed alone and found that we had come straight up to well-concealed, recently evacuated Jap positions. A mess tin of tea was still warm. Whilst our morale was low at this retreat, the Japs' had also broken.

I sent a party on ahead after we had crossed the Nanthayan Chaung. When I came in at dark I was greeted by a jubilant Peter Vaughan. The night before they had ambushed six lorries, killing over forty Japs, and had taken three prisoners. Hubert Skone came in much later in the night, bringing in the rearguard.

Vaughan's arrangements for our reception were excellent.

Guides led units through the dark to the bivouac areas he had chosen, nearly every man and all wounded receiving a mug of hot tea. Preparations had been made for the wounded, and before I came in Peter had sent out two platoons to relieve the stretcher-bearers.

By midnight we were nearly all in. A few stragglers who had missed their way in the dark came in next morning.

The Nigerians had made a light plane strip, a rather difficult one due to the smallness of the area, and evacuation of the seriously wounded started at dawn. We counted our casualties, and they were heavy.

Four British officers and sixty to seventy British and Gurkha other ranks had been killed. We had twenty missing although some turned up later and some were recovered wounded by patrols from the block. We had suffered about 150 wounded.

The Japs had lost very heavily, and that final bombing had been the last straw. They had also retreated from the field of battle. Patrols from White City who brought back some of our own and the enemy's wounded, reported very heavy Jap casualties. The Japs never attacked the block again. We had accomplished our task.

There was at least one amusing incident amongst all this carnage. Before the machine-gunning and when Ian was away to the right flank I saw some Japs talking at the end of a pathway. I seized on the nearest officer, which happened to be Capt. Rogers, who looked, and was, very young (he been lent me as a liaison officer from the Nigerians), and told him to take a platoon of Gurkhas and write off those Japs. He said, 'But, sir.' I said, 'Hurry, man, or you will miss them.' He said, 'But sir!' I stared at him and said, 'Get a move on! Don't stand arguing!' I thought that he might be frightened. He went off and did quite a good job. Later he asked me if he could go back to Spitfires. I then found out that he was a South African Air Force captain! However, he did a good job, and if they will wear the pips of an army captain they must expect things like that. Later, after we came out, he went back to Spitfires.

I heard a very good description of the Nigerian ambush by Charles Carfrae's column. As already related, the previous night they had only managed to get one truck, as a man had fired before he was ordered to do so.

This time they were all in their concealed positions along the road, every sort of weapon ready to do its duty – machine guns, rifles, Brens, discharger cups, grenades, Piats, flame-throwers – when they heard the noise of lorries coming nearer. Slowly the lorries chugged along, stopping every now and then, while the Nigerians, tense, watched and waited, every man's finger on the trigger. Then the first lorry came into view with shaded lights. It came up slowly to the stream and halted. It was close enough, but there were more behind. An officer got out and felt the ground for mines, and then waved the lorry on a little, and so on while 300 pairs of white eyeballs in black faces twitched at his every movement. Their fingers tingled on the trigger, but so did their backs at the thought of what the man who had fired too soon had received. Slowly the lorries came on as the officer proved the way, until the leading lorry was nearly past them, and five other silhouettes, each with its load of sleeping soldiers, were close behind. Up went the Verey light. Crash! as about 5,000 rounds of ammunition coupled with grenades, Piat bombs, and flame-throwers roared into the six vehicles. The Nigerians then charged into the flaming lorries, a few figures escaping into the jungle. These twelve Japs, so ingrained was the training taught to them at their training depot that 'When in doubt, dig', dug in pointlessly close by the road. Next morning they were rounded up and killed with, I think, only one Nigerian casualty.

We had not yet realized that the Japs were broken, and the sight of this ambush was a most welcome and cheering one.

The above account of our action gives, I am afraid, a very parochial viewpoint of what went on round about where I myself was. The Reconnaissance Regiment had borne the brunt of the attack with vigour and steadfastness which earned them very high praise. The Gurkhas suffered many casualties. Ian MacPherson's company, under his leadership, had been superb. While I went visiting during the battle, Francis Stuart, in his quiet unobtrusive way, kept the whole of Brigade H.Q. functioning as it should, and maintained unbroken the thread of authority which bound the separate operations of the force into an integrated whole. His calm quiet voice was invaluable in such a situation. I also remember that once when I saw Hubert Skone he indignantly remarked that, 'They have been grenading me quite hard. One landed just by my foot there, but didn't do any harm.' I was glad to be able to leave the rearguard with its possible troubles of disengagement in his confident hands while I led the column out of the maze on a different route to that which we had entered.

The final Jap attack on the block had been a very heavy one and had continued in broad daylight, resulting in a heavy enemy casualty list estimated at 300 to 400 dead on the wire. The colonel commanding the 24 Independent Mixed Brigade, after furious exhortation from his Army Headquarters to break the block, had himself led his troops in this final effort, and was found amongst their dead. The Japanese morale after that, coupled with the effect of our counter-attack, wilted right away, and they started to straggle back.

I kept Charles Carfrae's column blocking the road with Peter Vaughan supporting it, while the rest of us returned to safe harbour near Capt. Bell's hideout in the re-entrant near Nahpi. We had evacuated most of our wounded, thanks to the industrious efforts of the light plane pilots, who continued until that strip began to be sniped at by stray Japs. We then constructed a most difficult strip at Nahpi – difficult because there was no alternative – and later one plane, an L1, made a most marvellous landing on this quite steeply sloping strip and took out more casualties, the pilot returning until all our wounded were evacuated to Broadway.

The Nigerians soon reported many encounters with Japs trying to infiltrate past their road block on the Tonlon Chaung. One of Bell's rifle patrols counted a woebegone party of 400 straggling south close to the railway line. When the havildar and six men fired on them, most of them fled, dropping bicycles, kit and even arms behind them. Demoralization was complete.

The Reconnaisance Regiment had finished their campaign with a fine action, and were now proudly on their way to Broadway for evacuation to India. The Gurkhas were well-nigh tired out. The Nigerians kept up active patrolling and harassed the retreating Japs. The Japs then mounted machine guns along the path, and tried to cover their retreat. We retaliated by booby-trapping road blocks, and extensive booby-trapping of all paths and crossing-places of the Tonlon Chaung. We had previously laid quite extensive minefields along the chaung on all possible diversions off the already well-mined road.

Peter Vaughan finally asked me to withdraw his men who had had little rest, being awake at nights in ambush and patrolling by day. This I did.

I sent a company of Gurkhas to harass the Japs in the re-entrant just east of Pinwe where some of them seemed to be gathering. The company started the previous night, bivouacked, and were fortunate enough to have a Jap column stumble on to them, as they stood to in the morning. The Gurkhas caused quite a number of casualties, but, in their overwrought state, many of them disappeared up the hill-side, to come down later. I do not mind recounting their slight failures, as it shows our condition and it also enhances the greatness of the deeds that they were to do later.

So here we were, realizing that the remnants of a demoralized and defeated enemy were retreating past us, but too weak to turn their defeat into rout. The two Leicester columns of 14th Brigade were placed under my command. There had been some muddle over this, owing to wireless difficulties, and the fact that we had not the same cyphers. Rear Brigade was in the process of moving from Imphal to Sylhet, as was envisaged by General Wingate, as the threat to Imphal increased, and it was necessary to remove all who were not potential Jap killers, the garrison being now on air supply. We were just in the 'skip distance' (the gap between the range of the ground wave and that of the sky wave) of our wireless sets to White City, which had a high-powered transmitter, and Force H.Q. knew little of what was going on. In fact, because I had sent all our situation reports to White City for onward transmission, and because White City thought that Force H.Q. had received them direct, Force H.Q. never knew of the results of the counter-attack till later.

However, I managed to get Geoffrey Lockett's column directed on to Pinwe, and he came along with tremendous speed and vigour. Just when he was closing for an attack on Pinwe, which at that time was the Jap rallying point and lorry head, he received orders that he was no longer under my command and was to go elsewhere. In his anger at missing an action, he loosed off all his mortar shells into Pinwe before departing, fortunately causing quite a lot of casualties and confusion amongst some Jap lorries.

Peter Vaughan himself took out an ambush party on the Sepein road, but waited all night, and caught nothing. We could not get any air support at this time, and we were short of food. Booby-trapping of the track by the commando platoons was our most lucrative pastime until the Japs' machine guns kept them off. The Burma Rifle scouts calculated that between 1,500 to 2,000 Japs had withdrawn. We never caught any guns, but we thought that they had pulled up into the Nathkokyin re-entrant and were hidden there with a force guarding them. At this time we could not get air support, probably because of a change of airfields.

The Japs must also have been hungry, for during our nightly supply drops, some of which went wild in the difficult area amongst the hills in which we had chosen to bivouac, the Japs joined in and started to steal some of our food. The situation then was that there were two forces each about 1,500 men strong within half a mile of each other but each too hot, hungry and tired to fight. We were now less than they were, as the Reconnaissance Regiment had departed for home.

We had shot our last bolt. I was tired, sick and irritable. I regret to say that I sent a message to General Lentaigne saying as he had taken away the Leicesters from under my command, at the crucial juncture when we might have turned defeat into rout, I could not hold myself responsible for failing to complete the destruction of the Japs. I did not realize that, because of the wireless difficulties and mistakes, he was not fully in the picture, nor did I know till a long time later that his headquarters and the whole base organization was in the throes of a move. Communications with India remained bad for some time due to this move, and, as it says in the Bible, 'Evil communications corrupt good manners.' On April 25th, after blocking or harassing the road behind the Japs for nine days, with weary hearts and aching limbs, we wended our way slowly up the 3,000-foot hills to the cool and safety of the Kachin village of the Gangaw range.

With the West African Brigade we had already blocked all communication to 18th Division from March 16th to April 26th.

CHAPTER FOUR

THE CHANGE IN PLAN

During this attack by eight battalions of the Japanese, supported by air and artillery, all Special Force's energies had been rallied to defeat them.

The Japs, having hurled themselves again and again at the machine guns and mortars of White City for fourteen days and having finally been attacked in the rear, had retreated from the field of battle, and White City was no longer menaced. This had been due to the combined efforts of battalions from nearly all the brigades, and to the tremendous support given by the Air Force.

But the monsoon was now imminent. Broadway had been judged by the experts to become unusable in the monsoon owing to its low-lying situation. The air effort required to make it weather proof with the aid of pierced steel planking was more than South-East Asia Command could afford, now that their hands were still full combating the Japanese siege of Imphal. Aberdeen, whose field was on paddy, would become inoperative after the first rains. Indaw airfield was only fair-weather, and therefore not now worth capturing. General Stilwell's advance had been held up while his communications were threatened. Now that the threat had decreased, he was on the move again. Our stranglehold on the communications of the Japanese 18th Division facing him had not had its full effect because they, not having to fight, could to a great extent live off the country and so not draw much on their reserve supplies. The importance that they attached to our stranglehold may be judged by the ground and air effort that they made to break it. We had also, by destroying two of their battalions, helped to weaken the division. The only leakage now was via Bhamo to Myitkyina where the Morris Force was reducing, if not stopping, the flow of supplies.

One school of thought in S.E.A.C. still wanted us to move

out to the Chindwin and complete the destruction of the Japs on the Chindwin front. Slim, who had developed a jealous dislike of Wingate, never understood the Chindit's role and method of operations, also now wanted the Chindit to help him out of his difficulties at Imphal and Kohima.

However, General Stilwell had at Quebec been promised our help in getting him forward, and was adamant that we should be retained on his front. His ambitious and finally successful scheme to capture Myitkyina by air and land was due on about May 15th, and he was not willing to surrender any of our brigades. 111th and 14th Brigades had been doing good work on the Jap communications to the Chindwin, but we were now to concentrate on helping to take Mogaung, the key town where the Ledo road meets the Mandalay-Myitkyina railway.

It was decided that we must have an all-weather Dakota field close to the block in order to evacuate wounded. As no such field could be found near White City, the final decision was to place a new block within easy reach of the light planes which would now be based on the American airfield on the Ledo road.

The new plan was therefore as follows:

77th and West African Brigades would remain responsible for White City. 111 Brigade would establish a new block on the road and railway north of Hopin. 14th Brigade would move up in support. When the block was established, White City would be evacuated. 16th Brigade would fly out of Aberdeen and Broadway, after which the two fields would be abandoned. The West Africans would take over 16th Brigade's animals to bring them up to strength and make them fully mobile.

Later this plan was modified in that 14th Brigade remained with the West African Brigade at White City, while 77th Brigade marched towards Mogaung.

During the time we were in the hills from April 26th to May 2nd, I gave way to an appalling fit of depression which Francis did his best to assuage. I sent vehement messages to General Lentaigne on the shame of giving up General Wingate's plan – messages which eventually passed the borderline, and became insubordinate. Francis stopped many of these. I was suffering, I think, from strain due to the thought of giving up Broadway and White City when we had won through after so much loss, and the change in Wingate's plan. I had also an attack of malaria, and had been shocked by hearing of the deaths of Lieut.-Col. Richards, Paddy Ryan and Paddy Dermody in hospital, bad news which until then had been concealed from me.

General Lentaigne was extremely generous to me during this period, but finally had to pull me up by threatening to sack me if I continued to send such messages. At that time I had received the following message from Force H.Q.: 'Confirm your troops physically capable one more effort and subsequent walk out to American Roadhead. 14th Army consider your troops now finished and should be flown out.'

I received from Skone, who had also picked up the message: 'If C.O.'s opinion required my opinion same as 14th Army. If an effort vital to success of operation then effort can be made but *not* considered advisable.'

On the 30th, I walked to Naman and flew to White City to consult the commanding officers of the South Staffords and Lancashire Fusiliers, who confirmed Skone's opinion. Eventually I sent a signal: 'Regret 14th Army appreciation correct. Recommend South Staffords, Lancashire Fusiliers, 3/6 Gurkhas and Advance Brigade H.Q. be flown out from Broadway. Cannot answer for King's and 3/9 Gurkhas.'

After lying awake all night, and having had a long talk with Bobbie Thompson who was more fit and cheerful and whose advice I have always respected, the following day I qualified my last message by sending on May 1st:

'Due to probable difficulties of obtaining aircraft for flying out quite prepared to march out via Mogaung to Stilwell's roadhead. If, however, flying out from Broadway does not in itself harm Special Force operations, and can be planned as properly scheduled operation, recommend withdrawal that way sooner than lose men through sickness in Hukawng valley. Will support any decision utmost.'

Bobbie had feared that we might be left waiting, waiting for planes at Broadway, and eventually the majority would have to walk out anyway.

At about that time I was asked the strength of the three battalions and Advance Brigade H.Q. for a fly-out. It was 2,277 all ranks and 313 animals.

Our casualties in these battalions and my headquarters to

date, not including Nigerians, Reconnaissance, King's and 3/9th, totalled 46 officers, 10 Viceroy commissioned officers, and 692 other ranks, killed, wounded and missing, and 279 sick evacuated (mostly since the relief of White City) who it was felt would not be able to march. Our only reinforcements had been a few officers. We still were potentially a fair-sized fighting force, but we needed a good long rest.

On May 2nd I received a signal from Lentaigne: 'Am making endeavour to evacuate 25, 20, 50, 38, 80, 36, 63 columns (includes the three battalions) and Advance Brigade H.Q. from Broadway. Let you know 0800 hours May 3rd.'

Next day the decision had been made: 'Until Chindwin front cleared impossible send fresh troops to hold area in Irrawaddy valley now dominated by us. Special Force role is to assist Stilwell capture and hold line Mogaung-Myitkyina.'

In recounting this series of messages I have departed from the chronological sequence of events. We had marched to the top of the hill where we organized a good recuperative supply drop, as we all, especially the outsize Nigerians, were suffering from lack of food. One of the reasons for this had been the disorganization due to the change of our rear base, and it is a compliment to the whole organization in our rear to record that it was the only time during this campaign that we went really hungry.

I had heard, before meeting them, many jealous disparagements of West African troops, mostly by foolish Indian Army officers. One of these *canards* was that they could not march up hills. On the way up the 3,000- to 4,000-foot Gangaw range in the great heat before the rains, I watched the Nigerians closely, passing them during halts and watching them go by. The only Africans who were not cheerfully marching up in good order, and who tended to lag behind, were those who were carrying the British N.C.O.'s heavy packs as well as their own.

I do not think that there is much wrong with the African as a soldier. If he could have British officers who grew up with him, as happened in the Indian Army, if his fighting traditions and exploits were properly publicized and commemorated, if there was a real desire of the white residents of Africa to have him as a good soldier and to be proud of him and fond of him, as was the case in India, he could be as good as the finest Asiatic troops who have ever been under our command – and, in this generation, more loyal.

The Africans are not all saints, however. When our supply drop came at last on the top of a mountain ridge, much of it fell far down the hillside and had to be collected by the Gurkhas and Africans. During this collection when a man was hungry and on his own, a few Gurkhas and many more Africans succumbed to what was, with us in Burma, one of the greatest crimes – pilfering food. They were severely punished. At one time when the medical officers were looking for their stores, they found one large African sitting under a banyan tree eating and greatly enjoying biscuits spread with blood plasma, which he thought was jam.

Everywhere in the hills we found evidence of Musgrave Wood's, and, to a lesser extent, Bell's excellent Kachin organization. The Kachins were rabidly pro-British and had been organized in accordance with General Wingate's directive.

In my own operation instructions, before the fly-in, I had stated:

PROPAGANDA

In the initial stages the propaganda to put out is that the Japanese are cut off in the north, that we have not won the battle yet, but we hope to retain any part of the country which we capture. Anyone may help us who wishes to do so, and we will reward him, but we cannot guarantee at this stage to protect his family and village. Any man who shows his worth may be given arms, but this will be done on a limited and controlled scale.

Every opportunity will be taken to show our strength in air, weapons and riches, and in making out that the Jap is poor in material and strength, that he gained his ends when we were occupied elsewhere, but that his time is coming as soon as we wish to turn the heat on him.

We are sorry that we had unavoidably to leave Burma for a while but that it was only a temporary measure. Every effort will be made to exaggerate our numbers and strength whenever it is necessary to show ourselves. We do not seek to call for volunteers to fight the Japs, but that if anyone wishes to help us and shows that he can do so, we are willing to use him.

We must never be niggardly in our rewards or purchases. As regards the Japanese granting Burma independence, the line to take is 'How independent is Burma now? During the Jap occupation Burmese cannot even travel over the countryside unhindered. The Japs only gave you independence because such a grant of independence (which is only an airy phrase) would be an embarrassment to the Allies when Burma and the rest of South-East Asia was rid of the Japs. The British Commonwealth of Nations would grant Burma its independence when it was ready for it, and could enjoy the results in peace and prosperity.'

This rather repetitive directive was written hurriedly to give a line of action for all from the Kachin Hills east of the Irrawaddy to the railway line, so that we should speak with one voice. It was merely the expansion of General Wingate's instructions. It was well received by the Burmese, Shans and Kachins. We were not going to woo them and make them feel important – that was beneath the dignity of the British people – but if they wished to join us it was up to them, and it would be remembered.

I was very sad at the thought of giving up this whole area, and we arranged to fly out any who thought that reprisals might be taken on them. In actual fact the Japs never occupied the hills nor the Kaukkwe valley, and so, with the extra clothes and riches our occupation had given them, our presence remained a boon to these loyal people. At the time, however, I could not foresee this, and it was one of the causes of my bitterness over the new policy.

The two battalions moving along the paths running along the high ridges adjoining the hilltops were welcomed everywhere by the Kachins. We eventually reached Tengaw above Musgrave Wood's lair at Naman. I had gone down to visit White City as already related, and Peter Vaughan, anxious as ever to get into a fight, had accompanied me. Hugh Christie joined us there. At Thayaung, where we had last seen Hugh Christie's 50 Column, he had nobly agreed to lend Peter Vaughan his 3-inch mortars and Vickers machine guns, providing the British mule leaders for the team, as

Peter Vaughan, although he had his crews, had no guns for them.

The Force deception plan for our advance north had been that we were on our way to attack Mohnyin. This was planned in the hopes that, while Jack Masters, now commanding 111 Brigade, was installing his block north of Hopin, the Japs would still be anxious about Mohnyin and retain troops there.

In view of this, and before his departure from us, Peter Vaughan was anxious to put in an attack against about one company of Japs at Ywathit, some five miles north of Naman. He was also anxious to try out the means of attack in the jungle often described by General Wingate, and actually put into effect against us by the Japs. The method was to advance as close to the Jap positions as possible frontally and, when they opened fire, to let one or two Vickers machine guns situated as closely as possible to them rake their position backwards and forwards and the trees around them for snipers, while another sub-unit envelops them around the flank. At a signal the firing would stop and the Japs were overrun before they had had time to get their heads up. The beauty of this method is that, with the aid of tracer and a fixed limit to the arc of the guns, the enveloping force can get extremely close to the enemy while the guns are still keeping their heads down. I heard later that the use of this method of attack was one of the main tactical reasons for the success of the German attack in 1918.

So I agreed with Peter Vaughan's proposal, especially as it would help the Kachins in the neighbourhood to subdue the Japs. I made one proviso: that the attack was not to be pressed home if after initial surprise it entailed heavy casualties, as the situation did not warrant it.

Peter Vaughan himself carried out a personal reconnaissance the evening before, and observed the enemy from within fifty yards of Ywathit. I had hoped that we should obtain some air support, but this had gone sour on us for some time. After Kachin levies had guided the column to the forming-up place by night, and the machine guns had been sited, the attack went in at dawn accompanied by a hail of machine-gun and mortar fire. Ywathit was occupied, and the Japs' quarters burned before leaving. The Japs, who numbered about ninety strong, and had two machine guns, suffered about thirty casualties whilst the Nigerian casualties totalled one killed and eleven wounded. The whole engagement lasted barely three hours. It was a very successful little action.

We were sorry to bid farewell to the 7th Nigerian Rifles. They had come to us fresh when we were feeling rather exhausted and battle-worn, and their enthusiasm for action, their cheerfulness and their willingness to learn had been a great help and tonic to us, and to me especially. They were to rejoin their brigade in the block. As we waved them farewell we told them that we would always supply them with a spot of blood plasma if they were hungry.

After receiving back their guns, mules and muleteers, Christie's column joined the Gurkhas on top of the hill. This column had done a tremendous amount of marching in dangerous areas, and although involved in few major actions had had a continued series of minor engagements, and was almost continuously under the strain of expected ambush or surprise attack. During our months of training in the jungles of India I had noted the Lancashire Fusiliers' capacity for long and hard marching, and also, partly because of their length of time with the brigade, their skill in the column bivouac and dispersal drill. I had therefore chosen them for the less satisfying, but nevertheless essential, job of harassing the enemy's communications to decrease his efficiency and to contain his troops in the north. They had been successful in this, but it was a great and continued strain without much visible return in seeing Jap dead, and, owing to the hard conditions in the great heat – conditions which were much harder in many ways than in the block where there was always an airstrip if you were hurt – they suffered more from disease and exhaustion and strain.

I had a long interview with Musgrave Wood before I went up the hill. He and his Burma Rifles and the few British troops with them, wireless operators, etc., were very anxious to remain with the Kachins. They had worked it out and considered that they could stay there all monsoon. One of the troops told me that he would prefer to stay rather than go back to India and do more training and peacetime guard duties. I felt for them and told them that I would put the matter up, but I could give them little hope of an affirmative reply. As I expected, the reply was that they could not stay indefinitely, but could remain, to move their headquarters and stores up to the top of the hills, which they did by elephant later, and if any Burma Rifles wished to remain he' could do so on half-pay. Some of the Kachin Burma Rifles who came from that area chose to stay.

Musgrave Wood, who was an independent type and who liked running his own show – a frame of mind in which I had every sympathy – had run a very good information service during the six weeks he had been installed, besides raising, arming and training the Gangaw levies. Twice the Japs had tried to eradicate him, but never found his cleverly concealed hideout. If they had, they would not have been too happy; Musgrave Wood had put down every sort of booby-trap device besides cleverly sited mortar and machine guns, to be used in its defence. His information on Jap dispositions and movements had been of great use to me in maintaining my peace of mind about the risk of an attack from the north.

CHAPTER FIVE

EVACUATION

I cannot say that we were rushing forward into the next phase of operations with banners flying and yearning for action. In fact, I am rather ashamed of my feelings during this period. The first rains of the monsoon were starting. Even up in the mountains Francis and I, with one ground-sheet below us and one above, had spent more than one uncomfortable night. Francis, who was much more ill than I realized, was still imperturbable but even his temper broke at times. Usually, however, he was a great comfort in difficult periods. When Joe Lentaigne and I were exchanging angry messages I was most disturbed, but Francis, who had been on General Auchinleck's personal staff in the desert, said that it was nothing to what generals said about each other there.

There is no doubt that commanders, however junior, who are conscientious and keen on winning the war, and who have consideration for those under their command, must feel strongly and emphatically about their convictions, and therefore are likely to express themselves strongly. In fact, one would have no respect for them if they did not. I therefore personally deplore the jackals who try to make material kudos out of the strongly expressed convictions of their superiors when they manage to find some trace of these long-since discarded verbal missiles. Joe's and my arguments were, of course, on a minute scale and of minute importance compared with those of whom I am thinking, but it did give one an inkling of the feelings of high-ranking generals, and an added consideration for them.

It was hot, wet and sticky as we moved slowly and fitfully along the valley. Now that we were on the move again I could not help thinking of the casualties we had had. I had received from Paddy Ryan in hospital a letter in which he could not disguise the pain he was in, but he wished us good hunting, and said that he had been proud to be with us.

I was told that he, Richards and Paddy Dermondy were all in the Special Forces Hospital in Sylhet under Matron MacGeary, who had looked after us the last year and who had nursed Wingate back to health after his typhoid.

After Wingate's death, this was one of the first of his structures to be torn down. These three, who had been undergoing penicillin treatment – the penicillin we were obtaining from the Americans as penicillin had not yet been allotted to the Burma theatre – were dragged off to the hell-hole Dacca, a most unhealthy place with a very bad reputation amongst the troops as a death centre, where, taken off penicillin, they had died.

This was not a very good omen as to how Special Force would be treated now that the influence of Wingate had departed.

Joe Lentaigne, however, having to take over in most difficult circumstances and having to follow on after such a great personality, manfully dug his toes in, risked his reputation, and later, I found, had done a great job for us in keeping us supplied and informed.

14 Brigade and the West Africans took over White City. The Black Watch had a fierce all-day action near Nathkokyin where they did very well. Aberdeen, with all its guns and stores, was evacuated, and later all the guns and stores of White City were also taken out by air. Geoffrey Lockett, who could hardly be persuaded to leave the place, and wanted to defend it himself, sowed every inch of it with booby traps and mines before he left. A year later two of our officers who visited the place found it completely overgrown. The Japs had tried to enter it, but there were signs of them having been blown up. Our officers managed to get in to visit the graveyard, which was overgrown but untouched. Probably a plethora of booby traps had had the same effect as I had experienced in 1940 when I was commissioned to booby-trap the Brighton and Worthing piers. We laid every type of trap, bluffing, double bluffing, treble bluffing, and then suddenly a seagull let one off. This made us jump, but then all the debris landed on another one which went up, and then another and so on, the booby traps playing leapfrog with each other as we rapidly backed down the pier ready to jump into the sea. However, they eventually gave it

up. But it did teach me a lesson, and that is not to place booby traps too close to each other. This is what might have happened in White City – it allowed our observers to get in unharmed.

Now that we could ride again, I missed Paddy Dermody, my groom, with whom I always used to ride in the old training days. We had formed a team which could throw grenades and fire rifles from our ponies. It probably would not have done much good, but it increased our confidence when we first rode around the area near White City. Paddy, who was known as Paddy by everyone in the Brigade including the Gurkhas, with whom he was a great favourite, had been, amongst other things, a jockey in Ireland. I used to ride the standard army way with my toes up and out at an angle of 45°. He was always advising me against this; any other rider, he said, could come alongside, put his foot under yours, and tip you off. Which he then proceeded to do, and I did.

He joined the Irish Free State Army, where he rose to the rank of sergeant. In 1940 he 'fell in' his platoon and took them on to the Liverpool boat; after landing in England, they all joined the King's Liverpool Regiment. He told me this once when we were out riding, but he never saw anything out of the ordinary in it. Wingate got him as a groom in the early Patharia days, and they had a high regard for each other. Paddy was with Wingate when he came back over the Irrawaddy and Chindwin. Crossing the Irrawaddy, the boat Paddy was in with Sqn. Ldr. Longmore overturned. Paddy said that he was helped to shore by a great friend of his, a Burma Rifle man, who let go of him when they could stand, but stepped in a hole and was carried away by the current and drowned. He often used to tell me that it was his duty to go back to Burma to fight for Burma in honour of the Burmese who had saved his life. He and L/Cpl. Young hit it off very well together because they were both romantic-minded, honourable, honest and fearless young characters, and became inseparable. Cpl. Young was never quite the same after hearing of Paddy's death. Young, however, could cheer up at times, such as when he had hung my recently obtained hammock-cum-mosquito-net-cum-shelter, and one end gave way in the night and landed me upside down in a tangled mass into a pool below. He laughed so much at my vituperations that he could not extricate me for some time.

I had said in a report after the 1942 campaign that 'weariness and lack of sleep makes cowards of us all'. I can give three instances exemplifying this state of mind during this period.

At Naman, there were two and a half battalions of British and West African troops. We heard a report, which was correct, that about 300 Japs were coming in that direction. We were in an excellent position and well protected against surprise. The West Africans were not at all worried and were ready for a fight. We, whose nerves were on edge, with the frailest of excuse went up 4,000 feet into the hills in the heat of the day.

On the east side of the hills Brigade H.Q. column had bivouacked well off the path into the jungle. That night some men, possibly Burma Traitor Army, possibly Kachins trying off their rifles, appeared to wander around us all night firing off rifle shots. I could not sleep. I visited the Gurkha sentries, who were unconcerned. However, before dawn I awoke the column and we saddled and loaded up in the dark and stole away. We were behaving as 'King of the Jungle' indeed!

At Naungpong, at the headwaters of the Kaukkwe, on May 15th, the brigade had concentrated. We had formed a defensive perimeter around the village. We heard a report that there were 400 Japs in a village five or six miles away. We were about 2,200 strong. It was with the greatest will power on my part that I succeeded in quashing the suggestions, and my own inclination, to go away. The report turned out to refer to a village of the same name forty miles away.

It can be seen how low we had sunk. Besides the reasons I have given I think that one other reason was that we had, for a brief while, thought that we were going out, and life became momentarily precious again. I have stated these views candidly. They were certainly evident amongst nearly all, from majors upwards. I think, however, that the junior officers, and men, who had had more of the risks but possibly less of the strain, would have been quite willing to have had a duffy. But there was no doubt that we wanted a rest.

After we had received the decision that we were to go on

for one more operation I still could not believe that we were in a condition to do so, and Hubert Skone, whose opinion I asked, agreed vehemently with me at the time.

I knew that the bone growth in his heel was hurting him when he marched, so I suggested that he should fly out to present our views and that he could catch us up later by air if necessary. Moreover at this time I had received a message from General Lentaigne that potential brigade commanders were required: were there any I could suggest? I had strongly recommended Claude Rome and Hubert Skone, and I thought that by letting Skone go out to see what the form was, I would be helping him.

So Hubert flew out and I heard no more, except that I thought that he had got a brigade. So later I promoted Freddie Shaw, much to Hubert's very natural disgust and fury as he had been standing by to come in. I received a sharp letter from him after the campaign. I managed to put matters right up to a point by telling the whole story to the Military Secretary himself, and he eventually got a brigade, but Hubert, who had no other interest but his Gurkhas and soldiering, never quite forgave me. Such are the difficulties of fighting when the only link is wireless telegraphy. Half our imagined troubles and grievances could have been put right by a few minutes man-to-man talk.

I did get such an opportunity on May 8th, when I strode off with grim determination and suppressed rage to Broadway to see General Lentaigne.

I was still simmering over the idea of giving up all our gains and marching north into a cul-de-sac between the Mogaung river, the flooded Namyin Chaung and the Japs, in the height of the monsoon. My battalion commanders had all separately expressed similar views very strongly to me. I walked with a section as escort and, in my preoccupation with my angry thoughts, I marched so fast and without halting that they could barely keep up. On arrival I was greeted warmly by the ever-loyal Claude Rome, who fed me with rum and tea. He was looking at me queerly. When I started to tell him what I came for he suggested that I waited till I heard Joe.

We talked for some time while I gradually cooled down and Joe explained the situation at Imphal and pointed out that co-operation with Stilwell was our only chance to prove the correctness of our theory. When I despairingly pointed out that we were going into a death trap, he said, 'I have not seen you like this before, Michael. If you really feel like that I will have to relieve you, which I do not want to do.' That brought me to my senses.

After fixing certain plans with Claude, Joe and I took off to meet the battalion commanders. Unfortunately on landing we turned on our nose and another plane had to be called forth to bring him back.

Joe had brought some bottles of rum.

After he had gone my officers clustered around me to ask if we were really going out. I said 'No. "Here's to the dead already and here's to the next man to die." ' That night over a roaring fire in the jungle we sang amongst others that old song the 'Calcutta Cholera Song' – sung also in the American Civil War and by the Royal Flying Corps – one of whose verses goes:

> Betrayed by the country that bore us,
> Betrayed by the country we find,
> All the best men have gone before us
> And only the dull left behind.
> Stand to your glasses steady
> This world is a world full of lies,
> Here's a toast to the dead already
> And here's to the next man to die.

One tall Gurkha officer told us that he had booked a houseboat in Kashmir for his leave when he came out. We immediately toasted to him as 'the next man to die'. Of the officers present, he was.

After a lot of rum and lugubriousness, we slept, and woke prepared for all that came. Our mental storm had passed. The moral of this is again that personal contact and explanation so often melts away all grievances. The visit cheered us all and gave us greater resolution to carry on.

The monsoon, however, had only just begun. Broadway was fully evacuated of all guns, ammunition and stores, and the light planes flew north to establish a new base at the recently captured Myitkyina airfield.

I worked out a plan for the capture of Mogaung; I estimated that I would need five battalions. However, it had been decided that the 3/9 Gurkhas and the King's would join Jack Masters with 111 Brigade to assist form his new block 'Blackpool'.

We were to protect the east side of this block by sitting in the hills above it, and giving such support as we could. This gave Claude Rome nothing to do, so he was going to fly out. But the wet weather settled down, the light plane strip remained out of order, and Claude fortunately for us, stayed in. I was always glad of his sound advice, but it must have been at times galling for him not to have had more opportunities for the action he liked; when he did get any opportunities, however, he made the most of them. I only heard later that he had practically led the charge in the counter-attack at Broadway, although his report gives no inkling of this.

The monsoon set in on April 10th, and movement in the hills, which meant climbing up and down 4,000 feet, was slow and difficult. Steps had to be cut for the mules, and sickness increased; before reaching our destination at Lamai two of our men died of cerebral malaria and exhaustion. From an enemy point of view the period was uneventful. The Japs never climbed into the hills, and only rarely entered the Kaukwe valley, and we would be given fair warning by the friendly Kachins.

We watched on a clear day quite a heavy air raid on Broadway. I think Jap planes, which could not make their assigned targets in India on account of weather, were sometimes redirected on to us. But it was fun seeing the bombing some days after our departure. I think that the deception boys must take some credit for it, as they had concocted some plot which told the Japs that we were going to do something quite different and not nearly so foolish; so they were probably convinced.

It is always a great fillip to the morale to watch enemy aircraft bomb a place where you have been and now are not. Another thing front-line troops always like is watching one of their headquarters being bombed or shelled. It would be an interesting experiment in psychology to order the bombing of your own headquarters by your own aircraft in order to restore the morale of your troops.

During this period White City was most ably evacuated by Brigadier Abdy Ricketts, who had taken over command of the West African Brigade. He had left England only a fortnight before. 53 Jap Division were now at Mawlu and Sepein concentrating for an overwhelming attack on White City. Abdy Ricketts directed some of his own and 14 Brigade columns on to Mawlu where they engaged the enemy while he evacuated every gun and heavy weapon by Dakota from the airstrip, and then stole silently away into the night, leaving White City inextricably tangled with booby traps.

The interrogation report stated: 'At dawn on May 1st the Independent Mixed Brigade (I.M.B.), plus 4th Infantry Regiment (53rd Division), advanced as planned only to find that the position had been evacuated only a few hours earlier.'

CHAPTER SIX

BLACKPOOL

From Lamai we could see the newly installed Blackpool block across the Namyin valley. I deployed the battalions in the following order:

The Lancashire Fusiliers from Teinlon to exclusive of Loilwaw; South Staffords inclusive Loilwaw to inclusive Pagunyang; 3/6 Gurkhas exclusive Pagunyang to the north.

Their tasks were first to clear the foothills of any enemy, secondly to harass any enemy using the road and railway by fighting patrols at night, and thirdly to mortar enemy gun positions.

The exhilarating sound of gunfire, as the Japs attacked Blackpool, swept away all our doubts and cares and we were ready for action.

At that time we had no thought of Blackpool getting into difficulties. The weather now was appalling, with thunderstorms roaring and flashing around us in the hills with very heavy rain. The battalions had great difficulty getting their animals and weapons down the slopes, and the South Staffords had to manhandle their heavy weapons down 3,000 feet as the mules kept slipping and rolling with them.

The South Staffords were the first to draw blood when one of their patrols crossed the Namyin Chaung and attacked Banmauk, where the Japs had some guns which were shelling Blackpool. Casualties were inflicted on both sides, after which the guns were moved. The Lancashire Fusiliers had some brushes near Teinlon. Here also they picked up 140 officers and men of 82 King's Column which, while crossing the railway on their way to Blackpool, had bumped the enemy. The column commander with the front of the column had pushed on, leaving the rest to their fate. The latter, after a confused fight in the dark, withdrew to Teinlon. Hugh Christie looked after them, but, before they could rejoin their battalion, the Namyin Chaung came down in spate and flooded the countryside; that and the enemy prevented their rejoining their battalion, so they stayed as an extra Lancashire Fusilier company until the end of the campaign.

Each battalion had received 40 to 100 reinforcements at White City, and these acted as a blood transfusion to the units, as these new officers and men were anxious to win their spurs and prove their worth, whilst the older ones, having told such tales of what they had done in the past, felt constrained to do it in the future.

The 3/9 Gurkhas managed to join Jack Masters in Blackpool without incident, and were a welcome addition to his depleted brigade. Jack Masters, who was a very intelligent and gifted Gurkha officer, showed a great example by his rapid march to instal the block, arriving there first with his Brigade H.Q. and then gathering the rest of his battalions around him.

The flooding of the Namyin nullified our efforts to help 111 Brigade. The Japanese-paid Shans in the valley removed all the boats, with the result that only one or two officer patrols managed to swim across and shoot up the odd Jap on the road or railway. One officer from Brigade who got across, became separated from his patrol. He later swam back in the dark and found himself covered in leeches. He could not pull them all off and had no cigarettes to burn them off. He walked to the top of the 4,000-foot hill where we were installed, and collapsed. After removing about fifty leeches from all parts on and in his body, the Medical Officer gave him a blood transfusion, after which he felt better.

111 Brigade had not the advantage that we had had of rehearsing our installation of White City before we flew in. The South Staffords had carried out a whole week's digging and wiring in Assam, and we had time to plan for every eventuality. We had been fortunate in that the Japs attacked White City with too few and too early, in their overweening belief in themselves.

Jack Masters was attacked strongly almost as soon as he had arrived. He had been given the task of forming a block between certain limits, whereas I had been able to choose, in my reconnaissance from the air, practically any place between Hopin and Indaw. Richards and I had sat for hours studying air-photos before our reconnaissance, and then we were fortunate in that the Japs were holding Nansiaung and so we were driven to using our alternative choice, Henu, which turned out to be better than anything one could have wished for. At Hopin the mountains run steeply down to the flat paddy, and unless one gets right in the middle of the valley one is bound to be overlooked. Jack chose a hill which was to some extent overlooked, and whose forward slopes were very vulnerable to artillery fire. Sitting up on our hill as armchair critics, Francis, Bobbie and I decided that we would have probably chosen the same place, but in the light of events it would probably have been better to have occupied a village in the middle of the paddy astride both the road and the railway. All the villages were on slight eminences above the paddy, they had all made bomb-proof shelters, and we decided that, although there could be no escape as the paddy surrounded the village, it would perhaps be better against artillery fire.

111 Brigade made a glider strip. Then, with the bulldozers landed by glider, they made a Dakota strip and got their guns in. Soon after, the Dakota strip was overrun and, either by gunfire or small arms fire, was rendered inoperative. This was not vital but it meant that wounded could not be evacuated. What was vital, however, was that the Japs surrounded the block with anti-aircraft guns and shot down or prevented the Dakotas from re-supplying 111 Brigade. This, coupled with a very heavy artillery bombardment and a full regimental (equivalent to our brigade) attack, was their eventual undoing.

After the initial attack the Japs withdrew. The block was not truly a block across the road and railway, but overlooked it at about one and a half miles' distance. The result was that the Japs continued to use transport on the road at night, and were using the rail for a shuttle train service between Mohinyin and Mogaung. It was most galling to be able to see this and do little about it. I used very strong exhortations to get the battalions to attack the railway. So strong were my exhortations that Ron Degg almost decided that he would soldier no more. The elements were running riot, and of over twelve determined attempts to cross the mile-wide floods, only one under Lieut. Wilcox, South Staffords, and Lieut. Adey, Burma Rifles, succeeded after three nights of exhaustive effort. They blew the railway line, but missed blowing the train, owing to the difficulty of keeping the mechanism dry during the crossing of the flooded Namyin Chaung and Mana Canal. It was a very determined and gallant effort. Later Lieut. Almond of the 3/6 Gurkhas also managed to cross, but alone. He stayed the night in Taungni on the railway, which was supposed to be held by 2,000 Japs. He saw five whom he engaged.

About half a dozen bedraggled Gurkhas ran towards a Lancashire Fusilier position one day shouting 'Major Calvert, Major Calvert', at which the Lancashire Fusiliers rather ungratefully fired at them. Fortunately they missed the lot. They turned out to be six Gurkhas from my column of the year before who after capture had been conscripted as forced labour to lead mules for the Japs. They had heard that I was about. They told us of heavy casualties suffered by the Japs in the attack on Blackpool.

On May 25th the situation at Blackpool looked grave. 14 Brigade was ordered to attack the enemy around the block and I was ordered to assist with at least two columns. The 3/6 Gurkhas by this time had moved north, as will be related later.

I had exhausted every method of helping 111 Brigade. I has sent every type of message to my battalions who were deployed in various flooded re-entrants along the foot of the hills. I sent my own élite brigade company under my Animal Transport Officer, Major Gurling, with orders that they must set an example. But after nearly drowning three, and losing a lot of equipment, even they were forced to give up. The rain had delayed 14 Brigade. The maximum we could do was the rather ineffectual mortaring of gun positions and individual efforts by officers. It was most galling not to be able to do more, but I am quite certain that it was not possible.

On the 26th, Blackpool fell from lack of ammunition and food and casualties from artillery fire. The garrison lost seventy men in one day from artillery fire alone on inadequately dug and exposed positions. It is a truism to say that troops cannot be shelled out of a dug-in position, but that depends on how well dug-in the position is.

As the result of a fine counter-attack, with heavy casualties caused to the enemy, most of the garrison escaped, but many wounded had to be left. The enemy made little effort to pursue. In interrogation after the war, they admitted losing at Blackpool one whole regiment from 53 Division. This division, elements of which we had already met at White City, had been ordered to destroy White City after the failure of 24 Independent Brigade. When they found White City evacuated, they had moved straight on to Blackpool.

Another reason, I think, for the failure at Blackpool was its too close proximity to the enemy's front. Immediately behind a front there is the divisional and corps artillery. Behind that are the reserves of infantry and artillery and much ammunition close at hand. Then there is a gap in which for many hundreds of miles, perhaps, there are practically no troops at all. This is the same in all theatres of war, and it is quite obvious to anyone driving up to the front from the rear. Now that gap is the best area for attacking the enemy's line of communication. If you get closer to the front you meet his reserves, who without much movement and inconvenience can be set upon you. Ground commanders who have a limited vision are always trying to get guerrilla or airborne or penetration forces mixed up just behind the enemy's front. This does no good as they are then easily destroyed. At Blackpool, the artillery was already present, and had hardly to make any move to start its bombardment – whereas at White City, which was about the right distance behind the lines, the enemy had to form a base, build up his artillery, and generally redeploy new forces, all the time being harassed and weakened by our lighter forces. On a long single line of communications it does not matter where one breaks it any more than where one breaks an oil pipeline or railway line. In fact, the farther away from his main centres one breaks it, the better. Any railwayman would much prefer to mend a bridge close to a large junction where he has his engineers, his material, his reconnaissance parties, etc., and where he does not have to make new administrative arrangements for the feeding of his labour force.

This principle was fully brought out when I was at Aandalsnes in Norway in 1940. There a single-line railway was supplying the British brigade seventy to ninety miles away. In spite of day-long bombing of the small station yards during the long daylight hours, our railway boys always managed to send a train up to the front and receive one back. There was one exception, when one enemy bomber by luck or good judgment dropped one bomb on the line about thirty to forty miles up the line. By the time that we had found out where it was, had organized a force to mend it and transport to get the material there, and finally mended it – which took the least time – forty-eight hours elapsed before a train made the complete journey.

So one can sum up. It is always wrong to direct forces operating behind the enemy's line in co-operation with the direct offensive of a major force, too close to the enemy's main force. It will always pay greater dividends if the penetrating force cuts the enemy's communications many miles behind the enemy's own reserves. He must then either move his reserves away from the main battle to free his communication, or draw troops from elsewhere, both of which can be easily resisted. Unfortunately if one is not in the main battles, the main forces cannot see farther than their noses, and do not realize, and later belittle, the results attained by those forces, as with strategic bombing. In fact, I consider that Air Force officers tend to be the best commanders or directors of behind-the-line operations, because they are mentally trained to see over the 'other side of the hill'.

Blackpool fell on the 26th. While this battle was raging other events started to unfold themselves.

On May 18th, I received a message: 'Myitkyina captured by Stilwell.' This turned out later only to refer to the airfield. The Jap garrison was not reduced until nearly two and a half months later. On the 20th I informed Force H.Q. that if my brigade was required for a definite operation I would like the King's back for it, as a brigade in open warfare, in order to carry out a three-battalion attack, needs a fourth battalion to guard its base and for relief. I also stated that my battalions were fully deployed down 4,000 feet over difficult country, and that I would require due warning of a change of role. On the 21st, Special Force H.Q., who were now installed next door to Stilwell's H.Q., informed me that General Stilwell was sending a column down the railway from Myitkyina on to Mogaung. He estimated the enemy was mainly concentrated at Kamaing and that Mogaung was weakly held. In actual fact the column from Myitkyina never started. I was also informed that the King's could not return to me until 14 Brigade arrived at Blackpool. Then the intention was, first priority to hold Blackpool, and secondly to advance north, 111 Brigade west, and ourselves east of the railway to attack the Mogaung area.

On my own accord I had sent the Gurkhas to reconnoitre towards Mogaung as I anticipated orders to attack Mogaung. They had reached Mansen.

Their information was that there were 4,000 Japs in the Mogaung area. This was supported by a 14th Army intelligence summary which stated that Mogaung was held by two regiments.

I therefore signalled Force H.Q. that I was chary of sending the 3/6th beyond Mansen in any strength without support. I received a reply that it was essential that they reconnoitre towards Mogaung to find enemy dispositions, and that General Lentaigne hoped soon to be able to give orders for a general advance of 77 Brigade, and one other brigade, on to Mogaung, in conjunction with a move of a column from Myitkyina. As it happened, owing to the Jap attack on Blackpool and prolonged resistance at Myitkyina, only 77 Brigade was to move. This could not be foreseen.

The weather, besides preventing our helping 111 Brigade and delaying 14 Brigade, had held up the Chinese advance on Kamaing.

I had passed the G.O.C.'s message to the 3/6th, emphasizing the importance of their task. General Stilwell in his message had evidently meant by 'reconnaissance' that the whole battalion should move on to Mogaung and fight for information. I took it to mean reconnaissance by patrols whose duty was to see and not be seen. This the Gurkhas had done. However, for a time, the 3/6th were moving more warily than I desired. In war I have found that there are always more reasons for not doing anything than doing something. This misunderstanding was to brew up into a first-class row of which I knew nothing until later.

On the 22nd, I suggested that I take the whole brigade to seize the high ground east of Mogaung, but events at Blackpool caused this to be cancelled.

Both the U.S.A.A.F. and R.A.F. in this terrible weather had persevered with their supply dropping to us in our difficult position in the hills. We had three more cases of cerebral malaria and tick typhus. Communications with rear brigade were held up for a time for a reissue of cypher books, copies of the previous ones having been lost and compromised by 83 Column while crossing the railway.

Colonel Rome, whom I had left at Naungpong to be flown out, joined me at Lamai, accompanied by Major Houghton, our senior doctor, who had also stayed to evacuate some sick by air. These he eventually brought up to Lamai with the aid of Kachin stretcher-bearers. Claude and I discussed the attack on Mogaung. Our first essential was to seize a base from which we could attack, as close to the town as possible. This base must be capable of being developed to include a light plane strip, a supply-dropping area out of range of enemy anti-aircraft guns, houses for the creation of a hospital, and protection by a screen of Kachin scouts.

I therefore sent him off to take charge of the Gurkhas and to move boldly forward over the hills via Wajit and Ngakah-tawng, and to seize and form a base for our attack at whichever place he thought most suitable. I would follow as soon as possible with the rest of the brigade.

I had appreciated from information received, and from study of the maps, that the Japs might hold the line of hills Wasu Wajit–Ngakahtawng–Lamun–Weyan. I therefore made this line our first objective, and suggested Wajit as our first base. I was determined to seize Tapaw Ferry, firstly in order to use it as a bridgehead for the column which was supposed to be coming from Myitkyina, secondly as a line of withdrawal from Mogaung in case we were pressed in between the river and the hills, and thirdly as a hospital area for evacuation by seaplane if light plane strips became out of the question because of the weather.

At Naungpong and during training, Claude and I had often discussed the best means of attacking as a brigade, and we came to the conclusion in the light of my previous attacks that we must plan on the following lines:

1. We must first seize and hold an area to form a base close enough to the objective so that battalions fighting on the objective can be economically supplied by mules from the base. If possible this base should be protected by one battalion. Attacking battalions could then leave therein their packs, sick, animals, etc., safe from enemy attack. The base must include, as I have stated, a light plane strip – or lake from which light planes with floats could operate – a good supply-dropping area which if possible should be an open

space where supplies could be quickly and efficiently collected, and which should be out of range of enemy anti-aircraft fire; and a village which could be used as a hospital area after cleansing and disinfection.

2. Good telephone communications throughout the base and to the Tactical Brigade H.Q. with the forward battalions, and on to the battalions.

3. If possible, a good observation post for visually directing air support on to the objective. This should be connected by phone to Tactical Brigade H.Q. for air support – and main brigade headquarters for instruction to the supply-dropping planes if necessary.

4. Before any full-scale attack was possible the base must be well stocked with ammunition and supplies, as the quantity the columns carried with them on the move was only sufficient for harassing tasks and driving in outposts.

5. The brigade would be converted from a column basis for movement, on to a battalion basis for attack. The fingers would clench into a fist. Also increased fire support must be obtained. If this was not possible by flying in artillery, heavy mortars must be dropped.

6. The flanks of the attacking force, and a wide area around the base, must be protected by what Wellington called 'a cloud of skirmishers', and in our case would be Kachins, organized and equipped by the Burma rifles under Taffy Griffiths.

7. Any *coup de main* tactics must be avoided as this would risk an undefeated enemy being able to surround the force seizing the objective, and, with the aid of light anti-aircraft guns, they could then starve the force into surrender.

As Claude and I had worked this out between us, there was little need for me to issue any detailed orders to him, as we were 'in each other's mind', which is the best form of communication there is. I knew that, released from his rather irksome defensive role at Broadway, he would advance with a vigour which would leave nothing to be desired. My confidence was not displaced and Colonel Rome's initial success put the brigade on such a good wicket that the enemy could only delay his own defeat.

I told Claude before he left that although I had not yet had any executive orders to move, and was still committed in the Namyin valley, I considered my tasks there were still-born, owing to the floods, and I would anticipate the G.O.C.'s orders by at once sending the South Staffords in support of him, first to Sumkrung and then to Wajit. My own brigade company would take over their role in the valley.

We were now starting to meet American influence. We found in the hills around Lamai that the Kachins had begun to be organized under the able leadership of Capt. Cummings and Lieut. Davis of the U.S. Army. Capt. Shaw Hamilton of the Burma Intelligence Corps, who had all along been attached to Brigade H.Q., carried out a long reconnaissance down to Kashankwawng to the south, and reported the hills entirely clear of any Jap influence. I met Lieut. Davis, who was to do very good work for us later on. He was of a type that one would normally expect amongst the British rather than the Americans.

He told me that he had come over to India on lend-lease inspection duties, but that this was merely so that he could get into some interesting job, which he finally managed. He had an interpreter who could not speak Kachin and could not understand English! In spite of this, he gained the complete faith of the Kachins in his area. He was quiet, calm and forceful, English-looking, I believe a high-ranking American polo player, and probably rather a playboy in between wars.

I explained our role, what we intended to do at Mogaung, and what I would like him to do. He was a man of few words; in fact, his interpreter could not have been a very busy man; and he went away and carried out his difficult task efficiently and calmly. Later he led his Kachins on a few attacks on the Japs around Wajit, and very definitely by his character and offensive action kept out any interfering Japs who wanted to investigate our flanks. He was a very fine type indeed.

Before leaving the area, I decided that I would try and make the Jap commander in the railway valley believe that we had come to stay. I surmised that, after his stiff battle at Blackpool, and his collection of booty, his natural inclination would be to rest on his laurels for a while in spite of whatever urgent orders he received from 33rd Army Commander to push north. I wanted to help him in this, and give him an excuse to stay, anyway for a little while longer while we rushed at Mogaung.

We therefore made up a haversack purporting to belong to my Signal Officer so that it would be more plausible if some drafts of old signals were found screwed away in his pack.

Inside, besides the usual junk one carries in a haversack, was a note from Signal Officer Major Pringle to me stating that he had now been over three months in Burma and had not shot a Jap yet. Could he please join one of the raiding parties one night, as he was fed up with sitting around at Brigade H.Q., and wanted some exercise.

There was a bit more, but that was the gist of his request. On the back of it I had written, 'O.K., but don't get into trouble. One good live Signal Officer is better than one dead Jap.'

The messages we left were mostly correct, innocuous ones, but included one which stated that two out of the three battalions at Broadway were to come under my command, and we were given the role of harassing Jap communications in the Hopin area during the monsoon. Initially these battalions would draw on the monsoon reserve rations held at Broadway, so as not to make their presence known by supply-dropping aircraft. Broadway had been stocked up sufficiently to last the monsoon without further supplies. The Allies hoped to make use of Broadway again after the monsoon. Shaw Hamilton and Taffy Griffiths also hinted at this to the Kachins in the Lamai area, and Shaw Hamilton spread the news on his journey south.

We then opened up one half of a field dressing and covered it and parts of the haversack and documents inside with 10 c.c. of blood drawn by my senior Medical Officer, Major Houghton, from a R.A.M.C. sergeant on Brigade H.Q. Also in the haversack were left some marked maps showing our dispositions as they were a few days before, Jap positions, one or two of Pringle's letters, and an already compromised code book.

Lieut. Wilcox, on his raid, succeeded in depositing the haversack realistically on the railway in the neighbourhood of Banmauk.

The minimum object of this deception plan was to deceive the local commander, if only for a few days, while we moved north. I considered that the deception might at least succeed for a time as I felt a written document would take precedence over reports by Burmese agents from the Kaukkwe valley. Incidentally one of the messages in the pack stated that we were receiving good information from Burmese agents who were in Japanese pay. I thought that this might sow seeds of doubt in their own agents, and the Japs might even shoot them themselves!

Whether this deception succeeded or not, I do not know, but I do know that no reinforcements reached Mogaung for some time, and a reconnaissance column of Japanese visited Broadway about three weeks later.

I have described this in detail as, being unable to contain the Japs in that area by military means because of the weather, I could only try to do it by guile. The Gurkhas, before they left, also staged a mortar demonstration on Sahmaw to keep the Japs happy in that area.

Colonel Rome had gone off like a shot from a gun on May 27th, the day after the fall of Blackpool.

At a later date I received the following signal from General Lentaigne:

'Stilwell has cut road at Seton [south of Kamaing]. Another regiment following up. You will take Mogaung with Brigade less 81 and 82 Columns [King's] and levies. Plan at your discretion. Ensure adequate ammunition. Give timings.'

This was what we wanted. My timings were unduly optimistic. I signalled that we hoped to put in our first attack on the hills east of Mogaung by June 1st, and start the final attack on Mogaung on June 5th.

Incidentally, as an example of an operation order, this message can hardly be bettered in conciseness and completeness. It is a worthy lesson to those whose operation orders contain windy verbiage and which appear to be written as a sort of apologia in advance so that if anything does go wrong, the staff officer can say it is not his fault. This message showed confidence and trust and willingness to provide anything which was asked for to the best of their ability. An order such as that delights a commander in the field and encourages him to do well.

We were having supply difficulties at this time in the bad weather, and the Lancashire Fusiliers had been out of rations for four days.

I relayed the G.O.C.'s signal to Claude, adding, 'Let cal-

170

culated boldness and haste be your watchword.' This was really an unnecessary spur to him, but I was feeling Wingateful.

Our hospital had been filling with sick and a few wounded. Malaria was breaking through the mepacrine tablet defence, and although we increased the amount to three tablets per day, it was not sufficient to overcome repeated new infections of malaria, or that was what my senior Medical Officer told me. Jungle sores were on the increase. Two cerebral malaria cases had been carefully nursed back to a state of convalescence, but we had two more cases either of cerebral malaria or tick typhus – I forget which – who were unconscious.

It was therefore a welcome surprise to receive about eighty Oriya Indian coolies who had left the Japs to join us.

These Oriya Indians come from the province of Irissa, south-west of Bengal, and used to work on contract as coolies on the Burma Railways. They would then return with their proceeds to their families. I had a soft spot for them. In the retreat in 1942, a Cpl. Serjeant, a Pte. Medally and myself got separated from the rest in an encounter with the Japs. We were part of a 'semi-warlike band' harrying the Japanese flanks. After being chased about a bit and having gone without food and water for some time, we eventually decided to swim the Chindwin. We retained two revolvers and one or two grenades, putting them in a large pack in which were placed or attached our empty water-bottles for buoyancy. Also in the pack were our boots and some of our clothes, and one or two other odds and ends. We chose a rainstorm to make our attempt, being far too thirsty to wait till evening according to our first plan, as we had lain all the very hot day right amongst the Japs who were searching for us. We saw a boat, jumped into it, and pushed off. It sank almost immediately, having a large hole in the bottom.

We next started to swim, but both Cpl. Serjeant and Pte. Medally had too many clothes on, and we had to return to shore. All this time the Jap sentries were fortunately sheltering from the heavy rain. After removing more clothes we set off again. Medally said that he was not much good. Cpl. Serjeant said that he could swim all right before he had had a touch of infantile paralysis. The Chindwin was about 400 yards wide at the point we chose, but with a fairly swift current. I am a fair swimmer, so I towed the pack whose buoyancy was negative. We started off all right, Medally on his back, and Serjeant swimming a sort of side-stroke with his right arm reaching out of the water as though taking a hat off a peg. I had to keep Medally straight, as often, if I took my eye off him, he had turned a full circle and was heading for our starting-point. When we were about half way, Serjeant said in a matter-of-fact tone of voice, 'Sorry, sir, I can't go on.' I told him to hang on a minute while I caught up with him. I could only use one hand, lugging the wretched pack along with me. I told him to hold on to the pack, and then, putting one hand underneath his armpit, we slowly made for shore. Unfortunately I must have ducked him once or twice, for suddenly I saw, a few yards downstream, our precious pack make one emergence like a turtle, and then sink for ever out of sight. On landing we had to hurry straight into the jungle as there were some hostile Burmese around.

We then took stock. I had a pair of shorts, a handkerchief and 1,000 rupees. Serjeant had a shirt and a pair of socks, Medally a pair of shorts and some wet cigarettes. We then set out to walk the rest of the way to India. It was getting dusk when we started. We slept together that night on a bed of leaves, covering ourselves with more leaves like the Babes in the Wood, but it was very cold, and nothing that happened to the Babes in the Wood ever happened to us. Next morning we tried walking in the jungle to avoid hostiles, but this was too prickly underfoot, so, when we reached a path we followed it, we knew not where.

We had had plenty of water, in fact our first action when the water of the Chindwin reached our mouths was to stand inconspicuously with our heads just out of the water drinking, as we were then very thirsty. But we had had no food for three days.

Our first food was some peanuts a refugee must have dropped. Then we found some bits of old chupatti some Indian must have thrown away. Our biggest find, however, was a heap of sugar swarming with ants. We shooed away the ants, reckoning our need was greater than theirs, and lapped it up.

Our water that day consisted of some green slime from a

two-foot-wide pool at one end of which the waters lapped against a cowpat. We strained some of the water with my handkerchief. That night we again slept together under the bushes, our wasted angular bodies letting in the draught everywhere. This episode had been the culmination of quite a long period of campaigning, much of it behind the enemy, where supplies had been fitful, so we did not start off with much reserve of flesh.

Next day we saw more signs of refugees but though we searched avidly with our eyes as we walked along, they had not thrown anything away. Every Burmese conscientiously removes thorns from a path, obeying some unwritten social law, so apart from rocky ground where the rocks and stones were sharp and hot in the sun, our feet did not suffer badly. That evening we reached the refugees. There we were, bedraggled, unshaven and half naked and only Medally could speak a little bazaar Urdu, but they immediately with one accord welcomed us, gave us blankets and even a mattress, laid us down and covered us. Then these Oriya Indians cooked some marvellous dal (lentils) and chupattis which we washed down with beautiful sweet tea. Next morning they insisted that we came along with them. But they said that they had been raided the day before and beaten by the Japanese who had made them give up their money, and had forced their womenfolk to give up some of their crude jewellery, so they said that we must dress as they did. So we put on clean sheets and sandals and walked very slowly along with them. It was very slow because not only were they carrying all their belongings including trunks and the odd mattress, etc., but also their grandfather and grandmother who were perched on the grandson's shoulders.

We skirted around one Japanese-occupied village. I peeped out coyly from behind my sheet to see the Japs watching us, and interrupted Medally's repetitive commentary, 'What a lark, what a lark, wait till I tell my old dad. What a lark,' with instructions as to what we were to do if the Japs came on us. My plan was for us to shriek shrilly and rush into the jungle where we would be prepared to defend our honour.

After a day or two the pace was too slow for us, and I thought that we might miss the British forces in Kalewa. So I gave the headman, in the presence of the others, most of our 1,000 rupees and thanked them warmly for looking after us, and with much embracing we headed north to Kalewa where, on arrival, my friends in 17 Division thought that I was shooting a hell of a line by arriving dressed as an Indian. Later a Major Johnston of the Marines and myself and one or two volunteers were sent downstream in a little white chug-a-chug motor-boat to collect stragglers. We went down until we were fired upon. We then pottered slowly around and with appalling slowness chugged against the current out of sight and range. We did pick up a few Indians but no troops. I tried to make some provision for my friends the Oriyas, but Kalewa was evacuated by then. I only hope that they got through.

The moral of this was that there we were, the great British nation, the rulers of the earth, being ignominiously pushed out of Burma, yet these poor coolies would still succour three white scarecrows, whom they called 'Sahib', at the risk of their lives, and without thought of gain. There was no hesitation. The welcome and offer of food and clothing were instantaneous and open-hearted. We hungered and they gave us food. We thirsted and they gave us drink. We were naked and they clothed us.

So I was glad to help these Oriya coolies, and they were a great help to us, acting as stretcher-bearers in the less dangerous areas throughout the rest of the campaign. Later, after some argument from India, they were flown out to India and from then on looked after. I told my Brigade and Force H.Q. my story of them, and they were well fed and well looked after. We had had food they liked – provided by an understanding Rear Brigade H.Q. – flown to us for them.

CHAPTER SEVEN

TOWARDS MOGAUNG

After withdrawing my defence company from the valley which was now commanded by Lieut. Rooke, under the fatherly surveillance of Major Gurling, the brigade Animal Transport Officer, Brigade H.Q., complete with sick and wounded, moved down to Pankaukyang, a distance of sixteen miles in one day, and down 4,000 feet of slippery paths. Next day we reached Tingmongyang, where we made a light plane strip to evacuate the wounded. On the way we had to build a bridge over a turbulent torrent to get our mules across. This we did by cutting down trees. Our mules knew us so well they would follow their drivers anywhere if the driver walked confidently forward and did not look back. That is the great secret with mules. Never look at them and pull. They are much stronger than men, but they also have a high opinion of their own intelligence and realize that they can do most things a man can do and lots of things he cannot. In fact, in their heart of hearts they only concede one point which they realize we can do and they cannot. So if you want a mule to do anything, do it yourself and he will follow. We used to have mule swimming races in our regattas in training. They can swim much faster than any man, and they really enjoyed this and went flat out to win. Mules can be some of your best friends in the world, but like all staunch friends they take a lot of getting to know initially. Anyway, throughout the campaign they supported us and were keen that we should win. In fact, in 77 Brigade when we say 'We' we include our mules and ponies. Once, at White City, we had had a luxury drop in honour of a victory, which included white bread, cheese, bully beef and stewed fruit, all great luxuries to us. Riding back on Jeannie with Ginger, my new groom, I met a Lancashire Fusilier with an enormous cheese sandwich about six inches thick. I made some comment on the size of the sandwich, and the Fusilier said, 'It isn't for me, sir, it's for Doris,' and smiled knowingly. 'Who is Doris?' 'My mule, sir. Named after my girl, sir. I always give my mule what I like most, sir, like I will give Doris after we are married.' I hope he survived and that Doris waited for him.

At Tingmongyang the Lancashire Fusiliers, with the 140 men of the King's Regiment, joined us. They had made a prodigious march from Chiropyang area up 4,000 feet and down 4,000 feet in wet weather, covering in two days about twenty-five miles. In that permanent rain and slime, after 1,000 men and mules have passed in single file along a path, the last files are often over their knees in mud. It was no mean achievement, and could hardly be called laggardly.

I draw attention to this because I found to my amazement later that General Stilwell had complained vehemently that our movements were slow, and that we were deliberately disobeying his orders. He took this up with the Supreme Commander, who had to send the extremely busy General Slim to Stilwell's headquarters at Shaduzup to smooth matters over. General Lentaigne, who probably had a better idea of the conditions, did not pass this criticism on to us as he was prepared to shield us from blame.

I had left an R.A.F. detachment, complete with two wireless sets and operators, and a small Burma Rifle party, at Lamai. Their job was to call for and bring down direct air support on any targets that they saw in the valley below, or that were reported to them by the Kachins. From Lamai one could see almost thirty miles north and south of the valley, and with Kachin agents' reports, it made an ideal observation post. We had a powerful telescope dropped to the party.

This detachment, which was commanded by F/Lt. Allen, Royal Australian Air Force, remained there for a month doing excellent work. His greatest success was to destroy a passenger train full of troops moving north. Presumably by then the Japs had repaired the blown bridges to the south, all of which were of small span. The P40s and P51s returned again and again on to the train, causing its utter destruction. The American fighter pilots got to know this station so well that, if they could not find the target that they had been sent out to bomb, or if, having dropped their bombs, they wanted to do a spot of strafing, they would fly near Lamai and ask if there was anything for today. Allen usually had some information for them.

Besides actually directing planes on to targets, this detachment gave us a continual supply of reports on enemy movements day and night, up and down the valley. At night the enemy used lorries with lights, trusting in the difficult weather conditions which made night interception exceedingly hazardous, so that with ordinary visibility from Lamai or lower down the hill it was possible to report on the actual numbers of lorries using the road. This method provided information far superior to any of the intelligence detachments scattered about Burma – brave and intrepid though the latter were – because, apart from sending information, the observation post could, by talking to the planes and by the use of gridded air mosaics of the valley, bomb pin-point targets, such as gun positions or concealed lorry parks. I considered that there is great room for development of this technique.

I had found by now that R.A.F. pilots, and especially their counterparts from the Dominions, when left alone with small detachments, were, because of the more individual aspects of their training, often better than Army officers in dealing with new situations, exploiting advantages and improvisation. The herd instinct ingrained in the average Army officer or N.C.O. who is always wanting 'to return to his company, battalion or brigade' when left alone and is always tending to look over his shoulder, does not seem to apply to the R.A.F. officers I have known in this type of warfare. Their individualistic attitude is an advantage. By self-control and self-discipline an individualist can always knuckle down to become one of a member of a team, and can, when necessary, shake off his shackles and become an individual again. But once a man has become like a sheep, it is very difficult to eradicate his sheeplike qualities. I had always preached on training that I preferred the officer who, when left on his own, did not say, 'My God, I must get back, I am out of touch,' but said, 'Thank God I am on my own. Now I can do what I always wanted to do and put some of my ideas into action. I'll show that bastard what I can do when I'm left on my own.' And he probably did.

I left another detachment at Tingmongyang under command of an R.A.F. officer, F/Lt. Burns, with about thirty sick awaiting evacuation, protected by Lieut. Davis's Kachins. My senior Medical Officer, Houghton, who was himself sick, stayed with them. The R.A.F. officer carried out his job efficiently and with Houghton, who was not going to give up, returned to the brigade three weeks later. It was necessary to leave an R.A.F. officer on the field, as without his persuasion the light planes, which were now under new and very strict management, would not land.

Claude Rome, with great speed and overcoming all obstacles of weather, marsh and enemy patrols, which he either drove off or avoided, reached Loihinche on May 31st. We had just received intelligence from Force H.Q. that the enemy either at, or coming to the defence of, Mogaung were between 4,000 and 5,000. I hoped, however, that my deception, coupled with 14 Brigade's successful action at the Kyusunlai pass west of Hopin, would keep the Japs in that area.

I had placed my demands for ammunition and stores for the Mogaung action. They included a request for 5,000 rounds of 3-inch mortar ammunition, but by the end of the battle we had used more than 60,000 rounds. Mortars in close country are far superior to 25-pounders. Field artillery has to stand so far back to clear the crest of the trees that it has to have special protection from marauders. There are only a few places where it can be sited, so it is not so flexible as a 3-inch mortar, which can be placed almost anywhere. Finally the missile arriving at the other end has about half the potency of a 3-inch mortar bomb. We were very much attached to our 3-inch mortars; they served us well.

I had chosen to follow a north-south route with the Lancashire Fusiliers rather than follow the same route as the 3/6 Gurkhas and South Staffords, as I expected them to meet opposition sooner than they did. In that case we would be in a position to outflank it and help them forward. However, we arrived at Wajit on June 1st after having to carry out a river crossing of the Padawng Hka. We were now in bad leech country. At ten-minute halts we would remain standing while the thin blind leeches, which had loped along to the path when they smelt our salty sweat, strained themselves out from the nearest plant, reaching blindly for us. At halts one would find half a dozen on one's legs, but the only thing we were afraid of was their capacity for getting into

178

orifices, which entailed extreme discomfort to the owner, as one or two of the men had found to their cost. I found that a sharp knock or tug would dislodge them even when they were only half gorged, and the hole in one's skin which they had filled with a non-congealing tincture soon closed and there was not much bleeding afterwards, in spite of what the pundits say. As a non-smoker I did not possess cigarettes, and I was damned if I was going to start smoking for the benefit of a lot of leeches.

The villages were the only leech-free areas in this part of Burma during the wet season, as the villagers had grown a plant around them through which no leech would go. Leeches would not go into lantana, so this shrub, which we all disliked so much, did have some use.

We used to bivouac on the outskirts of the village where there is usually a village green of some sort. The houses, raised from the ground on stilts, were usually quite clean, but underneath, where all the food and garbage was swept, chickens and pigs lived and fed. If one stirred up the garbage below one of these houses with a stick, the whole ground would become alive with hopping fleas.

All through the Kaukkwe valley we found villages which had been destroyed by the predatory Chinese during their retreat in 1942, and the Kachins here and in other parts feared and disliked the Chinese more than the Japs, of whom they had seen few.

On the march to Wajit, and on, we ploughed up to our knees and sometimes up to our waists through miles of flood and mud. Those farther back in the column suffered most. At Wajit a platoon patrol of Japs bumped and surprised a standing patrol of a platoon of Lancashire Fusiliers, who lost three killed. This was due to negligence and lack of vigilance, but soon, under the command of their company commander, Harrington, they recovered, and drove the enemy off. It woke everyone up to the fact that we were going into battle again.

On May 30th I received a message from Force H.Q. that a Chinese regiment was advancing south of Tumbonghka to co-operate in the attack on Mogaung, and that our job was to attack Mogaung as soon as possible to prevent reinforcements going on to Myitkyina, where the Japs were holding out in the town against overwhelming odds. If I found that opposition was too strong I was to withdraw into the hills, from where I was to exert the maximum pressure.

The difficulty, as I saw it, was that in this area the hills were all very steep, with marsh in between them, and that practically the only routes were along the paths on top of the knife-edged ridges. If we had a setback, a determined enemy could make things very difficult for us between Mogaung, the Mogaung river and the Tsanin marsh. The Chinese regiment, like all the other columns which were supposed to join me in a co-ordinated attack on Mogaung, was held up by difficult country and Japanese opposition, and did not join us for another three weeks.

The South Staffords under Ron Degg, pushing on behind the Gurkhas, met opposition at Ngakahtawng. Major Nip Hilton, a five-foot-high ball of fire who was an ex-sergeant-major, went straight at the Japs, who were about a platoon strong, and eradicated them. They then met stronger dug-in opposition in the Lamun area, but a sharp engagement, with the aid of mortars rapidly brought into action, eradicated that also. It must be remembered that the officers and men were wearing their heavy packs during these marches and very often during the fighting as well, and the total weight of their equipment was about 65 lb. Further, the whole column was strung out behind the vanguard, usually on an awkward ridge.

On June 1st, the South Staffords married up with Colonel Rome and the Gurkhas at Loihinche.

I had suggested to Claude that the best route for an attack on Mogaung was via Loilaw, and that his first job would be to clear Loilaw and the Tayok Taung feature. After arrival at Loihinche, however, he judged rightly that Loilaw was not the best route and that any attempt there would disperse the brigade. Another factor was that it was from that direction that the Japs were expecting us. He therefore asked permission, which I gave, to take the Lakum pass overlooking Kyainggyi and to form his base at West Lakum.

On June 1st, leaving the South Staffords at Loihinche, he attacked Lakum, drove out light enemy opposition, killing about ten, and took the enemy dug-in positions on Lakum pass, which were fortunately undefended. He was now

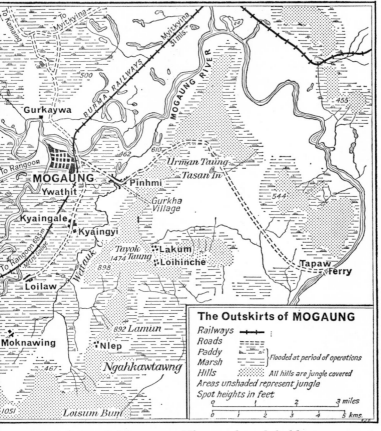

The Outskirts of **MOGAUNG**

Railways
Roads
Paddy
Marsh
Flooded at period of operations
Hills   All hills are jungle covered
Areas unshaded represent jungle
Spot heights in feet

within sight of Mogaung. His speed and boldness were
already paying big dividends.

The brigade had still to concentrate and form a base
before we could launch a full-scale attack. The enemy were
determined to oppose the concentration of the brigade at
Loihinche. Seeing that the forward battalions had circumvented them at Loilaw, they pushed to the east to the
Lamun area and dug in strongly on all the peaks over which

the path went, between Ngahkawtawng and Loihinche. We reached Ngahkawtawng on the evening of June 2nd. I sent a company that evening to occupy the hilltops above the village. Some enemy were sighted that night reconnoitring our positions.

I had sent the King's company to Lamun, a mile farther on, to occupy that village as a flank guard for our advance next day. I had also sent Capt. Butler – formerly Guides Cavalry, at this time a volunteer with the Lancashire Fusiliers – with sixty men to seize and hold the Tapaw ferry.

The main body started its advance at dawn in the usual tropical rainstorm, one column going along the top of the ridge, and one on the main path at the bottom. Before this latter column had gone very far it was fired on by four Jap military policemen. We had to put in a two-platoon attack through very thick prickly cane jungle before we had killed all four, to a loss to ourselves of one killed, three wounded.

Most of the main body had passed Lamun, and were heading left up the hill on the ridge, when firing broke out near the rear of the column. The King's company had evidently missed Lamun in the dark, and had bivouacked a few hundred yards farther along the path at the bottom of the hill. Lamun was occupied by some Japs whom they had missed. The Japs attacked the centre of our column where the Hong Kong Volunteers were guarding our wireless sets. A brisk action took place, the Chinese putting up a good fight and holding their ground, while Lieut. Rooke attacked with one of the brigade defence platoons. The King's company joined in the rear of the Japs, the remnants of whom fled, leaving seventeen dead. We had been fortunate in not falling into their trap. Lieut. Rooke was wounded in the scrotum and thigh, fortunately not too seriously; he carried on gallantly for some days before being evacuated. We also had about ten other British, Gurkha and Chinese casualties.

The head of the column reached the top of the hill and turned right along the crest. The Lancashire Fusilier company soon met opposition from a Jap platoon dug in on a jungle-covered knob with precipitous sides. After the initial attack had failed they brought up two machine guns and one mortar and pasted it backwards and forwards up and down ceaselessly, while two platoons crawled and climbed up the flank of the knob and, on a signal, as the fire ceased, threw their grenades and fell on the enemy at short range. The Japs left ten dead, the remainder fleeing. They had come to stay, and they were well stocked with food and ammunition. In the rain and muck the assaulting force had done well.

We carried on along the ridge until further opposition was met. This appeared to be one platoon reinforced by the survivors of the knob. The same tactics were applied, this time with the same success after a very stiff fight, the machine guns being brought even closer than before.

After this the reserve Lancashire Fusilier company came to the fore. The going was frightful with our heavy packs, up and down the precipitous little 300-foot hills which the Gurkha column's passage had made into a greasy switchback. Once a machine-gun crew with their mules slid all the way down one slope and found themselves amongst a lot of jabbering Jap survivors at the bottom. They insist that they got the gun into action before the Japs recovered from their surprise.

The third action was very similar to the first two. A misdirected mortar unfortunately landed amongst some of our attackers and caused casualties, including an officer.

The fourth occasion was complicated by an open field between us and the Jap position. However, David Monteith, who was now commanding the leading company, worked out a very clever plan of attack and eradicated them.

After 2-inch and 3-inch mortar fire as a preliminary curtain-raiser, and sustained searching fire by two machine guns for fifteen minutes, what was left of the Japs ran before the charging troops reached them. I can understand the Japs running when the machine guns ceased, as the experience at Kayin under fire of three Jap guns was one of the worst moments that I have suffered. In this case David had managed to get his two machine guns into action within fifteen yards of the Jap position! I paced this out carefully after the action.

Our casualties for the day had been 5 officers wounded, 5 British other ranks killed, 20 British and 1 Gurkha other rank wounded. The Hong Kong Volunteer casualties were counted amongst the British as, amongst other things, they received the same pay! I don't know what the logic of that statement is, but they were certainly British and proud of it as they were all born in Hong Kong, although many had Portuguese, English, Scottish or Chinese ancestors.

All these casualties had to be lugged along either by the Oriyas, or our own troops, who already had packs on. It was now 5 p.m., and we were all incredibly tired, but I was determined to make Loihinche that night, as I had reason to believe that we had defeated the Japs in the area for the day, and I wanted to join up with the rest of the brigade before the Japs dug across our path again. So, slowly, in the rain, with full packs and all our casualties, and having to manhandle many of our loads over slippery areas, we worked our way down to the flat again, and then up 1,200 feet to Loihinche. On the way I met Ron Degg. He had come out to help us when he heard our firing, but had arrived too late to join in the last fight. All that night the South Staffords helped the Lancashire Fusiliers up the hill with their casualties and their mules, and received them with hot tea at the top.

Hugh Christie told me that he was glad that I had been present to see them fight. Most of their previous actions had taken place outside the block when I was not present. The Lancashire Fusiliers had done very well.

With our overwhelming superiority in 2-inch and 3-inch mortars, Piats, automatic weapons and numbers, we had been able to inflict far heavier casualties on the Japs than we had received ourselves, but they had made a gallant effort to stop us and had certainly delayed and tired us. We claimed one officer and between thirty and forty Japs killed. They appeared to have been a nucleus of 18 Division Infantry, supported by odds and sods from the convalescent camp at Pinhmi, all from 18 Division. I would prefer to fight the infantry of 53 Division than the odds and sods of 18 Division.

This great division, which was giving General Stilwell so much trouble, had fought in Malaya and was the division which effected the landing and capture of Singapore. It had then moved up to Burma after the fall of Rangoon, and had gone through the Chinese armies on the east Burma front like a knife through butter, capturing Toungyyi, Hsipaw, Lashio, Bhamo, and Mytikyina in a very short time, a manoeuvre which broke organized resistance in eastern and northern Burma.

184

Since then they had remained in the north under their noted commander, Major-General Mutaguchi, and boasted that they would never leave north Burma but would leave their bones there. We were trying to gratify their wish. We had already taken some of the flesh off them by our blockade.

Capt. Butler, with the two Lancashire Fusilier commando platoons, accompanied by some Burma Rifles and Kachins, avoided our fight at Lamun, near which he had also bivouacked, and struck off for Tapaw in the morning. There, after a stiff little skirmish, he drove off the 'garrison' of ten Japanese, killing three. The only casualty in his party was himself, shot through the wrist. This he treated himself without reporting it, and stayed at his post.

George Butler had volunteered with David Monteith from the Guides Cavalry which, after active service in the desert, had been incarcerated in the North-West Frontier with little to do. They had a good colonel who sympathized with their desire to see some fighting, and gave them leave to do so for one season only. Butler had been one of the successful defenders of White City, relieving Ian MacPherson. He was a tall, taciturn type with a Trubshaw moustache. On his return to his unit he was asked what he thought about it all. His cryptic observation was, 'I did not know infanteering was so dangerous.'

Butler transformed Tapaw into a strong defensive position with barbed wire, punjis and cleverly concealed posts. A few days later I asked for the eight American ranger boats with their 22-h.p. outboard motors and their Sapper operators, to be dropped at Tapaw. This was successfully done without casualties, although one or two of the motors were damaged. I was told that some of the Sapper operators who had never parachuted before were asked whether they would do three practice jumps at Chahlala, in India, before the one into Burma or go straight away. They said, 'B . . . this, why do four when you only need do one?' They dropped accurately, accompanied by the ribald remarks of the next ones to go.

Outboard motors are like mules, they operate successfully and efficiently only if they know their driver, so it was essential that these drivers dropped with them.

Butler also made rafts in case we had to cross the Mogaung river in force or ferry across a Chinese regiment.

He patrolled as far as the railway north across the river but did not blow the line, as General Stilwell stated that he did not want it damaged.

Although this detachment did not from then on have much excitement, its presence was a great comfort to me.

CHAPTER EIGHT

THE CAPTURE OF PINHMI

I arrived at Loihinche on 2nd June to find that Claude Rome had taken the Lakum pass, and when I arose on the morning of the 3rd I watched the initial supply drop for our assault taking place in the plain east of the pass. A Burma Rifle platoon was on Tayoktaung. Leaving, for a while, one company at Loihinche until Lieut. Davis's Kachins could ensure that all the Japs, except stragglers, had left the hills. I moved with the rest of the brigade to Lakum West to join Claude. The battalion held the high ground occupying previously prepared Jap positions.

Our supply-drop area and Lakum itself were being shelled intermittently by the Japs from Mogaung. We soon brought the Mustangs on to where we thought the guns were and on to the two villages of Kyaingyi and Kyaingale, where it was reported, and later confirmed that there were trucks and a vehicle workshop.

We could now see the whole of Mogaung town and plain before us. We were well dug in along the ridge, the marsh protected our immediate rear, and the stalwart Davis would give us any warning of forays into the mountains to turn our flank. The question was, how best to attack Mogaung, now just over two miles away, out of range of our mortars.

One of the South Staffords officers reported seeing a 4.2-inch mortar in Cawnpore Arsenal which would have the necessary range. I sent a personal message to Joe Lentaigne asking for a couple of 4.2-inch mortars, stating that even if I could not take Mogaung on account of the intervening floods and marsh, with these I could harass it day and night. He signalled back that he had asked 14th Army but that they had stated that this was not a 4.2-inch mortar theatre!

I reported that an officer had seen one in Cawnpore. Joe

immediately sent an officer there and in a couple of days two 4.2-inch mortars, one English and one American, had been dropped to us with ammunition. They also obtained all the 4.2-inch mortar ammunition in India, which was not much.

These were a great asset. We took a little while working out their range tables and method of firing, especially the American one, which had a rifled barrel and which none of us had seen before.

Soon we were harassing the Japs at odd hours all night, while the Air Force harassed them during the day. Diaries showed that we killed at least one battalion commander and his adjutant while they were carrying out their nightly rounds. By placing the mortars behind the hills, we ensured that the Jap garrison in Mogaung could not hear their noise of discharge but only a whirring sound just before the bomb landed. The British mortar, at long range, was ideal for harassing; it was inaccurate, and neither we nor the enemy knew for certain where it was going to land within a radius of at least 500 yards. But it had a very good lethal effect as it burst immediately on impact. The American mortar was much more accurate and had the advantage of slight penetration effect, which was most useful when used against Jap dug-outs, which could not be too deep or have too much overhead cover in that low-lying country. The result was that we used the British mortar for harassing at night, and the American for destruction or neutralization of strongpoints. As we could spare only one team to fire both, this Cox and Box method suited everybody except the Japs.

But this did not solve the problem of capturing Mogaung. Mogaung was a difficult place to attack. On the north was the 400-yard-wide four- to six-knot Mogaung river which curled around the rear to Tapaw ferry and into the Irrawaddy. This river was bridged at Mogaung by a damaged, but partly repaired, girder railway bridge which took the railway on to Myitkyina. To the west of Mogaung, the twisting Namyin Chaung, now in flood, ran through low-lying country from Hopin past Loilaw to its confluence with the Mogaung river at Mogaung. To the west was the range of hills of which we now occupied one sector. But between the hills and Mogaung ran the Wettauk Chaung, also in flood, from the neighbourhood of Loilaw to Pinhmi, and then through a series of wide marshy lakes called 'Ins' to the Mogaung river. There was a steel road bridge at Pinhmi which took the Tapaw ferry-Mogaung road over the Wettauk Chaung just south of the first 'In', the Pinhmi In. Loilaw, where the railway to Mandalay crossed the Namyin Chaung about four miles south of Mogaung, closed the only gap between the Namyin Chaung, the Wettauk Chaung and the hills. There was a good road from Loilaw to Mogaung. This route, the only one on which we would not have to cross a water gap, was the way which the Japs had expected us to attack. But it would have meant attacking along a road banked up above low-lying country and marsh, with little cover.

Strangely enough, although all units which first started to fight in Burma disliked the jungle and complained about the poor visibility, having been in the jungle for a while they were now subject to agoraphobia, dislike of open spaces.

Sitting on the Lakum pass I tried to plan my attack. To our front was the Wettauk Chaung, about thirty yards wide, which my night patrols reported as unfordable. Beyond, looking from above, there appeared to be little cover in the paddy and marshland, apart from the cluster of trees around the villages of Kyaingyi and Kyaingale. My first idea was to make a bridgehead over the Wettauk Chaung to our front, seize Kyaingyi and Kyaingale, and use them as bases for the attack on Mogaung proper.

This would leave the left flank open to an attack from Loilaw where 500 Japanese were reported, and on the right flank the Japs could use the Pinhmi bridge to bring troops over the Wettauk to attack our base at Lakum from the hills. Further, a shortage of Sappers and assault troops was a factor against making an assault crossing. Only one Sapper officer out of seven now survived with Brigade, the remainder having been wounded or gone sick.

So far there had been no signs of anything but an improvised defence of Mogaung, backed up by some artillery and anti-aircraft guns in Mogaung and to the west. There was therefore a possibility, with the Japs disorganized and without proper command as they appeared to be, that we could march straight into Mogaung without much opposition, and seize it. But this would mean leaving at least one battalion at

Lakum to guard our sick and wounded and our stores and mules. It also risked being surrounded by anti-aircraft guns – as had occurred at Blackpool – and being starved out. During the monsoon it was too hazardous to carry out supply drops at night, as had been done at White City, and in the daytime Dakotas circling around three or four times to drop their stores accurately would be chicken feed for the Jap anti-aircraft gunners. (These gunners actually turned out to be a highly inaccurate and rather miserable lot of Hong Kong and Singapore Brigade R.A. Sikhs who had volunteered or been conscripted into this job by the Japanese.) Such a course also counted on our being relieved by the quick approach of a Chinese regiment, which, in spite of promises dangled in front of our eyes like a carrot before a donkey, seemed quite unlikely. There was also little point in occupying a strategic position, leaving an undefeated enemy in the neighbourhood, when by defeating that enemy in detail – which seemed at the time a likely possibility – the strategic position would fall like a ripe plum into our hands.

As I ruminated, staring into the distance, a young Gurkha, one of the new reinforcements, who was drinking out of a water-bottle, came into my view. He suddenly realized that I was looking at him, and a look of guilt came over his face. He quickly took a tin of chlorinating tablets out of his haversack, picked out two and swallowed them, washing them down with a draught of water. He then smiled at me with a self-satisfied air. As one of these tablets is meant to be dissolved for twenty minutes in a two-pint water-bottle full of water, I hope that taken *neat* they did not do irreparable damage to his inside.

After discussing the plan of attack with Claude, I decided that it was essential to clear the hills first and then make our axis of attack the Tapaw–Pinhmi–Mogaung road, with, if possible, the Pinhmi bridge a secure crossing over the Wettauk. Our right flank would thus be secure on the Mogaung river. Then if we were driven back, we would be driven on to our supplies and, if the worst came to the worst, on to Tapaw ferry.

This plan may appear to be too cautious, and perhaps a *coup de main* would have been successful and saved us many casualties. But it must be remembered that we were a Long Range Penetration Brigade without artillery, whereas the

Japs possessed artillery, and the memory of the fall of Black-pool was fresh in our minds.

So our next job was to clear the hills. We knew that there were some Japs in a Gurkha village one mile north of us, as most of the Gurkha population had come to tell us so. All over the hills of north and eastern Burma are Gurkha villages which were established after the Burmese wars of the nineteenth century, when the Gurkhas, who had fought in Burma at that time, were given grants of land. These Bur-mese-Gurkhas – for most of them have intermarried with the Burmese – are a very fine type. My orderly in 1942 and 1943, Bahadur Singh, was a Burmese Gurkha. Apart from being an ex-soldier and ex-policeman, he had the great ad-vantage of speaking Gurkhali, Burmese, Urdu and English. He was also an extremely good batman, and was a godsend to me. He did not come in this campaign: he was sick. The Gurkha population of the village was of great assistance to us later in the collection of supply drops and as stretcher-bearers.

I therefore gave orders for the South Staffords to attack along the ridge and the Gurkhas to attack along the eastern edge of the hills, the rate of advance being governed by the Staffords.

The Staffords cleared the hills as far as Pinhmi, having to eradicate three platoon positions in turn. They used the tactics which the Lancashire Fusiliers had found to be so successful on their advance to Loihinche. The enemy did not fight to the last.

I also sent one company of Gurkhas, which was under the command of Capt. Butler (not the one at Tapaw) to try to seize the pass where the Tapaw road crosses the hills. Butler succeeded in this most creditably. He moved cautiously through the jungle at the bottom of the range until most of his company were within grenade-throwing distance of the Japanese, who were occupying a strongly dug-in and barbed-wired position at the top of the pass. At a given word everyone threw his grenade, and fired his weapon into the enclosure, and then, with a great shout, attacked and over-ran it practically without loss, killing about four to five Japs out of a total of about forty, the remainder fleeing.

The Jap officer was the first to recover. He drew his sword and tried to rally his men to charge and retake the position.

But Butler had guarded against the possibility of a counter-attack by armoured vehicles and had placed a Gurkha covering the road with a Piat. As the officer turned to charge, the serious-minded young Gurkha fired his graze fuse Piat bomb and hit the officer in the belly. The officer and the counter-attack rapidly disintegrated.

This was a most important gain. The Jap position was wired in better than I had seen elsewhere in Burma, and might have caused us endless trouble. The garrison appeared to have been made up of orderlies and convalescents from the Jap hospital at Pinhmi, but it was an easy position to hold, and I gave great credit to Butler and his boys for their success.

Ron Degg, after working his way along the hills to Pinhmi, heard from some locals of ammunition dumps on the western slopes. He sent down his commando platoon who, led by a local, blew up two large dumps. These made a magnificent explosion which was heard way across the valley to the hills west of Mogaung where 111 Brigade and the West Africans were now making their presence felt. Ron Degg finally cleared the highest peak, Uhman Taung, where the Jap artillery observation officer was killed, and his telephones taken over by us.

The Japanese telephone line is much better than ours; it is lighter and more easily laid. We always used it in preference to our own. On the whole our arms and equipment were better than the Japs. They especially preferred our 3-inch mortar, many of which they had obtained in Singapore and Hong Kong and Burma in 1942, and our boots. It was strange that while we were experimenting with Japanese boots and shoes, the Japs would always, whenever they got the chance, take the boots off any of our dead and wounded and wear them. Personally having worn in Scotland, Australia, Burma and elsewhere, all sorts of types of boots which various commando-type organizations were trying out, I always came back to the British Army ammunition boot. The Indian pattern was no good, and all our brigades were fitted out with the Australian or South African pattern which were best. Where the Japanese equipment was better and more useful than ours was in mess tins, water-bottles, telescopic sights and maps. Their mess tins had lids, could be suspended over a fire and were designed for cooking. Ours

7. *The Author with, centre, Squadron Leader Bobbie Thompson, R.A.F. (now Sir Robert Thompson) at Broadway.*

8. *Sappers preparing a bridge for demolition at Henn, White City.*

9. *Mustang (P. 47) Fighters – Bombers of No. 1 U.S.A.A.F. Air Commando, the Chindit Artillery. They had a longer range than R.A.F. fighter-bombers, so were used almost exclusively for deep penetration support.*

are designed to act in lieu of plates and are quite useless. Practically all our troops were equipped with Japanese mess tins by now. Their water-bottles were a great improvement on ours, but just before the war ended, the War Office had designed a water-bottle on Japanese lines which was very good. Their telescopic sights were designed not so much to magnify, but to clarify. I am not certain of the optical principles involved – something to do with extracting only certain of the rays through a prism – but whatever it was, it appeared to clear away all haze and make objects stand out more clearly and the results were very good. As for maps, it was purely a question of printing. The maps they used were identical copies of our own ordnance survey maps. But whereas the ones issued to us were in only two colours – black with brown contours – in theirs the forests were green, the paddy yellow, the rivers blue, and the roads red.

The most vital thing to know in Burma was when one changed from jungle to paddy. In our maps as printed, one could not tell without the most minute inspection. In theirs, as printed, it was obvious. After three years of importuning, the Geographical Survey people in Delhi eventually agreed to put the paddy in yellow. They complained that it meant one more process which was expensive. But the original surveyors gave very much more detail on their maps than that. Streams which were perennial were all in blue to their source. Where they became seasonal, the blue ceased. If Bernard Fergusson's brigade had been equipped with properly printed maps they would not have got into such trouble in Indaw for lack of water, and Indaw might not have fallen. The conservatism of the ordnance survey branch at Delhi, who refused to accede to the pleadings of the practical people who had to fight on the spot, was responsible for this and many other defeats. The Japs, realizing the value of the coloured maps they had found in Maymyo when we left, continued to print them in colour. I and all my battalion commanders and most of the company commanders made use of the Jap maps in preference to our half-finished products.

On the subject of equipment, there are one or two other important points to mention. In 1943 we had been an experimental brigade and many new types of equipment were tried out on us or invented by us. This year we were, to all intents and purposes, an experimental force, and much of what we found out to be useful was adopted by the remainder of the Army in Burma.

In 1943 we had started the 'wearing of the green', everything green – handkerchiefs, vests, pants, mugs, towels, backs of maps, toothbrushes, handles, everything – and it was a punishable offence to have anything white on you. I was one of the first to start this, having a tunic made of some green velvety whipcord type of curtain cloth which I bought in Bombay. This year we had tried out inflatable groundsheets, like lilos, but they were not much of a success. We were given some impregnated mosquito veils which later were adopted by the rest of the Army.

The American hammock was one of the greatest successes. I have already mentioned this, but I consider that it is so important as to be worth emphasizing. It consisted of an ordinary hammock made of waterproof material. Above it, and connected to the bottom by mosquito-net walls, was a waterproof sheet. The entrance was through a zip-fastened aperture in the mosquito net wall. The whole weighed $6\frac{1}{2}$ lb., and if properly slung, kept one completely dry, in the heaviest monsoon rain and wind. Underneath there was a pocket in which one could put one's rifle and other stores. As a boy I used to camp out in one of those light cotton tents which did not keep out heavy rain, but diffused it into a fine mist so that it did not fall heavily on me. If I had had a hammock of this nature, how much better off I could have been. One cannot, of course, so easily cook under its shelter as one can in a tent. Another disadvantage is that during shelling you feel extremely naked slung up in the air between two trees. When shelling started near our Brigade H.Q. at Mogaung, Bobbie, Francis, Taffy and myself would discuss whether we should get out into the cold rain and get into our three-foot-deep water troughs, which our slit trenches had then become. Then suddenly the Jap would get the range, a shell would fall near, and there would be four splashes into our cold baths, accompanied by others from our orderlies and the rest of the Brigade H.Q. Later, when I was not in it, my hammock and pack was hit and a beautiful green pair of folded pyjamas was riddled with holes. I was very proud of these pyjamas, but when L/Cpl. Young became sick and was evacuated, Charley, my new Chinese orderly, reckoned they were no good, and threw them away.

Other useful items of equipment which we had but which were not in general use were a balloon-silk waterproof bag which fitted into the pack and, besides keeping everything dry, acted as a flotation unit when swimming (it was also used for getting water for mules); an anti-gas wallet which was very useful for keeping personal belongings, like letters, dry, and as a tobacco pouch for those who smoked, and Air Force escape food packs as issued to the R.A.F. when flying over Burma. (These are a very useful emergency ration, and besides that, have compasses, medicine, etc. I see no reason why all troops should not be issued with these in future.) We relied entirely on the American K. ration, supplemented by extra tea and sugar as our basic ration. After victories we would receive a supplementary luxury issue of bully beef or M. and V. – both of which were highly esteemed by us – stewed fruit and sometimes white bread and rum. From the Japanese we would sometimes capture rice, tinned salmon and tinned steak and kidney pie, which was most welcome. From the Burmese we would buy rice which mostly went to the Gurkhas, and the odd buffalo or pig. Compared with the previous years, rations were delivered regularly and we suffered no great hardship. Perpetual K. rations were a hardship; they only are designed to be eaten for a week at a time at the most, but as the music-hall song says, 'You'll get used to it', and it is astonishing what one's body will get used to.

Since reaching Lakum we had been receiving good supply drops, with the result that we could bring down heavy mortar fire on all the Japs seen and on Jap positions before attack. One hundred to 200 rounds on a Jap platoon position before an attack was quite normal, as well as intermittent harassing fire on such Jap positions as Pinhmi bridge. Eventually the Japs did not dare move about much by day, owing to our observation from the hills and their fear of our bringing down the fighter bombers on to them.

I moved my base to a Gurkha village soon after it had been taken, as we found it possible to make a light plane strip for the evacuation of our wounded. The Jap artillery, directed from the artillery observation post that we had now eliminated, had found the range of Lakum and caused some casualties in Brigade H.Q. and the hospital, and had set alight some flame-thrower fuel which had, in its turn, destroyed some of our ammunition.

The light plane strip was soggy but capable of use in what

fine weather there was. Later Bobbie Thompson or one of his officers, probably an Australian, had the brilliant idea of having some coconut matting dropped, with the result that they fashioned an excellent mat wicket which allowed planes to land and take off in most weathers. If the ground under the matting became too soggy for use, they changed the wicket to one side. Brushwood was placed under the matting, which was found to be an improvement, and after one plane had failed to take off in time and buried its nose in the marsh, fortunately without casualties, the R.A.F. put a bump at the end of the strip. Then, if the pilot had not taken off by the end of the strip, the plane was bumped into the air willy-nilly.

The pilots were not initially told of this bump, nor of its original composition – dud wet mortar bombs. This strip was another example of R.A.F. pilots' ingenuity and resource. General Wingate's insistence on pilots accompanying the brigade had certainly paid a great dividend. Personally I would far prefer to have two pilots on the ground directing nine in the air than to have twenty-seven pilots helping us in the air with none on the ground.

On the night the South Staffords blew the dumps, the Japs made a very inefficient attempt at a counter-attack. About sixteen of them advanced in file at night along a path down which a machine gun was aimed. They left about half of their number behind them as corpses.

I next ordered the Lancashire Fusiliers to attack Pinhmi village itself. The attack started late in the afternoon, guides having lost the way to the forming-up areas. After difficult fighting in lantana shrub, they evicted some Japs guarding ammunition dumps. They had an uncomfortable night holding their gains, but finally cleared Pinhmi village in the morning, finishing up by holding the line of the Wettauk Chaung to the Pinhmi In. The bridge itself appeared to be strongly held. It was unfortunate that the attack the previous day was four hours late in starting, otherwise they might have managed to seize the bridge before the Japs occupied a position around it. This bridge was to give us much trouble.

In between Pinhmi and Pt. 610, where the Gurkha Butler was still in possession of the pass, there was a concealed general hospital. It was long before we discovered how large it

196

was. Besides innumerable huts and wards hidden in the jungle reaching down to a landing stage on the Pinhmi In, the hill behind was later found to be honeycombed with dug-outs. The night before we had taken Pinhmi we had heard lorries moving up and down over the road which we had mortared. We realized now that these were evacuating wounded. The Lancashire Fusiliers were the first to send a platoon to clear the area. At the doorway of the first ward that they entered, the leading man was shot through the head by a bedridden patient. The result was that the Fusiliers threw grenades in. In another ward, as they came up, they heard an explosion. Five Japs had crept off their wooden bunks and put their heads together round their one and only grenade, and pulled the string. This had been effective.

Later I sent a company of Gurkhas through, and they had one man shot and one wounded. So they finished off a few more Japs. Many of the patients had apparently tried to escape by swimming the Pinhmi In, for we found their clothes alongside. They may, of course, have decided to drown themselves. A little later, one of our officers thought that he would like a bath there. He put his leg in, and almost immediately it was nearly black with leeches. So those Japs who waded and swam across could not have had a pleasant time. Some tried to go down the Mogaung river in rafts, but Fusilier Butler dealt with these at Tapaw ferry. Others took to the jungle and increased the revenue of the Kachins, to whom I paid one rupee for each Jap right ear.

We were fighting hard to our front, and I could not spare units to try to clear the extensive hospital in our rear. A fortnight later when I did send a unit, they found about thirty to forty Japs in advanced stages of starvation, lying amongst the dead and rotting. Some even then resisted, but most died of advanced malnutrition, our doctors being unable to revive them. About eight remained alive, and at least one of them, who had lost his leg, was so incensed at the way that they had been left by their doctors and orderlies to die, that he said that he would fight for us.

Our capture of Pinhmi included twenty large dumps of ammunition, one field general hospital, one field hospital complete with excellent equipment and drugs (which our doctors acquired) and about fifteen lorries. Capt. Brazier and a Nesei were flown in, and I received from our prisoners quite a lot of 'hot' information about the defences of Mogaung. I placed our escaped Gurkha prisoners from the 1943 campaign to guard the Jap prisoners until they could be evacuated.

The Jap prisoners on the whole lived up to their precept of death rather than dishonour. Lieut. Satrai, who was captured on the first attack of White City, was flown to a hospital in Assam. He kept asking to be interrogated, and then shot. When he found that he was not going to be shot, he asked to see the matron and the C.O. of the hospital, thanked them for their kindness and said that it was dishonourable to live, and that he must die. He then turned his face to the wall and, although forcibly fed, within five days he was dead. A post-mortem could discover no cause of death.

Another of our prisoners choked himself by eating his blanket. Those that were evacuated were first securely trussed before being put in a light plane, otherwise the pilot would not take them – which was understandable. They were then deposited at Broadway before being transferred to a Dakota. There was a lot to admire in the Jap, and there is no question – I do not think that any front-line soldier would disagree – that given the same equipment as us or the Americans, they would be amongst the finest and most dangerous soldiers in the world.

Apart from the attempts to block our path north of Ngahkawtawng we had not yet encountered any real co-ordinated defence. The Japs were strong in artillery, which, belonging to 18 Division, was good, and we were shelled daily. The loss of their observation post on Uhman Taung made their shelling less accurate. Their infantry defence to date consisted of isolated platoons or less, sticking on to a feature or around a dump, well dug in and provisioned, but with no attempt at siting for mutual support. The result was that we could liquidate each position in turn. Around the dumps, for instance, there would be two or three men dug in and well concealed guarding each dump. We would have to clear each party one by one. It took time, and they caused us casualties before they were killed. But, in these small numbers, they could not look in all directions at once. It was therefore possible to hold them from one direction and attack and kill them from another.

My appreciation was therefore that there was, as yet, no real co-ordinated defence, but that every man had received an order to stick to his post, being promised reinforcements soon.

Our casualties were mounting. Since the beginning of the advance from Lamai to the capture of Pinhmi, our casualties by May 6th were:

Officers: 5 killed, 13 wounded.
Other ranks: 53 killed, 166 wounded.

With our superiority in weapons and men we calculated from the number of bodies counted that we had killed between 150 to 200 Japs, not including those killed in the air strikes and mortaring in the Mogaung plain. The proportion was too even for our liking, but every Jap, unless he was surprised and thrown off his balance, seemed determined to kill one of us before he himself was killed, with the result that he did not disclose his presence or open fire until our chaps were right on top of him, when he could not miss one man at least. This was one of the reasons why I ordered the use of as much machine gun and mortar preparation as possible before an attack to try to redress the balance in our favour. Fortunately, being on air supply, we never suffered any shortage of ammunition. This advantage, however, was often offset by Jap shelling. As everywhere, once our chaps were in their trenches, shelling caused little or no casualties: it was the first surprise salvo which caused the casualties. These occurred usually at dawn and dusk. At night the Japs were afraid of our spotting their positions from the gun flashes. By day they were in fear of our air strikes. At about 5.30 p.m., therefore, as at White City, they would start their hate, and, as at White City, I ordered that teas should be made at 4.30 p.m. so that everyone would be in his trench at 5.30 p.m. The result was that the man cooked his meal between 4.30 and 5 p.m., ate it, baled out his slit trench, and sat there until dark during the Jap shelling. He then got out and carried on his normal duties. Of course, there were variations, and, now that the base was protected from artillery fire well behind the hills, there the more normal routine was followed.

It may seem a paradox to state that being on air supply we had no shortage of ammunition. It is a tribute to the hard work and good organization of our rear base, and the more than conscientious performance of their duty by the R.A.F. and U.S.A.A.F. transport squadrons whose pilots were averaging 300 hours' operational flying a month at this time; and is is a fact that supply by air results in a more plentiful amount of ammunition *when required* than the more archaic method of supply by lorry. Firstly, if one trusts the air supply implicitly as we had all grown to do, one does not have to carry about large 'just in case' reserves. Sufficient quantities of small arms ammunition and mortar ammunition for any offensive or defensive to last at least five days with the most liberal expenditure, can be supplied by air within twenty-four hours by normal demand, or in an emergency, within six hours of the request. Whereas in land supply the request and the items of supply have to go through so many middlemen and are then subject to such interminable delays due to road or rail congestion, that at least three days' notice is required for abnormal demands. Secondly, air supply is completely flexible, the supplies can be switched from one unit to another unit which may be in trouble 250 miles away, using the same planes from the same base at very short notice.

All units do not require the maximum at the same time; but in land supply, dumps have to be made for these peak periods, whereas in air supply the dump for all units within a 250-mile radius can be at the air base. The result is that no unit suddenly requiring a lot of ammunition ever goes short.

Thirdly, a point I have touched on already: delivery is made direct to the consumer – that is to the unit actually firing the ammunition, and not to some accounting unit controlled by a staff officer who is not in the picture, and who sends forward what he thinks the battalion will need. The battalion, in our case, had its quartermaster at the air base; he remained under command of the battalion commander, and he would soon hear from his C.O. if what he had asked for was not produced at once. This system worked very well and with the minimum of friction. Any method whereby some strange newly constituted body at air base sends forward what it thinks the battalion needs is impersonal and therefore inefficient, wasteful and doomed to failure. It is essential that units or formations have their own representative at air base to whom the air-base depots make delivery on paper, whilst the goods themselves are loaded on to the plane. The unit or formation in the field requires only a minimum of its 'Q' staff with it if it is supplied by air. Their only job is to make demands and organize distribution, but they must have someone at air base to translate those demands into supplies put on to planes in light of what is available. To have these people in the field is just making up so much more weight of food to feed useless mouths. I would prefer that weight to be ammunition.

A British division nowadays totals about 20,000 men. About 10,000 of these or less are potential enemy-killers including the lethal parts of infantry battalions and artillery and reconnaissance regiments; Royal Corps of Signals, which are essential; a certain number of the Royal Engineers, because the fewer the trucks in a division, the fewer the engineers required to get that division across country; the essential staff officers; the essential medical personnel excluding a large proportion of the ambulances which are not essential with air evacuation; and the essential workshops for repair, which, in turn, can be reduced as the number of vehicles is reduced. The remaining 10,000 are lorry-drivers and distributors of supplies and their barnacles, and units carrying around 'reserves' of supplies. All these 10,000 become redundant when the division is on air supply, because supplies are delivered to the unit by air, and distributive services are not necessary. They are therefore not required in the field, and the division becomes a streamlined, hard-hitting formation much stronger than before, since it does not have to weaken its offensive strength by detaching units to protect a mass of people who cannot protect themselves. An analogy is that of a well-trained boxer in good condition who can afford to take the offensive with both hands as he can afford to take the odd blow in his stomach without harm; and an untrained boxer with a paunch who must keep one arm on the defensive to guard his stomach.

Any commander who has once tasted the wonderful freedom given by air supply cannot easily reconcile himself to return to the fetters of road supply, any more than a man who has once tasted the untrammelled liberty of a free country would voluntarily surrender to the thraldom of totalitarianism.

In my brigade the number of those who were not potential Jap-killers numbered less than 5 per cent of the brigade; or if one adds mule-drivers, all of whom were interchangeable with men in the rifle companies and were so changed for rest or recuperation if they had been wounded or sick, the proportion would then be not more than 12 per cent. Nearly all our distributive and 'Q' staff were in India. The 14th Army staff, seeing the large number there, thought that we had a wastefully large staff, not realizing that because they were centralized, which always makes for saving, in overall numbers we had far fewer staff per fighting man than any unit in Burma.

The question that must arise in everyone's mind is: agreed that air supply can be a saving and gives magnificent mobility and flexibility, what about the enemy if he has air superiority? The only answer I can give is the same as that of Field-Marshal Montgomery when speaking of any other form of offensive: 'We must win the air battle first.'

An alternative is supply by radar-directed V.2. More air effort should be made to drop explosives to people on the ground who can efficiently use them rather than to drop them indiscriminately from the air.

I do not advocate air supply for the whole of an army, but only those fighting formations who are actually fighting – especially in the offensive; and in all forms of 'extensive' warfare where communications are negligible and the area is vast. It is not often realized that the Burma front, from the Chinese theatre to the Arakan, was longer than the Russian front. The area was vast and the Jap air force could not be everywhere at once.

CHAPTER NINE

ATTACK ON MOGAUNG

We were now faced with the crossing of the Wettauk Chaung. The Lancashire Fusiliers had been unable to take the Pinhmi bridge by a *coup de main,* although they did manage to get one or two people on to it; and I asked Hugh Christie to try again. Here I made the grave mistake of not reconnoitring myself. It would have meant crawling on my stomach in the mud to the river bank, and then being very careful of snipers. I told Hugh Christie to support his attack with the maximum amount of covering fire by mortar and machine guns, and to use smoke, and we would obtain an air strike.

This air strike, which I had especially asked not to land on the bridge but on the embankment on the other side where the Japs' posts were, was extremely accurate, one bomb landing on the embankment, knocking out one Jap position. The Fusiliers tried to cross the river, but it was too difficult and they received casualties. I had seen David Monteith that day. He was commanding the attacking company. He looked extremely tired and old. He had been placing a 2-inch mortar in position to put down a smoke screen. He then walked back and was shot through the head and killed. His fatigue had made him negligent of his own safety.

It had proved impossible to seize the bridge by direct assault, and the Fusiliers had received quite heavy casualties in the attempt. The difficulty was that the road leading to the 150-foot bridge was in the clear view of the Japs who had burrowed into the embankment on the other side. We had to find some other route to Mogaung. I should not have ordered this attack. If I had reconnoitred myself, I would have seen how little chance of success there was. The moral is that it is essential for the commander to see for himself, always. There can be no exceptions or compromises.

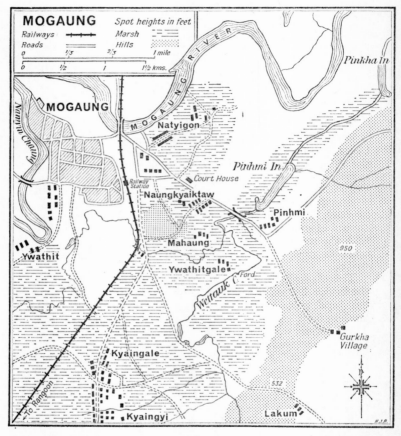

The rain had ceased for a while, the floods decreased, and one of our patrols found a ford over the Wettauk south of the bridge. I knew that unless we hurried, Jap reinforcements would reach Mogaung, if they had not already done so. That day I had been sitting up near a South Staffords mortar whose officer was stating that being right up near the top of the hill, and with the use of extra secondary propulsive charges, he considered that he could increase the range from a maximum of 2,700 to over 3,000 yards without bursting the barrel. As I was sitting there I saw through my glasses about two companies of the enemy marching down the open road near Natyigon. The range was over 3,000 yards. But I asked the mortar officer to see if he could land one amongst them. Putting the maximum charge he dared on to the mortar bomb, he fired and it landed plumb into the middle of them. At that moment six Mustangs appeared through the clouds. I shouted to him to put down smoke, and got on to the air observation post by phone and told them to tell the planes to go down straight on to the smoke on the road at once. In less than a minute the Mustangs were diving straight on to the troops lying in the open. After dropping their bombs, they kept up a low-level strafe round and round until they had no ammunition left. As we heard later from Jap diaries, it was part of a new battalion of 53 Division just moving in and the planes caused heavy casualties. Their reception must certainly have surprised them.

I decided to attack with two battalions up, the Gurkhas and the Staffords, with the first objective Mahaung and the railway station. I still hoped that we might forestall the enemy reinforcing Mogaung, and I was prepared to take risks. So at dawn on the 9th, the Gurkhas leading, we splashed through the Wettauk and along a flooded path through the marsh. The Gurkhas pressed on well, and were soon in a position to deploy for the attack. I halted Brigade H.Q. and the defence company on a T-junction of tracks to protect their rear and form a base for casualties, etc. I sent one company of the Staffords to reconnoitre to the right and try to clear Naungkyaiktaw woods. Our long column had been fired on en route but not enough to cause delays. We were all on tenterhooks at the possibility of entering Mogaung during the next twenty-four hours.

The Gurkhas, by some excellent fieldcraft and tactics, surprised the platoon holding Mahaung, killing twelve, and captured it. Those Japs who took shelter by the railway embankment were accurately mortared and later bombed, so that their casualties were probably higher.

The Staffords company, under Major Nip Hilton, also went forward most aggressively, crossing one chaung up to their necks in water. It must have been well over Nip

Hilton's hat. They encountered the enemy in a bamboo clump near Ywathitgale and, after some stiff fighting, with repeated counter-attacks by the enemy, finally killed most of them and drove the rest out.

On hearing this I dispatched Ron Degg with the rest of his battalion to take over that area and clear Ywathitgale itself. This he did, finally reaching the Pinhmi-Mogaung road.

On the way up I realized that the flooded way we had come could never be a reliable line of communications from our base to the forward battalions: any more rain would make it impassable for mules and probably also for men.

Therefore, on hearing at midday that the Staffords had reached the road, I decided to change my original plan. I left one Gurkha company at Mahaung under Capt. Fearfull Smith, whose duty it was by offensive noise and action to give the impression that that was our main effort. I gave him the task of harassing the enemy from Kyaingyi to Mahaung for the next twenty-four hours.

I decided to leave Brigade H.Q. where it was to give him support and act as a flank guard to the Staffords.

I ordered the Staffords to put a strong block on the road facing both ways. I ordered Freddie Shaw to operate from the South Staffords' block and to attack the Japs in the rear on the Pinhmi bridge. Hugh Christie I told to engage the Japs from the front while the Gurkhas moved up.

Thanks to the zeal of all ranks, the plan worked admirably. By the time I had issued orders and the switch had been carried out, it became too late for the Gurkhas to attack. But we found that Ywathitgale was an important administrative H.Q. and telephone centre, and its capture helped to confuse the Japs as to our intention.

During the night twenty Japs walked unconcernedly into the Staffords' block, leaving twelve dead behind them in the morning. A few also bumped into Brigade H.Q., and sustained casualties. Fearfull Smith created merry hell all around him, penetrating Kyaingyi and also to the Mogaung railway station.

At dawn the Gurkhas attacked Pinhmi bridge but were thrown back. Freddie Shaw then put in another attack which entailed their advancing through the marsh up to their waists in mud and water. After a hard fight, they took the bridge, killing about thirty-five Japs and capturing one medium machine gun and two light machine guns. Our casualties had not been light.

This was a very creditable effort by the Gurkhas, their jemadars and subahdars putting up an especially good show. The Japs were in excellent concealed positions high up on the 15-foot embankment leading to the bridge, surrounded by a sea of marsh and mangrove swamp. They could never have expected that the battalion could cross the marsh in force other than by the road, and it was only due to the offensive spirit of all ranks that all obstacles were overcome. Leaving Fearfull Smith to carry on his depredations for another twenty-four hours, I switched the whole brigade on to the axis of the road. We were now securely established along the axis of the road, two battalions up and one in the Pinhmi bridge area.

We heard later that the Japanese considered that their Pinhmi bridge garrison had done a very fine job in holding us up for three to four days.

It was now June 10th. Our total casualties in the encirclement and capture of the Pinhmi bridge were about 130 killed and wounded. I was still pressing the battalions on as hard as I could, to forestall Jap reinforcements. But without knowing it I was already too late. It was the forward elements of two battalions that we had seen arriving on the day we mortared and bombed them. Between the 10th and 12th the remainder and two new battalions arrived.

If we had managed to rush the Pinhmi bridge that first day, or found the ford earlier, we might have entered Mogaung before the new battalions. As it was, we had a long way to go before its capture. In retrospect, taking the wider view, it might seem that this would end up in our favour, Mogaung now lost its usefulness to the enemy as a road or rail centre as we overlooked the bridge, while the town itself became a bomb trap wherein at least four Jap battalions were destroyed. This sentiment would not have been much comfort to us at the time, and, even seen in retrospect, the balance was probably against us, as our continual attacks eventually virtually destroyed us.

I was increasingly anxious about my southern flank, and was importuning Brigade for some news of any of the columns or regiments which were supposed to be co-operating in the attack on Mogaung. Davis had forestalled at least one attempted raid through the hills, his Kachins killing about twenty Japs. But now we were vulnerable from flank attack along the plain, though admittedly they would have to travel through the difficult marshes that we had traversed.

I was still pushing my wretched battalions to try to win the race. On the 11th, the day after the capture of the bridge, the Lancashire Fusiliers, who relieved the Gurkhas, attacked the Courthouse triangle. This was a triangle of trees and shrubs bounded on the south side by the Pinhmi road, and on the north side by a cart track, with its base on a stream which our forward troops had reached.

The Fusiliers, after a long protracted fight carried out under the able command of Major Harrington (Hugh Christie having a poisoned leg) – a fight which lasted throughout the whole of a very hot day, and in which they used every one of their remaining rifle platoons – out-manoeuvred or killed the forty or fifty Japs dug in in that area. The enemy left ten dead. Our casualties were small, being one officer and two other ranks killed and eight wounded. The Fusiliers again used their superior fire power and greater strength to make the Jap position untenable. They had the satisfaction of capturing three dual-purpose 3-inch anti-aircraft guns which had been shelling us. One had been damaged by bombing, the others were in good condition, but their breech-blocks had been removed. We tried to get these into action as they were of British make, but similar breech-blocks did not reach us in time.

At the same time as the Lancashire Fusiliers attacked I had sent the Staffords towards the north to clear the area from the road to the river so that our right flank at least would be secure. They had a hard time. They avoided the obvious path, but, thinking of their previous success, ploughed and cut their way through the swamps, covering four times as much ground as they need have done. As they emerged, tired and exhausted, into the open near the river bank, they were engaged by a well-entrenched enemy. The Staffords attacked, but in spite of making some progress, they could not hold their ground. I had come up to see how they were getting on, and seeing that they had had quite heavy casualties, and were losing more in their exposed position, told them to consolidate farther back. Capt. Archie Wavell, son of the Field-Marshal, who had flown in as a reinforcement and was now commanding a company, asked permission to put in one more attack, as he now knew where the Jap positions were. It was getting late, and with Ron's concurrence I agreed. Archie put in a good attack and held his ground, but did not quite reach the river. During this attack he was wounded in the wrist, his hand only just hanging on. He applied a tourniquet and bound it up, then seeing that he was the only officer alive, put all his company into position before he reported his wound. That night Chesshire took off the rest of his hand. It was a plucky show and a very fine example to his troops.

It was essential to capture this position on the river, otherwise we occupied a vulnerable and insecure salient. Therefore, supported by the South Staffords, the Gurkhas went into the attack next morning. After a very hard fight against fresh troops, they were successful, and our right flank was firmly established on the river. The railway bridge was now in full view only 800 yards upstream, covered by our machine gun fire.

I had now the remains of all three battalions up with our southern flank and our communications with base guarded solely by the platoons of my brigade defence company. One platoon was in Ywathitgale, one platoon at Pinhmi and the third platoon at the pass over the hills to our base. The Hong Kong platoon only was protecting our base and the light plane strip.

On June 13th, all battalion commanders came to see me and said that however much they were willing to go on, these last series of attacks in rain and mud had exhausted their men and their casualties had reduced their numbers of fit men per battalion to a little more than a company strength each. Throughout our whole front except on the river bank, we were confronted with 400 to 600 yards of open paddy between us and Mogaung. On the river the Japs and ourselves disputed the possession of a long straggly village stretched along the bank.

Jap artillery fire had increased and was more accurate, and digging into the paddy and marsh afforded little protection. We had lost the race to Mogaung by 600 yards. I decided, therefore, to consolidate and wait either until we recovered, or until reinforcements reached us. How I wished that I had the King's (Liverpool) Regiment now!

The total attacking strength of all three battalions put together was not more than 550. Of these many had been wounded at least once, and nearly all had suffered or were suffering from malaria, jungle sores or trench feet. The worst of the lame or sick or battle-exhausted had long been interchanged with the mule-leaders. But mule-driving was no sinecure. The road as far as Pinhmi was reasonably dry, although occasionally shelled. From Pinhmi to the supply-drop area the path was ankle-to knee-deep in slush. The battalion mule convoys had to go up and down the two-to three-mile route two or three times a day transporting rations and ammunition. This route was also harassed by infiltrating Jap snipers.

At the base I had nearly 250 wounded awaiting evacuation, half of them stretcher cases. Now that we had lost our own light plane force and were dependent on General Stilwell's planes, the evacuation situation had become chaotic. At Tingmongyang, where I had left some wounded, planes refused to land, and only after two of those waiting had died did an American sergeant-pilot, strictly against orders, land and, after several trips, evacuate the lot.

There was some excuse for this attitude. In the latter stages Cochran's light plane force had been rather profligate in their expenditure of planes owing to accidents on landing. This was due to two main causes. First of all we, on the ground, as the monsoon made landing conditions worse, were asking the light planes to land on strips which became more and more difficult.

Secondly, the light plane pilots had had a long innings during periods of great strain and some of them were either getting careless or not caring what happened to the planes. But later, when I was to see the large number of planes in the rear areas apparently being used solely for liaison or not being used at all, I could not help feeling that the maximum was not being done to evacuate our wounded. There was an outstanding exception: an American sergeant-pilot, a silent man, who used to fly in to us against orders. I think that he was the same man who had flown into Tingmongyang. He would fly backwards and forwards from Myitkyina, an over-all distance of seventy miles, in any weather, averaging nine or ten times per day. His maximum was fourteen sorties in a day. He would never leave his plane and never switch his engine off. He just went backwards and forwards from dawn to dusk, evacuating wounded. It was a stupendous effort, involving 700 to 1,000 miles in a light plane per day, and on behalf of us all I salute him.

One day at my Tactical H.Q. near the forward battalion, I received a message from General Lentaigne which was to be placed in my hands by an officer. It was to the effect that unless Archie Wavell was evacuated that day, I was dismissed from commanding my brigade.

This was the first time I knew of Archie not having been evacuated. In fact, I was so busy fighting the Japs that I think I had forgotten about him altogether. Evidently what had happened was that his parents had received a message that he was dangerously wounded. This was normal routine, and having a hand off came into that category of wounded. The Viceroy and Lady Wavell had flown to Assam to meet him when he was evacuated. Archie, however, who saw lying around him men wounded and in a far worse condition that he was, had refused to be evacuated. The plane kept coming back to fetch Archie, but he had been adamant, and nearly sixty men were evacuated, many of them had lain there weeks, before I turned up and forced him on the plane.

There was more to it than the fact that he was the son of the Viceroy. From a map our position must have looked very serious. We were hemmed in all around. There were at the time 200 wounded on the ground. Our offensive had ceased. Our left flank was bare, apart from the gallant Davis and his cut-throats. Wingate had preached the gospel in the first campaign that wounded may be abandoned. It was not known that we had discarded this theory, and that it would be the last thing we would do, as the wounded knew. Besides all that, the campaign for revolution in India was on, with the so-called 'Indian National Army' fighting on the Jap side. It was feared that if they could lay their hands on Archie, they might try by torture to influence the Viceroy. Therefore it was imperative that he should be flown out. Evidently other messages had been received that he should be flown out, but as they were judged to be an administrative matter, they had not been shown to me.

Young Archie earned the undying gratitude of very many of the men by his thought for them, and he probably saved many lives as well.

I used to go around and visit all the wounded periodically, especially after the elation of a success, in order that I could be sobered up by seeing what it meant in the end. There they were under a leaky improvised shelter, lying in two rows on the ground covered in blood-stained parachute cloth. We had had a surgical team flown in by now, and they worked in appalling, but unavoidable, conditions of mud and rain.

A man wounded would first be treated on the spot by his battalion. Then he would be carried back as far as Pinhmi by his battalion stretcher-bearers. There Chesshire and Thorne would treat him. After that he would almost at once be carried on in the rain to the base by the Oriya Indians or Burmese Gurkhas, or Sikh stretcher-bearers. He would wait his turn, according to the seriousness of the case, before being seen and operated on by the surgeon, meanwhile tended by other Medical Officers and looked after by less seriously wounded men.

If light planes were available, he would fly to Myitkyina that day – or the next day. If not, he might wait days before evacuation. If he had a flesh wound he would stay at base, helping tend the more seriously wounded, and then rejoin his battalion. Only the seriously wounded were evacuated. At Myitkyina he would be treated again as necessary, and then flown by Dakota to our new hospitals in the northern Assam valley near Ledo.

The fact of having this air evacuation sustained the morale of the troops, and the selfless, ceaseless work of the battalion Medical Officers, Major Houghton, and the surgical team, reassured them that all that could be done was being done for them.

We had now about fifteen escaped prisoners of war, mostly Gurkhas, who had either been living concealed in the area, or had been conscripted by the Japs for menial duties. These were joined by two anti-aircraft gun crews of the Hong Kong and Singapore Brigade R.A., whose guns we had captured. They were an emaciated, miserable lot, completely resigned to whatever fate was due to them. I asked them what fate they would expect from the Japs. They said that they would have been shot, but that their only excuse was that they had been led astray by Jap promises. One of their objects in volunteering was to get back to their homes and families in India. These men are mostly Sikhs recruited in India for a term of service in Hong Kong and Singapore.

There they had been an efficient, but always unreliable unit, being cut off from their homes and liable to every sort of subversive propaganda. Many remained in Singapore or Hong Kong or went farther afield as taxi-drivers, and they are to be seen all over the East in that capacity. I told them that I had known their units in Hong Kong and Singapore before the war, when they were efficient and accurate gunners. I had noticed that under the Japs they had been very inaccurate when firing at us. I considered that this must be because in their heart of hearts they did not want to shoot at us. I would therefore temporarily give them the benefit of the doubt, and not shoot them (of course I had no jurisdiction or inclination to do so in any case), and they must now, in penitence, serve us as stretcher-bearers succouring the wounded. They would get whatever food we could offer them, but I would not guarantee that it would be right according to their religion. I also stated that on their return to India they would be brought before a tribunal to be judged for their treachery, but that if they served us well I could put in a good word for them. They did serve us well, but they never smiled. I did put in a good word for them. They were treated leniently.

Colonel Rome with his Broadway staff ran the whole administrative side of the forward base. It was necessary to appoint an acting D/Q, Major Marshall and a staff captain, Carroll, for the assessment of demands and distribution of supplies as received, as well as the administration of the polyglot community at base. This community included, besides British and Gurkha and Chinese, some West Africans who had lost their way and finished up with us, Kachins, Burmese, Gurkhas, Oriya Indians, Sikh gunners and about fifteen Jap prisoners. In our brigade we always went on the assumption that if you give orders loudly in English they are obeyed, an assumption which has good basis of success. Throughout the British Empire all soldiers understand orders such as Quick March, Halt, Advance, and words such as Reveille, Retreat, Stand to, Officers' Mess, Latrine, Bandook, Char, and all types of other ranks' slang. Even the Japs found that soldier's English was the best *lingua franca* with the various inhabitants of the conquered British Empire in the Far East. It is only when he gets north and west of Suez that an English soldier finds it difficult to make himself understood. Soldier's slang has been made up after generations of contacts with Eastern and African peoples, and while so many of his words have their derivation from the languages of Asia, he has also enriched their language in words for objects which they had not known before.

The Sikh gunners had given us encouraging reports of the condition and morale of the Japs. They were short of food. They had rather lost faith in their commanders, especially the units of 53 Division, who since their arrival in Burma had lost heavily against us. They were being worn down in numbers and morale by the constant bombing and mortaring. Very many of them were sick, and the capture by Geoffrey Lockett of their quinine supplies had made conditions even worse. They were short of ammunition, and the news from the Pacific depressed them. This made us feel a bit better, so I asked battalion commanders to let our troops, who were working and sleeping deep in mud and were constantly shelled, know that the Japs reckoned that we were better off than they were. I do not know whether that was much consolation, but it may have been. It was at this time that I was getting seriously perturbed at the wastage due to trench feet. I therefore sent a signal to Force H.Q. asking them for 1,000 pairs of gumboots if possible, but if not, a smaller number of them for those who were in the worst situations such as being up to their knees on sentry all night. I received a reply saying, 'It is the medical opinion that the wearing of gumboots injures the feet, and that the best insurance against trench feet is to keep the feet dry'!

We were cheered up during this doleful period by messages from the G.O.C., and from the Supreme Commander, Lord Louis Mountbatten. His read: 'Confidential. Supreme signal begins. Convey to 77 Brigade my greatest satisfaction in splendid achievement of penetrating to Mogaung. This success after many weeks' hard fighting and marching shows clearly excellent fighting spirit of brigade to which I would like you to send my personal congratulations. Ends.'

We liked that. The only reason I could think of for Force H.Q. classifying the signal as 'confidential' was to prevent the Americans from knowing of it. The Japanese, as shown by diaries and later by their interrogation reports, were our greatest admirers.

At this time, as I have mentioned, we were confronted with an open stretch of paddy 400 to 500 yards in depth between us and the strongly dug-in Japanese positions along the railway line from the railway station to the Mogaung bridge. Patrols had identified about eight strong bunkers, each held by twenty to thirty men. These were bombed daily. On the Mogaung river bank the Jap positions were farther forward and only about 200 yards from the nearest Gurkha positions. On one occasion some thirty to forty men in broad daylight, presumably part of a new unit, moved up to the forward Jap positions. They were promptly enfiladed by machine guns and mortars. Later that day after some heavy bombing, the Japs gave up the position, leaving nearly thirty dead.

On our left, 400 yards away, we were well observed by a Jap position at Naungkyaiktaw. Our patrols at night used to cut their telephone lines and fix booby traps to the ends, as the position included a gunner observation post, and we were finding their shelling far too accurate, losing ten to fifteen men a day from it. The figures of 550 men fit to attack was rapidly decreasing by these casualties as well as by malaria and trench foot. Malaria cases, unless bad, did not leave their battalions, so that by any normal standards the 550 men would be considered far from fit. All three battalions used to send officers to base to see that no sick or wounded stayed there longer than necessary. In actual fact persuasion was rarely necessary; the spirit of the men, with their resolve to defeat the Jap at all costs, was so amazing that they would return without, or even against, the doctor's orders, still with their wounds unhealed. During our final attack I was reproving a South Staffords man who had not kept up with his section. He said, 'Take a look at this, sir,' and undid his trousers, showing a bandage covered in new blood on his thigh. 'My wound's broken open again. The bullet's still in, but I wanted to join in this last attack.' I was to meet that man later and he reminded me of it.

Young Lieut. Wilcox of the South Staffords was the outstanding example. He had been an A.A. gunner officer during most of the war, and only when they started disbanding the gunner units and transferring the officers and men to the infantry, owing to the great shortage of infantry reinforcements, did he get his chance of real action. He was wounded early on at White City in the thigh and shoulder.

He recovered there, except for stiffness where the bullet had injured the bone. He was one of the few to get across the Namyin Chaung and blow the railway near Blackpool. At Mogaung he was shot through the neck just below his chin. In a day or two he was back with his unit, with a plug of gauze which went right through, and with which he would clean the wound, using the gauze as a pull through.

Later he was shot in the head, the bullet passing along his scalp so that one bit of the scalp fell over his ear. I saw him lying on the ground and thought him finished. His scalp was sewn up, and a day or two later I met him coming back for more. I sent him back with orders to be evacuated at once, and I think he was. I believe that he took part in fourteen separate platoon attacks, and any platoon commander knows what that means. At that time he was, as far as I remember, the only remaining subaltern of the South Staffords who had originally flown in. All the rest were dead or wounded or evacuated. He was awarded the D.S.O. and American Silver Star, and I hope that he will be remembered not only for what he did and the example he showed, but also as a worthy representative of all the other subalterns who did not last so long.

When we were not actually attacking the enemy, it was essential to maintain pressure on him, to retain the initiative, and to continue to impose our will on him, as otherwise I feared a resurgence of offensive spirit with attacks on our vulnerable communications and lightly defended base. All battalions were told to patrol actively and offensively. They sent out fighting patrols which would shoot up and grenade enemy positions every night. Other patrols penetrated into Mogaung and waylaid Japs moving about at night, the only time when they thought that they were safe from observation. These patrols left booby-trapped Jap equipment and food lying about. They pin-pointed nearly every Jap position of importance for bombing next day, or in anticipation of our final attack.

We usually got the best of these patrol encounters. The Lancashire Fusiliers had one action near Naungkyaiktaw where they killed eight Japs for the loss of one officer and one other rank. To make up for our weakness in numbers, we made the most of our material strength. Mogaung and its approaches, all now in range of our 3-inch mortars and the indirect fire of our machine guns, were constantly harassed. Captured Jap diaries showed that this constant harassing had a most deleterious effect on their morale.

Joe Lentaigne told me later that, at this time, my reports were alternately cheerful and gloomy, which was a bit disconcerting for him. I think that the reason was that when I looked at our condition and situation, and after talks with the battalion commanders, I tended to be gloomy. But when I thought of the condition of the Japs, or when Brazier or the Nesei translated a captured diary, I felt optimistic and cheerful again. This may seem a feeble excuse, but I have never managed to feel gloomy for long, and if I ever saw a straw of optimism floating along, I would certainly clutch at it. In our hammocks and our comparative freedom from shelling we at advance Brigade H.Q. were much better off than the battalions. The battalions, sleeping by their flooded trenches which they had to tumble into as soon as shelling started (many of our casualties were caused by people waiting too long), were never dry. Their only consolation was that the mud was at least comparatively warm.

For us in hammocks, this mud business was not too bad. One slept naked under a blanket in the hammock; the only nasty period was putting on wet and muddy garments in the morning. Of course, there was no change of clothing, and most of us wore the same clothes throughout the campaign. My green pyjamas, which could be worn during the day, were my alternative to a specially-made green corduroy tunic and badly dyed corduroy slacks which, after two campaigns, have still much wear left in them.

On the 14th, I sent out Capt. Andrews of the Burma Rifles, a 6-ft. 4-in. black-moustached officer, with his Burma Rifle patrol to the north bank of the Mogaung river. I told him that I never wanted to see him again unless he returned with at least one Chinese regiment. I also ordered the Tapaw ferry detachment to bring around six ranger boats with outboard motors up-river to Pinhmi so that we could transport the Chinese across if they arrived on the northern bank. The Charon boys found a route up the various 'Ins' from the river to the landing stage at Pinhmi where they harboured.

I sent a signal to Joe Lentaigne stating that owing to casualties, sickness and especially trench foot, we could not hold our present position indefinitely. I received the reply that I was not to take any undue risks which might write off what was left of the brigade. If absolutely necessary I could withdraw to the hills to await the Chinese, holding a bridgehead over the Wettauk at the Pinhmi bridge. I also sent Claude out by air to report personally on our predicament. He saw Joe and General Stilwell, who promised to speed up the Chinese.

On the 15th I ordered a general withdrawal from Pinhmi for rest and recuperation, each battalion to leave an active screen in our present position. Half the withdrawal had taken place when I received a jubilant message from the Gurkhas that the Japs had withdrawn in front of their sector.

I stopped our withdrawal and our patrols followed up the Japs. We found that they had only withdrawn on the riverside sector to conform with the rest of their positions which were just in front of the railway line. Some of our troops following up slowly got caught in the Jap defensive fire, and it was only with the liberal use of smoke that we extricated them in daylight, with some casualties. But the enemy had given his new positions away, and these were promptly bombed. We advanced our positions about 250 yards along the river bank so that we could more easily neutralize the railway bridge. We thinned out the forward position so that each battalion could in turn rest in the Pinhmi area.

General Lentaigne had offered me a Bladet party of flame-thrower personnel which I eagerly accepted. An officer and twelve men dropped in complete with flame-throwers.

The 'Bladet' Force had been formed by General Wingate, and was under the command of Major Blain who had been my sergeant-major in 1943. During the early part of the campaign, as I have previously mentioned, they used to be landed by glider in areas south of Indaw, blow up the railway, and then be snatched out again in their gliders. They were all parachutists, and the detachment was dropped in to us.

We were still losing men daily from accurate shelling directed from Naungkyaiktaw on our flank. I estimated that there were about forty to fifty Japs there, and decided to eradicate them.

My plan was to use to a maximum our material strength in order to save casualties. Major Strong, the tactical investigator, had told me that they had worked out that if one puts down on to a position the equivalent of $\frac{1}{3}$ lb. of explosive per square yard, the men in that position are completely dazed so that an attack immediately afterwards finds them easy meat. There were certain qualifications, such as the depth they were dug in, the duration of drenching fire, and the time within which the attack takes place.

I worked out that on the Naungkyaiktaw position, which was easily identifiable as it was at the end of a peninsula of jungle jutting out into paddy, 400 mortar bombs in a short period should suffice. So my plan was as follows: One company of the Lancashire Fusiliers would take up a position across the isthmus leading to the peninsula, to block any escape and act as a reserve if the main attack was held up. The assault company would move into position in the paddy in the dark, on the enemy side of the peninsula where our patrols had reconnoitred. They would be reinforced by all our flame-throwers and Piat teams. Just before dawn, down would come 400 3-inch mortar shells thickened up with 2-inch and 4.2-inch bombs and machine gun fire. After ten minutes' bombardment the attack would go in, the machine guns sited to catch the Japs if they got into the open. The previous evening, the American Mustangs would carry out a good raid on the position as a loosener. The major purge would occur at dawn, the flame-throwers acting as the enema.

Intercommunication was by telephone reeled out to both companies from where we could watch. Two machine guns went forward into the attacking company to give close support if held up and for consolidation. The South Staffords would be in general reserve.

Half an hour before dawn on the 18th, the mortars opened up. Each of the eight mortars had been given a task on which they had ranged the previous night. I was sitting with Hugh Christie on a bank on the road where we could get a good view. One 'over' hit one signaller beside us in one cheek of his bottom. Our first phone message was from the 'isthmus' company saying that some of the mortar bombs were falling rather short. This was due to a Netheravon mortar instructor officer who was our worst mortar officer, but who thought that he knew too much and had not ranged his mortars the previous night. The rest went well. Half the area was overrun before the Lancashire Fusiliers and King's were held up at first light. The flame-throwers in the dark looked an impressive spectacle and had a good moral effect, without which we probably would not have had this initial success, but some of our men said that they tended to light them up as they attacked. After the usual tense period when the reserve platoon was put in around the right flank, a mass of enemy, to our surprise, broke east and then ran all round the paddy to get back to the railway station which was 400 yards to their west. Our machine guns from the court-house area caught many of them in their fire.

The morning ended with the company striding up and down the paddy as if they were snipe-shooting, killing Japs who were crawling or hiding in the ditches. My active brigade major, Brash, and I thought that we would take a short cut across the paddy to join them. Accompanied by L/Cpl. Young, who always faithfully followed me, we started, and then were most rudely fired upon by a Jap machine gun from the railway station area. I was in an elated mood that morning, and had already jeered at the more sensible Brash for wanting to go round by the woods. I could never refrain from laughing at him slightly, with his large red beard and slightly plaintive suggestions. The Japs must also have laughed because there we were running a few yards, being fired upon, and then flinging ourselves down again. I was helpless with laughter, as Brash suggested other alternatives in his soft voice, but all the time following me. 'I knew we shouldn't have done this, sir.' Everybody in sight stopped to watch us, and by the time we reached the Naungkyaiktaw wood I was completely exhausted by laughing, running and flinging myself on the ground. I beat Brash to it, and he came in complaining that he had been right, and we should have gone round by the woods.

We joined in the shooting, standing on chairs to kill off any Japs seen crawling away. The Fusiliers and King's were busy cleaning up the substantial dug outs with flame-throwers and grenades. Instead of a platoon, the Japs had numbered over 100.

At twilight that day, as the Fusiliers were finishing cooking their evening meal in their newly won positions, a patrol of seven men came in, heaved a sigh, laid down their rifles and took off their equipment. It was only then that one of the Fusiliers saw that they were Japanese. A rush for weapons ensued, and the Japs were soon all overpowered and killed. They were a patrol who had been away for twenty-four hours and did not know that their position had been captured. Seven more Japs were discovered in that area next morning and four were killed.

I think that apart from the effect of the bombardment and the flame-throwers, the main surprise effect had been the direction of attack. This method of filing out into the open, forming up and attacking from an unlikely direction had proved very successful, as it had done on our first attack on Mawlu. We calculated that we had killed about seventy out of the 100 Japs. As our attacking force was only seventy, the isthmus company not having got into action until the end, it fully proved the effect of surprise, attained by shock of material, and the unforeseen direction of attack.

Our casualties were sixteen killed and thirty-eight wounded, more than half of which I regret to say were from our own mortar bombs. In that sea of mud it was difficult for a mortar base plate to hold firm and keep the mortar on the target. At night quick corrections cannot be made. The use of the telephone in the attack had been very successful, allowing the battalion commander to talk to his company commanders, who were right forward with the attacking troops, and resulted in the stopping of the recalcitrant mortars which were shelling them. The King's company, now reduced to a platoon in strength, had done very well and borne the brunt of the attack.

One of them spoke to me afterwards, 'Well, we've proved ourselves now, haven't we, sir!'

CHAPTER TEN

MOGAUNG CAPTURED

At 5 p.m. on June 18th the enigmatic Andrews appeared in my shelter and announced that he had a Chinese regiment waiting on the other bank of the Mogaung. He gave me no details of where he had found them, how he had persuaded them, even how he had spoken to them, but he had got them.

We had all come to take these wonderful Burma Rifle officers for granted. You would say, 'Bring me six elephants', or 'a river', 'a steamer', or 'a Chinese regiment', 'fifteen bullocks', and they would look at you from behind their moustaches, salute, disappear followed by a worshipful company of Kachins, Chins or Karens, and then appear with whatever you wanted. They certainly lived up to General Wingate's tribute that they were the finest body of officers any unit had ever possessed. It was only after 1942 that they attained this uniform high standard after much weeding out of 'dead end' regulars. Then we saw the true Burma Rifle officers, the men from Steel Brothers, Bombay Burma Corporation, Irrawaddy Flotilla Company and the like. A very fine body of men who still believed – and expected all other British to believe – in those old-fashioned virtues, honesty, truth, courage, unselfishness, modesty and duty – duty to the men they commanded, and loyalty to their King and Country. In my opinion three main factors had contributed to this: first, the excellence and essential goodness of the men whom they commanded, especially the Christian Karens; secondly, their lonely life which gave time for meditation; and thirdly the example of their predecessors who carried down the great attributes of the British of the Victorian era.

The 1st Battalion of the Chinese 114th Regiment started crossing that evening in our power boats. I allotted them an area, and our Hong Kong volunteers immediately came into

222

their own as interpreters and liaison personnel, and were of great assistance both in smoothing over difficulties, and in establishing mutual regard by finding out what each form-ation had been doing. Cpl. Young discovered later that the regimental commander's English interpreter was a cousin of his. One or another of my men found a relation. This all made for good co-operation, and although most of my men spoke only Cantonese they could make themselves under-stood to most of the troops, who were Honanese from Cen-tral China and spoke Mandarin and some Fukinese from Fukien.

The commander of the 1st Battalion, Major P'ang, re-ported to me first thing in the morning. He was a tough little Haka from Kwangtung, and had been fighting every year for the last fifteen years. He was a true soldier, and any soldier in the world would have got on well with him. I have seen his type in the French Army, in the British Army, in the Russian Army, and in the Italian Army, a type which has more in common with any soldier of any age than he has with the civilians of his own country. You can see them throughout history – Alexander's phalanx commanders ('fought from Alamein to Peshawar and back'); Roman cohort com-manders ('By Jupiter, sir, I remember when I was in Londi-nium, the gels ...'); Belisarius' boys ('Of course Belisarius was always done down by those bloody politicans ...'); the Saracen desert rats; Genghiz Khan's cavalry officers ('I lay you five Christians to one that my horse will jump that yurt'); ('Old Cortes knew how to solve the Indian problem'); ('Always keep your stomach warm and your powder dry, my boy, and you won't get any of these new-fangled diseases in the East'), and so on. The true professional soldier, who is a soldier, and not a civil servant in uniform, has not changed throughout history. It always amuses me that, after having got the Germans to fight our battles for us as mercenaries for so long a time, we now reproach them for their 'disgraceful militarism'. I suppose that we shall do the same with Gurkhas when a Gurkha dynasty takes charge in India.

The Hakas are similar to the Celts, the descendants of an aborigine tribe which inhabited South China before the Chinese invaded the area from the north. The more adven-turous of them, like the Celts, as the pressure of population increased, migrated overseas. They are the forebears of the

Polynesian and the Maori in New Zealand, having many of the same customs and habits. They are a darker, tougher race than the Cantonese, but not quite so alert and bright. There are about 30 million of them spread along the South China coast, and most of the fisherfolk, with their much admired navigational capabilities which their ancestors must have taken with them into the Pacific, are Hakas. As one of my troops in Hong Kong explained to me when I was questioning him, 'We are same-like Scotch.' Their language is different from the Cantonese in that it has nine tones against the Cantonese seven and the Mandarin five.

Major P'ang's battalion was considered the best battalion of the best regiment of the best division in the Army, with the result that he usually led the way. After many years of campaigning, this had made him cautious and frugal in the expenditure of the lives of his men. This at times is a virtue, but at other times frugality at the wrong period causes greater loss spread over a longer period. I showed him our open southern flank as I took him around our positions, and he promptly placed a company on the hills at Lakum to protect it. We were all most impressed throughout by the business-like efficiency and commendable speed with which the Chinese got into position.

The 2nd Battalion of 114th Regiment arrived with the Regimental H.Q. during the 19th, and were rapidly ferried over. During this ferrying, as we were taking their guns across, some argument arose and nearly caused a fracas between our Charon party and the Chinese gunners. They did not like seeing their guns go over alone, and, like true gunners, wanted to accompany them. Our Sappers were having enough trouble with the river in full flood, and refused to let them on. Language difficulties were the cause of the altercation; it was soon solved on the arrival of a Hong Kong Sapper

I met Colonel Li, the commander of the regiment, and was impressed. I took him around the whole scene of operations, and he asked just the right questions all the way: 'How did you capture the bridge?' and on explanation: 'Your Gurkhas must be very brave.' When I pointed out some dead buffaloes and said, 'Jap patrol', he looked at me and laughed, obviously having had the same sort of reports. I was quite proud of our work, and it was like an engineer or

10. *Japanese trucks ambushed by the 7th Nigerian Regiment.*

11. *7th Nigerian Regiment ambush position.*

12. *Light plane landing at White City. The picture was taken from the railway line. White City in the background.*

13. *British 'Bunker' defence at White City. Overhead cover constructed from railway lines, railway ties and vegetation for camouflage. Manned by Vickers machine-gun covering barbed wire.*

artist showing a kindred spirit around his creation. He instinctively asked how we managed to overcome difficulties which only the expert would have realized were the real difficulties. Colonel Li was no sycophant, and we differed in our methods as will be shown later, but I respect him as a soldier and as a friend.

It was on the 20th that I took Li and his operations groups around. At my suggestion, they wore bush hats, looking rather comical in them as they were small men: there was a chance that the observing Japanese may not have realized their presence. I had reoccupied Mahaung as soon as P'ang's battalion had arrived. Colonel Li relieved it on the 21st with an infantry company, with the prompt result that it was announced in the situation reports that the American Chinese forces had captured Mahaung. This was not due to Li, but to an odious character whom I still had the displeasure of meeting.

The Chinese 75-mm. battery of artillery was sited in the Pinhmi area with its observation post alongside ours at the top of the hill, and with forward observation officers with our forward battalion. The 3rd infantry battalion of the 114th Regiment had been left as a block on the railway near Gurkhaywa just north of Mogaung. Some Japs bumped into them on the night 18/19th, but were soon driven off.

Now that my southern flank was protected, and we had artillery, my thoughts naturally turned to a final offensive for the attack on Mogaung. My battalion rifle company strength was not at all encouraging. They were: Lancashire Fusiliers and King's Regiment, 110 all ranks (not including sixty or so at Tapaw), South Staffords, 180, Gurkha Rifles, 230. I explained my predicament to Colonel Li and told him that in the state my troops were in, if they did not attack soon there would be none left with which to attack, owing to casualties through sickness and shelling. Colonel Li was very sympathetic, and said that he would do his best to relieve the pressure. I was disappointed at the time, therefore, when he sent his 2nd battalion off to take Loilaw. This they did after a sharp little engagement, obtaining some booty in the shape of some anti-aircraft guns which were protecting the bridge, and some trucks.

It was here that our methods differed. These Chinese battalions had been fighting year in year out as far back as they could remember. They realized that if they were not fighting in one place they would be fighting in another, so what the hell was all the hurry about? Further, a Chinese regiment or division is centred round its artillery. Once you lose your guns you really cease to be a division. One can always get more troops, though trained troops were very scarce. But if a divisional commander lost his guns, no more would be given to him, and he usually lost his division to a general who had some guns. This, of course, was not the case while they were under Stilwell, but the habits they had grown into could not be changed in a year.

The Civil War in China, which had been going on almost continuously since 1911, is analogous to the Thirty Years War, or the Wars of the Roses. The commander did not say, 'Let's win the war this year or next year', but 'What town shall we take this season?' After having made all the necessary movements, the town surrendered with honours, or, if they put up too much resistance, was sacked with rape, loot and arson, and that was the end of the season's fighting. After that there were the crops to be gathered and the question of obtaining good winter quarters. In that manner fighting in the Civil War in China had fluctuated backwards and forwards, and both sides were exceedingly clever at it. They tried to stand up man for man against the Japanese in Shanghai in 1937–38. I was there at the time and, because I spoke a little Cantonese, and incidentally got £50 for passing an exam in it, I could go over and watch the fighting. It was as hard and as bloody as I have seen anywhere in the world. The Chinese were very brave, but lost nearly half a million of their best troops, trained by General von Falkenhausen, as opposed to the Japanese acknowledged losses of about 100,000. From that time on, Chiang Kai-shek deserted the principles as taught by von Falkenhausen and went in for the principle of 'an army in being' analogous to our 'Fleet in being' theory. His central army did not allow itself to take part in mammoth battles in which the fate of China could be changed in a day. Much of the fighting was left to the local war lords, who were in turn defeated or went over to the Japs. Even at their one victory at Taerchwang, when von Falkenhausen had manoeuvred about four Jap divisions into an impossible position without supplies, the greatly superior Chinese Army would not attack until it was too late, and only succeeded in annihilating one Jap division. This policy, and the Allies which he was always trying (like us) to involve in the war, led to Chiang Kai-shek being on the winning side in the end. Fabius Maximus Cunctator had nothing on him. This policy had bitten deeply into the Chinese strategy and tactics. It is by no means a reflection on their courage, which I have always admired. It would be quite wrong to suppose that they are not good soldiers. In fact, the Japs learnt a tremendous lot from them, especially the art of camouflage. This was ingrained in the Chinese; I remember on one occasion behind the lines in 1937 I saw a peasant walking along with a cow which had a leafy branch attached to it. I asked him why, and he said it was to conceal his cow from the bloody Japanese aeroplanes.

I met von Falkenhausen's aide (who walked two paces to the rear and one pace to the left of his general when walking down a street) soon after Taerchwang. He told me that having manoeuvred the Japs' division into a trap and then not being able to get the Chinese to attack, von Falkenhausen became so desperate that he did not speak to anyone for four days until such time as they attacked. Out of the hundreds who tried and failed, only three Europeans in history have successfully commanded Chinese armies in action – Gordon, Falkenhausen, Stilwell – and they have all nearly shot themselves in desperation. To appreciate Stilwell one should read Gordon's account of his times in China. China is the graveyard of all military reputations.

Since the end of the 1939–45 British war (and I call it that because the British group of nations were the only ones to fight from the beginning to the end, the first to declare war, and the last to make peace), the Chinese Kuomintang stretched out its neck too far into Manchuria, where it lost its army. Once an army is defeated in the field the rapid occupation of territory becomes a matter of course, administrative difficulties being the only curb on its speed.

The Japanese Army for the first two years of the war considered that the Chinese were the best troops that they had to fight. At that time their order of precedence was Chinese, Australians, Americans, British, Gurkhas and Indians. Later the order was changed as each country in turn learnt to fight them on tropical terrain.

Naturally, having some little knowledge of the Chinese

Army, and with the excellent services of our own Hong Kong interpreters, we conversed and dealt with our Chinese opposite numbers. But with the Chinese units were some American liaison officers. I had had no notice given to me of them, and did not know what their function was. There was an extraordinary American lieutenant-colonel, a type, I suppose, which each country throws up at times. He had very little knowledge of the Army or fighting, but was a great blusterer. He would sit in my shelter spitting all over it to show that he was tough, calling the Chinese cowards, calling on us to attack, and saying that he represented General Stilwell and the United States and the Statue of Liberty and one or two other things. But he never made any constructive suggestions that I am aware of. His junior officers were always apologizing to my officers for his bad manners and his general odiousness. He never went anywhere near the forward troops as far as I remember, but this was explained by the excuse that the Chinese would not allow the liaison officers to go forward as they felt personally responsible for their safety. He was probably a very brave chap, and I tried to do everything to meet him half way and be affable, and wasted a lot of time with him. One day, feeling tougher than usual, he blew his nose on to the floor of my office shelter. One of his officers, who were all very reasonable, excellent chaps, told Francis Stuart that they were hoping to shoot him, as he was such a bad example of the United States' officers. He was an appalling person by any standards.

These liaison officers did not appear to have much knowledge of warfare – and indeed they admitted it: as far as I could see, their only job was to report direct to General Stilwell's headquarters what the Chinese were doing, and what they needed. It was only later that I was told that they were supposed to act as liaison between us and the Chinese. It was much more satisfactory dealing with Colonel Li direct as he and I understood each other, even if we did not always agree.

The Chinese discipline was good, except for their labour units who carried supplies, cooking gear, etc. These were some of the most genial thieves I have ever met. While we shared the supply-dropping area, supply drops became a sort of catch-as-catch-can between us and the Chinese until Colonel Li got rough with some of them, and shot one or two who had run off with some money dropped to us. One Chinese did literally attempt to catch a free drop in the heat of tussle, but with fatal results.

On June 21st, my night patrols came back bubbling over with the information that they had moved right up to the railway line, and had met no opposition. I thought that the Chinese movements around their flank might have forced the Japs to withdraw.

Accordingly, with our mortars ready with smoke bombs, I ordered a probing attack to be made. Our patrols went forward fast and confidently across the open. But the Japanese were still there, and, after holding their fire until our men were almost on to their position, they opened up. We had the greatest difficulty getting the survivors back under cover of smoke, and some gallant rescues were made by men running out to help or carry wounded back. It cost us dearly, with little material gain to us or loss to the enemy, and was the worst mistake, in my opinion, that I made in the campaign. We lost one British officer, four British and six Gurkha other ranks killed, and one British officer, six British and nine Gurkha other ranks wounded. We learnt of some new positions which were heavily bombed and mortared. I had brought up the 4.2-inch mortars close in order to try and knock out some of their positions and to extend our harassing area to the Japs west of the Namyin Chaung. We had located some gun positions there which the Mustangs bombed. One Mustang was shot down.

That evening we were granted some of the most intensive air support that we received in the campaign, obtaining over seventy sorties from the aircraft allotted to Stilwell. These pilots were eager to help us on, as they could see the material advantage of their bombing by our advance. They would come back again and again if the weather was fine enough, many of them carrying out four sorties in a day. Even the photo reconnaissance squadron would come over when they had nothing else to do and help us by bombing the Japs.

Mogaung was truly a death trap for the Japs, and even with regular reinforcements they could not maintain their strength in that area. In their diaries they howled to their gods, like some Old Testament prophet, bewailing the appalling fate that was theirs from the ceaseless bombing and mortaring.

Our bombers were using both blast and delay-action bombs. The blast bombs would clear the ground of all foliage and flimsy houses, often revealing the Japs' bunkers. The delay-action bombs would blow up the larger brick buildings and, penetrating, destroy the bunkers. At least two bunkers were wholly destroyed that day.

Colonel Li saw me and said that he was going to put in an attack from the south next morning: could we make a diversion? I agreed to lay down a mortar concentration at dawn with much machine gun fire. Accordingly, at dawn we opened up and drew all or most of the Jap defensive fire on to us. The Chinese attack, which consisted of only one company and did not have much weight behind it, was abortive, and soon petered out. They did, however, infiltrate between two Jap positions and were now close to the Namyin Chaung itself. The Jap artillery was becoming more active with some heavy stuff shelling us from a long distance. The Chinese guns countered fairly well. I sent a message to Joe Lentaigne that day saying that operations were proceeding well, and that the only danger lay in the Chinese spreading themselves too wide, and not having sufficient strength left to attack Mogaung itself.

Also on the 22nd the 3rd Battalion, 114th Regiment, crossed over the Mogaung, having handed over the area north of the river to the Chinese 113th Regiment. I had hoped that Li would use this battalion to attack Mogaung. But when I visited his headquarters, he told me that he was going to send the battalion off on an outflanking movement to cross the Namyin Chaung between Ywathit and Loilaw, and then move north to complete the encirclement of Mogaung by closing the western approaches. I argued with him that we would only get into the same impasse as had occurred in Myitkyina. There, after Merrill's Marauders had made their brilliant march to seize Myitkyina airfield, coinciding with a landing of a Chinese division by Dakota, the position had deteriorated into a stalemate. The Japs held out in the city, from which they could shell the airfield. Morris Force closed the gap by moving up to the bank of the Irrawaddy on the other side of the river. They tried to hold their positions there, but were very vulnerable, and the Chinese took so long in capturing Myitkyina that Morris had to withdraw more than once. At this period the Chinese had over 40,000 troops investing less than 4,000 Japs. Instead of concentrating at one point and breaking through, the Chinese were content to make a tenuous circle all around Myitkyina, with the result that in no place were they strong enough to attack, and Myitkyina was not cleared until after three months' siege.

I knew that my troops could not last much longer in the field. Li told me that he thought our troops were bunched up too close together and that if we spread them more we would have fewer casualties and could rest more of them at a time. There was some truth in this. As commanders get tired there is a tendency for them to wrap their battalions or companies around them for protection. I had found myself doing this, and had resisted it. The Chinese, on the other hand, is a great individualist, and if he is told to stay in a place even with a very few others, he will do so and sell his life dearly. The British and, to a lesser extent, the Gurkhas, like so many Europeans and European-trained peoples, have a herd instinct and like to brave dangers together in a crowd. But whereas the British and Gurkhas are prepared to attack the Chinese is not. He likes to surround, invest and shoot his enemy when they are standing up and he himself is in a hole. It is much cheaper this way, but it does not win wars. Battles are finally only won by the forward movement of one side against the enemy and by the destruction or surrender of that enemy.

The Chinese – and I like them for it – would almost prefer to take a position by a subtle trick than by a straightforward action, even if the latter is likely to be more successful. I remember, in Shanghai, wondering why the Chinese had erected a large matting screen around a section of the main road. Then I found them digging a huge hole. They then put light wooden boards over the hole, and studiously and carefully remetalled and tarmacked the road over it. This took about a fortnight. They then pulled down their road block and attacked the Japs. After a little fighting they all ran away followed by a Jap armoured car which promptly fell into the hole, to the great glee of the Chinese dancing around above it.

Anyway, after long discussion I told Li that I was considering attacking next day, and that I would let him know. I discussed the matter with Claude, who told me that it was my responsibility, and mine alone, and that he would not give an opinion. I again felt the loneliness of command. The battalion commanders were not keen, but on the other hand they did not think that they could keep their troops in the field much longer. While we were discussing, I received a message that the Chinese had occupied the railway station area. This would protect our left flank during our attack, and so I made the decision to attack. There were few orders to give out as we all had discussed the plan for attack several times before. I arranged artillery support.

The plan was quite simple. Natyigon and the Mogaung bridge were the key positions in the defence of Mogaung. Once this line had fallen, the rest of Mogaung was untenable. That evening another seventy sorties of planes again battered Natyigon. I decided on a night attack on a two-battalion front with the Lancashire Fusiliers and the Bladet detachment of flame-throwers in reserve. The limited objective would be the line of the railway embankment from the railway bridge to the station. As soon as this objective was taken, all platoons would dig in, facing all directions. At dawn mopping-up would be carried out. There would be an initial barrage of 1,000 3-inch mortar bombs from all the battalion mortars which were brigaded. The 4.2-inch would concentrate on special strong points, such as the Red House position.

That evening I went around our front-line positions alone. I talked to Michael Almand on the river bank. He was full of confidence, and told me his men were in great heart. I saw preparation for attack with men priming grenades, cleaning their weapons, mortars registering, guides being shown the way to lead their platoons to the start line in the dark, flame-throwers being filled, men writing last notes on scraps of paper, mules stocking up the ammunition, and the Medical Officers preparing their instruments so that they could get at them easily by the light of a lamp.

Standing behind a bush near the most forward position in the courthouse, searching with my field glasses the Japanese positions, I heard a very young South Staffords corporal giving out his orders. He had his back to me and did not see me. It was a moving moment and one which I will always remember. Having made my decision, naturally doubts assailed my mind. Then I heard his clear voice saying to his section of men, some of them many years older than he was,

'Well, this is it at last. We attack Mogaung tonight, and once we've taken it the Brigadier says we are through. We are attacking with the Gurkhas on our right. You all know what is in front of you. First there will be a very heavy bombardment lasting fifteen minutes from 3 to 3.15. At 3.10 we start advancing across this here paddy. We advance across killing any Japanese we meet, and then dig in the railway embankment by dawn. Take plenty of grenades to throw down them Jap bunkers. We have the call on the flame-throwers which will be moving a little way behind us. The Lancs will be in reserve . . . Remember we must get to that embankment and stick there. Remember that Mills here will take my place if I go, and if he goes, Lofty, you will take over. You can keep line by watching the tops of the trees which run along the road here. But remember, don't stop until you feel the old railway line. Then dig in fast. The Brigadier says that Winston is watching us, and hopes that we take the first town in Burma. Dusty, you will be on from eight to ten tonight, and . . .' St. George, I thought, for England!

I had given out an order of the day saying, amongst other things, that all the world was watching us, and the British and Mr. Churchill hoped to see that we would take the first town in Burma to be recaptured. At the time I really thought that this was true, not realizing that all Britain was thinking about was what was going on in Normandy, and if their thoughts turned to Burma at all, they did not see beyond Kohima. My order was not an appeal to sentiment, but was a sincere belief that we must do our stuff and uphold the honour of the British Commonwealth in the field of battle, and I am not ashamed of holding those views. And my more than decimated, diseased, starved, weary, mud-soaked troops fought to defeat an enemy who dared to consider that he was better than they, and fought in this forgotten corner for the British Empire and for all that the word British meant to them, as their forebears had fought for generations, just doing their best according to their beliefs.

I established my tactical H.Q. forward near the 4.2-inch mortars. Francis, now very ill indeed, insisted on being carried down in a stretcher to watch the capture of Mogaung. 'After all, I have waited long enough to see the capture of Mogaung, and as I am not dead yet, I am damn' well going to see it.'

233

I did not sleep that night, wondering whether I was right. I felt lonely, as it was my decision unshared by anyone else, except for the comforting words of the ever-faithful Francis.

Three o'clock came, and the mortars started, answered immediately by an intensive shell-and-mortar barrage by the Japs. I was hustling the 4.2-inch mortar teams to fire more quickly until they reached a tremendous rate of fire, one bomb going down almost before the other had come out. All our forming-up places, headquarters and starting lines were heavily shelled, causing many casualties. The troops moved forward out of this fire close up to our barrage, which suddenly stopped. I moved up and cursed a man who I thought was malingering. He said that he was doing his best to catch up but he had been shot in the leg. I saw one of the flame-thrower men hit and be set on fire. 'Oh God, I can't . . .' came a cry from the flames. By its light I barely missed stumbling over one man who had been cut clean in half just above the waist, the sector of his body looking like a sectionized aeroplane engine with its red and yellow wires.

The Gurkhas on the river, led by their young officers who showed a complete disregard for death, soon captured the railway bridge and all their objectives, linking up with the Staffords on the left. Michael Almand had started off many yards ahead of his men, and almost single-handed had killed all the Japs in one strongpoint. At another, when his men were held up, he himself directed the flame-throwers into the loopholes. He was everywhere at once, and an inspiration to his men before he was wounded twice.

One strongpoint was dug in underneath a house, and all loopholes were covered with expanded metal grilles through which grenades would not penetrate. Under covering fire the flame-throwers, which had a range of about thirty feet, were put on to each loophole in turn, the Japs screaming inside as they were burnt, struggling to get out. But there was no way out. Over twenty Japs died there. There were similar actions at other of the Jap warrens.

The Staffords had in many ways a more difficult task: their advance had to be made across 500 yards of open paddy before they reached the enemy positions. Unless they captured some by dawn, they would be left in the open at the mercy of the Japs. On the right and centre they successfully reached the railway line, by-passing one or two Jap positions. But at dawn they came under terrible enfilade fire from a previously unlocated Jap strongpoint in a house at the junction of the Pinhmi road and the railway. This position had about twenty men in it with a machine gun. It was causing heavy casualties to the Staffords and I ordered their left company to swing back, as men on the rail embankment were being picked off from behind without being able to do much about it. Under cover of smoke this company withdrew 200 yards. The Chinese had *not* occupied the railway station. This was a figment of the imagination of our wholly irresponsible American lieutenant-colonel. The result was that our left flank was in the air.

I brought up the Lancashire Fusiliers, who now consisted of only one company. Ron Degg, Hugh Christie, Freddie Shaw and myself met in a huge crater close to the grilled Japanese, some of whom were still screaming: we could smell the odour of cooking flesh. At one side of the crater lay Michael Almand where he had been placed by his men. He was lying on his side, with his right arm shattered, and wounded in his side. He asked me how the battle was going. He did not turn his head or open his eyes. I said that we were winning. He said 'Good.' I asked him if he had had morphia. He said no. I sent for some, and it was administered, and later stretcher-bearers carried him back. He died that night. He was later awarded a posthumous Victoria Cross. Another Gurkha got a V.C. that day.

We turned everything that we had on to the Jap positions. From Naungkyaiktaw the Fusiliers fired 200 mortar shells on to it, three or four machine guns swept every window from a distance of 300 yards, the Staffords' Piats and anti-tank grenades were knocking holes in the wall, flame-throwers were starting on to it when the garrison fled over the railway line, but not before a Gurkha machine gun caught some of them. They left six dead in the house.

It had paid for my H.Q. to keep right close up with the battalion commanders, as then I could quickly help them by bringing to bear the reserve of fire under my command. Our casualties were sixty dead and over 100 wounded. There were over sixty Jap dead visible, and many more in their warrens. Their one unidentified position had caused almost half our casualties.

I visited the railway embankment and saw the young

corporal and some of his section sprawled there dead, still holding their position. St. George had killed his dragon. But he himself had died.

By 12 noon, all objectives were in our hands. As we dug in the Japs started shelling again. We found that they tended to occupy substantial two-or-three-storeyed houses as a protection against our mortar fire. Fortunately the afternoon was fine and soon Mustangs silenced their guns, and bombed the new targets we indicated; throughout the day with intense and accurate bombing and strafing, they kept the Japs from consolidating. One large house was within seventy yards of the railway line. A wing of Mustangs demolished this while we lay and bounced up and down on our stomachs on the railway embankment, such was our confidence in these excellent American pilots.

The battalions were absolutely exhausted and finished. Both Freddie Shaw and Ron Degg stated they could never attack again. Freddie had tragically lost two officers, including the young Butler, who, thinking the position had been taken, walked over to the Staffords along the railway line, and were killed by the Jap machine gun at the level crossing. Stagg, Staffords' liaison officer with the Gurkhas for the day, was also killed in the same way. He was a good friend of Degg, who was desolate at that loss with the others.

I gathered my Brigade Defence Company, and the animal transport personnel of Brigade H.Q., and under Major Gurling they advanced with commendable speed for 400 yards beyond the railway line, brushing aside all opposition. They were now within 400 yards of Namyin Chaung, the western boundary of Mogaung. They came under heavy fire from the left flank, so they dug in with their right flank on the river and their left flank in the air. There they spent an uncomfortable night, subject to Jap counter-attacks and infiltration.

There were one or two interesting details of the attack which I now heard. The defenders consisted of the remains of a battalion of 56th Regiment, and a battalion of 128th Regiment of 18 Division. An entry in a diary stated that they were on their way to the Imphal front and had been deflected north. Morale of 128th Regiment was low, but that of the 56th Regiment was still high and they mostly fought to the last. One officer, when his position was taken, stood up and blew his brains out. The South Staffords, on comparing notes, thought that one party had come out with their hands up to surrender, but this was so unusual that our troops, not expecting it, automatically shot them. Both the South Staffords and the Gurkhas had indulged in hand-to-hand kukri and bayonet fighting.

Mogaung was now ours for the taking, if we could find anybody to take it.

One absurd incident occurred that day. Major Brash (who was acting as my mobile brigade major) and I visited the level-crossing house to see where the Japs had held out. The South Staffords were digging in behind it. We went up the stairs and entered all the rooms, after which we went round the downstairs rooms. As we entered one small room a rifle shot went off. We leapt to one side. I was in one of those moods where Brash's pained comments sent me into fits of laughter. He said, 'There's a man firing at us.' We moved across to look out of a barred window when there was another crack, and some plaster fell from the wall. 'It's somebody in the house, I can smell cordite.' I laughed more. I thought that I too could smell cordite. We drew our revolvers and looked around the ludicrously bare room while our troops just outside carried on digging unconcernedly. I crossed over and there was another crack. It was absurd. It reminded me of those silly cartoons where one sees a circle of smoke and the bullet knocking a man's hat off. The courageous Brash went to the door, and there was another crack, as he leapt in the air. I regret to say I dissolved into laughter. 'But this is serious, sir, there's a man shooting at us.' We could not get out of any of the windows as they were heavily barred. I tested the bars, and called over one of the old bearded N.C.O.s and asked him to look around. He was tired, and did not take it very seriously, having heard my laughter. He said that he would search around the house. He shortly returned to say that they had walked all round and found nobody, and that it was all right. As he was speaking Brash moved to the window, and there was another crack and he leapt again saying, 'I'm hit!' A bullet had gone clean through his calf. I told the corporal that we were going to run out of the house, and that his men must make some sort of demonstration as we did so, but I did not know what. He said that he would take his men round the house again, so soon after he had gone we dashed out with Brash hanging on to my shoulder. I put him on Jean, and he rode back. Jean was still mobile. Brash was very soon in circulation again as the bullet in his calf fortunately missed everything important and merely made a neat hole through it. Later that evening one of the corporal's men was relieving himself on a pile of masonry and noticed a body under it. He pulled the bricks away and the body suddenly leapt to its feet and started to run, but he clubbed him and shot him. This Jap sniper had lain in a covering of bricks a few yards from the door of the house. He was naturally in a very restricted position and could have only just seen our legs as we walked across the doorway. It was so ridiculous, but an end to a hard day, and I was in that slightly elevated mood which comes after a victory, but before the eventual depression.

I had now 176 wounded awaiting evacuation.

The next morning on the 23rd, I brought the Lancashire Fusiliers on to Gurling's left. The Chinese that day, advancing in a slow, cautious, methodical manner, succeeded in reducing some slight opposition at the railway station, and joined up with the Lancashire Fusiliers about 200 yards west of the station. They also occupied Ywathit to the south of Mogaung but were held up by fairly strong opposition on the other side of an open marshy area.

On the 24th Colonel Li came to see me and stated that it was a hopeless task trying to attack from the south as the country was open and covered by strong Jap positions. I had gone around that sector during the morning also trying to find a way round, and I agreed with him. So he asked permission to attack through the Lancashire Fusiliers with his 3rd Battalion. I agreed at once.

On that same day we had killed fifteen more Japs in mopping-up operations within the part of the town that we had captured. I had also sent a platoon of Gurkhas over the river to hold the north end of the bridge. They eradicated, without loss to themselves, about ten Japs dug in rather pointlessly in the jungle. Just before, I was standing at the southern end of the bridge discussing with Freddie whether we should send a platoon across when I noticed a soldier walking across the bridge. There were quite a number of Gurkhas with us at the time and no one took much notice as we thought that it was a Chinese. He walked on, hesitated. We shouted O.K., and waved him on. He came within about 100 feet, and I took a look at him through my glasses, and immediately yelled, 'He's a Jap. Shoot him!' As I did so the Jap realized what he had walked into. There was nearly 200 yards of bridge behind him. I saw the horror come into his face; then his good training asserted itself and he got down on his knees to take a shot before he ran, or to take one of us with him. The Gurkhas' rifles blazed as he fired, and he fell down wounded and was soon dispatched by the Gurkhas.

It may be wondered why every Jap is nearly always killed, and so few taken prisoner, even though wounded. The reason was that in the early stages so many of our men had been killed or wounded by wounded Japs feigning death that one's first tendency was, as with a wild beast, to make certain that the man was dead before closing with him. Strong, our tactical investigation officer, could not understand, when he went around examining corpses for the purpose of statistics to see what they had been killed by, why so many Japs had bayonet wounds in them. He found the reason was that few men would pass a Jap lying on the ground without sticking a bayonet in him to ensure that he was really and truly dead and would not shoot them in the back.

That day we captured a typical 'Good soldier Schweik'. He was a bewildered little Jap who had just recently arrived on draft to Burma from Japan. He was told to join his unit in Myitkyina. He had wandered up there rather leisurely, staying a few days at various transit camps en route. When he arrived at Myitkyina, his unit was not there, and the chaps did not know what to do with him. They made him cook, but he was so bad a cook that they sent him away. He became an officer's batman for a while, but the officer had been killed on patrol. He stayed around for a while, but feeling that he was not wanted had wandered down south. He had not the slightest idea of the situation, where he was, of the geography of Burma, or of the organization of the Army. He was very glad to be captured as he had lost his way in the jungle and had felt lonely and neglected, and was glad to meet his fellow men again. A simple fellow, a very human type which exists in every army. It was comforting to meet him in the 'death or glory' Jap army.

We were now being shelled with greater intensity. That evening, the 24th, we heard on the B.B.C. news that the Chinese-American forces had captured Mogaung. My officers and men were enraged and I was pretty angry myself. Of course it was the American colonel, who with his own wireless set direct to Stilwell's H.Q., had given them this news. Colonel Li, on hearing of it a day or two later, through one of the Hong Kong Chinese, came straight over to my H.Q. and, in front of the American lieutenant-colonel, apologized for that announcement and said, 'If anyone has taken Mogaung it is your brigade, and we all admire the bravery of your soldiers.' He said this with great dignity, looking me in the eyes as we both stood there; he then bowed, saluted and left.

But Mogaung was not yet taken. On the 25th it was planned that Gurling, the Lancashire Fusiliers and the Chinese would attack at 2 p.m. It was then that the Chinese announced that they would start the attack. I told the Lancashire Fusiliers to await signs of a Chinese advance and to arrange close liaison with them. The Chinese did not attack until 5 p.m. The Lancashire Fusiliers went boldly forward. They surprised twelve Japs having their meal in a dug-out and killed them. One platoon reached the Namyin Chaung on the other side of Mogaung but found itself isolated and therefore returned. Men at this time, when they knew that they would soon be flown out, were not taking the risks that they had used to. Gurling also went forward, but was soon held up by enemy in a big house. Some U.S. Mustangs were called upon to reduce it. 'O.K., we will skip bomb it – we will put a bomb through a window.' Flying very low, six of them had an attempt at it. The fifth put its bomb through the window, killing the occupants, and Gurling took the house. The Lancashire Fusiliers started unaccountably to withdraw. They said that the Chinese had gone forward and then withdrawn.

By this time, Major Brash and Cpl. Young had both been sent off by me to find out what was happening. Gurling sent a message saying that he was being enfiladed. I went forward and found the forward Chinese positions. In my best Cantonese I asked them to attack, but they grinned and said that they had no orders. So I asked for covering fire, but they did not understand. So I borrowed a Bren from them and showed them what I meant. They were hugely delighted but would do nothing. I moved to one side where I could see down a road, and saw some Japs running across. I fired the Bren off in their direction. Not having a very good view I went forward a bit and fired ahead of where Gurling was. Gurling later said that he wondered who on earth was firing and politely said that he thought that it might have done some good. I again saw a cluster of Japs about 200 yards down the road, fired, and I think that I hit some of them. Anyway we now got a lot of stuff thrown at us. One mortar bomb landed near the Chinese post. When the dust cleared away I gave the thumbs-up sign which I had found so useful in Shanghai. They answered, grinning. I signalled for some ammunition and they brought me over half a dozen magazines. I fired a bit more, and then changed to the other side of the road, as the Jap grenades were landing rather close. I saw some more Japs, or I thought I did, and fired at them and found someone firing back at me. I had left some of the magazines behind but one of the Chinese came forward and threw them across the road to me. I then loosed off one magazine after another in every direction forward except at Gurling. Quite often I saw some running Japanese and did my best to hit them. It was a comfort firing because one could not hear the shots back. After finishing off the last magazine and deciding to evacuate I leapt to my feet, seized the Bren by the barrel – a searing pain in my hand as I let go of it with a cry – the barrel was nearly red-hot. The Chinese roared with laughter, shouting to their fellows in nearby positions what the joke was. I then picked up the gun more gingerly by the handle and ran back to their crater where they all surrounded me laughing and patted me on the back, and thought that I was absolutely crazy. I went off to tell Gurling, who had suffered a number of casualties from the Japs, to fall back a bit, as now he was being enfiladed on both flanks. Also that evening the Japs hurled every sort of shell, numbering over 500, at us.

Evidently the Chinese attacked as a cover solely to leave two men concealed in the rubble of Mogaung to spy at the Jap position. All that night they lay there watching the Japs who came out of their holes for food and relief. By morning the two were back with their report pinpointing the Jap positions. Then the Chinese with their very accurate

American 4.2-inch mortars carefully bombed each position from close range, knocking many of them out.

That morning I relieved Gurling's troops, of whom as Brigade H.Q. personnel I was proud but who had now had about enough after three sleepless days and nights in a precarious position. I relieved them with the ever-faithful 3/6 Gurkhas. Freddie, who had said that his men could never fight again until his battalion was re-formed, volunteered to have another go after seeing the state that Gurling's troops were in. That day the Chinese and the Gurkhas stole forward and, without much opposition, reached the Namyin Chaung. Mogaung was taken. The hectic Jap shelling the previous evening must have been their swan song to cover their withdrawal. It certainly caused casualties and lowered morale.

On the 26th and 27th the Gurkhas mopped up and killed another two Jap officers, one warrant officer, and sixteen other ranks hiding around the town.

Mogaung was the meeting-place of the Ledo road and the Burma railway. It was one of the objectives laid down at the Quebec Conference. It was the first town in Burma to be retaken. Its capture had cost my brigade nearly 1,000 casualties. There were no inhabitants – not one. With no population there was no administrative problem in its capture. All was destroyed except some of the more massive pagodas. We were in touch at last with India by 'road' – a straight clearing in the jungle covered in two feet of mud.

We rested and the full shock of the number of our casualties hit us. I remember no elation – just the feeling of lying down after a terrible march.

Looking back on it I remember our first quick march thirsting to avenge Blackpool . . . the terrible exhausting day with the Lancashire Fusiliers overcoming five little strongpoints . . . the clearing of the hills with 'Gurkha Butler's' great success . . . Pinhmi and Pinhmi bridge . . . David Monteith's tired eyes as he went off to carry out orders that he knew were impossible . . . the crossing of the Wettauk Chaung with Fearfull Smith's depredations on the railway and Nip Hilton's attack across a swamp . . . the capture of Pinhmi bridge by Freddie Shaw . . . John Harrington and the Courthouse triangle . . . Wavell securing our flank on the Mogaung river . . . the King's and Lancashire Fusiliers who took Naungkyaiktaw with fewer men than the defenders . . . the arrival of P'ang and Li to take over the protection of our left flank from us . . . the premature advance and the extrication of our men . . . the attack on the railway . . . Lieut. Almand . . . Gurling's attack with Brigade H.Q. and the final result. Four long weeks of striving in a sort of miniature Passchendaele.

We would never have come anywhere near to success morally, physically or materially without the ever-present U.S.A.A.F. who supplied us, and, in the Mogaung death-trap, probably destroyed more enemy than we did. They used to come over cheerfully again and again with the quiet drawl, 'What's the target?', pilots flying over six sorties a day in all weathers and conditions. And there was the American light plane pilot who quietly and without knowledge that he was doing anything special flew his plane interminably to evacuate our wounded.

Elation! I had no elation, no satisfaction, no positive emotion – just to lie down for a while and rest.

Nearly the last shell of the battle landed between our 4.2-inch mortars which were situated close together behind the railway embankment as I had only one team available to man both mortars. Both barrels were damaged beyond repair. Strangely enough they represent the antithesis of the British and American military character. The British tend to be more precise, more accurate with greater penetration effect, and more liable to knock things out. The Americans are less accurate, therefore unpredictable and more dangerous, especially to troops in the open; they have greater killing power and require far fewer orders to get into action. Our characters, like our mortars, are complementary to each other, and the combination is irresistible, but usually there has to be a catalyst to make that fusion possible. Is that catalyst danger, war, a good commander, common aims? I do not know. I only know that we do not just combine naturally, and Lieut.-Col. Bluster, the American liaison officer, and myself were an example.

All we had as a catalyst were the Chinese whose traditional role is to play one nation against the other. I do not think that Li did this and I really, honestly believe that Lieut.-Col. Bluster was just one of those types with whom it is not possible to co-operate on a friendly basis. He was deeply imbued with anti-British sentiment – which, in itself, is no crime in a free world – but he made no attempt ever to submerge his anglophobia for the common good. He was a throwback to the eighteenth century and still blindly believed what his history books told him about the 'English' being the source of all evil. You could no more reason with him than you could with a drunk – and, as one does with a drunk, I tended to avoid him and deal direct with Li. He was the logical outcome of General Stilwell's anglophobia; but whereas Stilwell was too good a soldier to allow this to blind him militarily, Bluster was not even a soldier. I could produce Englishmen as ignorant, as obstinate and as blind in their own conceit and petty illusions learnt when they were six; but it is not normal for them to be chosen as liaison officers – officers selected to represent their country and its people. Lieut.-Col. Bluster fortunately only represents, if at all, a small section of Americans who appear still to be smarting over a 150-year-old argument which they won.

He was a big, commanding, broad, blustering man, every inch an officer. When he came to talk to me I would walk him along to the Courthouse triangle where the odd Jap would try to snipe us. He looked so much more imposing than I. But unfortunately the Japanese are bad shots, and I would return sorrowfully home with him while he told me how to fight.

CHAPTER ELEVEN

THE RETURN

Wingate would have been proud of you.

I felt indeed no elation now that it was ended. We had been told that once Mogaung was taken our task was done. My troops had fought every day for a whole month since first we had pushed off the Gurkhas from the Lamai area. Our casualties from the beginning of the Mogaung operation tell their own tale:

Killed: 17 officers, 238 other ranks.
Wounded: 30 officers, 491 other ranks.

This was over one-third of my force and does not include the very many sick, and those who died later in India.

I might quote Wellington, 'The next greatest misfortune to losing a battle is to gain such a victory as this.'

It can be said that we had too many casualties; if that is true, it would be my fault. But one would have thought that it could never be said that my troops had not fought hard. Yet that was what was said by General Stilwell's staff. Even Stilwell says that our condition was bad, as we did not know how to look after ourselves compared with his Marauders. The Marauders had done a very great job and I, for one, have the highest opinion of them. But they did not live on K. rations only for four months on end. They had periods of rest safe behind their own lines where their nerves could relax. They obtained reinforcements, I believe. Yet, by June 15th, they refused to fight any longer, as too much had been asked of them again and again, and they had been squeezed dry. I tell this only to make partial excuse for some of my actions during the next few days; they cannot be condoned, but there is some justification for them, in the perspective of our four months' fighting, of our casualties, of our sickness, of our scanty rations and the psychological effect of that communiqué about Mogaung from Stilwell's H.Q. which reached us through the B.B.C.

On the 27th, I sent a long message to General Lentaigne reporting that Mogaung was now taken, that I was handing over to Colonel Li and was going to move to Pinhmi and reorganize and rest. I had also sent a message earlier on: 'Mogaung having been taken by Chinese, 77th Brigade is proceeding to take Umbrage' (with invented map reference). I was told – but I think that it is one of those stories – that this message was given to General Stilwell's intelligence staff who announced that we were going to attack a village called Umbrage whose location they had not yet managed to find on the map.

We received some very fine messages of congratulation from Joe Lentaigne and from members of his staff, the other brigades and from Scottie. One, from Derek Tulloch, I particularly liked: 'Wingate would have been proud of you.'

We had a thanksgiving service at Pinhmi. I prefer thanksgiving after battle to prayers before. Unless they are very humble, I think that mass prayers for victory before fighting tend to be hypocritical in that one claims that one is in the right. In my opinion it also savours of unfairness. Thanksgiving afterwards when the survivors feel humble and have something to be thankful for is more sincere. Few of the troops attended. This may have been because they did not know of the service, or they may have thought that I was being a bit of a hypocrite; or they may still have felt that almost tangible bitterness in the atmosphere of a month-long battlefield dotted with their comrades' graves.

Next day, while the battalion was cleaning up, I went by boat to visit George Butler at Tapaw. It was quite eerie scudding down with the current between jungle-covered and possibly Jap-covered banks, and I was thankful when we arrived.

Butler gave me a great welcome. I inspected his very well-kept and well-fortified area. His troops had been kept supplied with much produce by the local populace. They had captured or killed a few stray Japs, but otherwise reported that there were no Japs between us and Myitkyina. I rode back that evening on Jean, glad to get into a gallop, and tried to free my mind of the worries, regrets and bitterness that now seemed to be haunting it.

F/Lt. Harte returned from his long sojourn up at Lamai where he had done so well and kept us so fully informed.

In my reaction I was haunted by the thought that I had caused too many casualties for the glorification of the brigade, and possibly for the vanity of being able to say that we had taken Mogaung. Of course, the whole battle, including the fighting by the Chinese regiments, had contributed to its capture. We had shared with the Chinese the honour of actual entry, but as Tolstoy says in *War and Peace*, commanders preen themselves on their victories which may have been caused by some quite extraneous accident such as a smile of a sweet girl to some troops going into action.

We unfortunately had met no sweet girls, and were forgetting what they looked like. It had been fighting or preparing to fight, or resting after fighting, morning, noon and night, and any spare time was spent in resisting the elements or discovering that one had another new disease. As I heard Pte. Dodds of the Worcester Regiment, who was with me in the walk-out in 1943, say to his chum when they were lying hungry and tired in the heart of the jungle, 'If I saw the most beautiful blonde in the world, taking off her clothes, all naked and standing in front of me, giving herself to me, I would say' – with a wave of his hand – 'Take her away, and bring me a tin of bully.'

I returned to find a message to say that we were to advance down the railway to Hopin. I refused. I was asked to send even just one company. I said that if I counted every rifleman who could stand, I could hardly muster a company. Back came a message: 'How many fit men have you?' I answered 'Three hundred.' 'Why don't you advance with them?' 'We were promised that there would be no more fighting after Mogaung was taken.' 'This would not mean fighting, but just an advance so as not to lose the initiative gained by the capture of Mogaung. Surely you could send one company down.' I sent a company towards Loilaw, but it did not go far. I also sent a message: 'I have only 300 men all told. Do you want me to form the King's Royal Staffordshire Gurkha Fusiliers?' I received no reply. This had taken a few days. The now dying Francis was evacuated at last and promised that he would see Stilwell and Joe Lentaigne and explain the position. I did not know that he was dying. I believe Chesshire knew, but realized that nothing could be done about it. He had tuberculosis in the guts, and had had it, and I think knew that he had it, all the campaign.

I sent a long message to General Lentaigne in order to strengthen his hand against the great pressure being put on him by General Stilwell (who was still frantic because Myitkyina had not yet fallen). I said he could show General Stilwell all my personal signals, and that I was prepared to take the consequences. I was not going to ask any more of my men. I was haunted by the fact that we had been the willing horse, and that I had allowed them to be flogged until they could hardly stand. I was not going to put them in a position where they might break and spoil their magnificent record. I am not saying that this would have happened, but they were all in a state in which it would have been quite unfair to ask more of them. I was prepared to take on my own shoulders any blame for not fighting.

I received a message to say that 36 Division was at last arriving, and that we were to wait and hand over our mules and arms to them. I was loath to hand over the valuable mules and ponies which had served with us so long and which were battle-trained and part of our team. I wanted them for next season. I explained this, but was told that it was impossible. It would be madness to fly in mules for 36 Division and fly out our mules, and the Air Force certainly would not do it.

I sent a message that we could not wait any longer for 36 Division. Now that the tension had ceased and reaction set in, men were going down like flies with malaria, dysentery and other fevers, and the death rate went up. My medical officers advised me to get off the scene of battle.

We were then asked whether we preferred to go to Myitkyina or Kamaing. There was a great fear amongst all ranks that we would be asked to take Myitkyina. We had a phobia about Myitkyina, and I weakly gave way to this. I said Kamaing. I sent one or two of the battalions across the river to Gurkhaywa in anticipation of a move. I also arranged with Colonel Li to meet the Commander 112th Regiment, who agreed to relieve my brigade.

Next day, I received a message to leave our mules at Mogaung, and to march with the rest of the brigade to Myitkyina, where we would be flown out. I then did a very foolish thing. I shut down all wireless sets and marched to Kamaing, having arranged that 112th Regiment (Chinese) relieved us. This was totally wrong of me, and my disobedience of an order was not even justified by success. The route to Myitkyina would have been far easier and our evacuation far quicker and simpler, apart from the fact that we would have met 36 Division and established good relations with them. This was never done, and all they heard about us were the malignant lies told them by General Stilwell's staff.

Lieut.-Col. Bluster now had a marvellous time. He sent back messages saying that we were cowards, yellow, deserters, walked off the field of battle, and we should all be arrested, etc. Most of the misunderstanding between General Stilwell and ourselves had been engineered by Bluster's misrepresentation, and now he felt justified. Amongst other messages received by us was one asking the relative number of our casualties and those of the Chinese 114th Regiment. It was about 800 to 30 south of the Mogaung river. But I will admit that as we moved north we found signs of very hard fighting north of Mogaung, especially in the area around Tumbonkha. All this is written as a record, and so that others may not make the same mistakes. This is what occurs when allies fall out, and I swear that one man only was mostly to blame, although I am quite prepared to admit my unjustified disobedience of an order.

I went to say goodbye to Li. He was not in his headquarters. I asked his staff to pass on my message of farewell and good luck. I moved my H.Q. across the Mogaung river to Gurkhaywa, where I summoned the headmen of all the villages in the district. There I received the following message from Colonel Li.

Dear Brigadier Calvert: I heard you were about to leave yesterday, and when I went to bid you goodbye at your H.Q. you were gone. I enjoy fighting alongside you, and am sorry that you have to leave because of casualties. My regiment and I really admire your brigade's gallant action and your men's spirit. We unanimously think that you and your brig-

ade are very brave. Your four months in Burma reflect credit
to the British troops. I sincerely hope you will come again to
fight the common enemy after your brigade has been
refitted. The 112th Regiment have part of their troops here
today, and we will try our best to push on and kill more Japs.
Good luck. COLONEL LI, *Commander 114th Regiment*.

I am glad to state that later Colonel Li was awarded the
O.B.E. and Major P'ang and Capt. Su the M.C.

I had been a bit annoyed by a message to Davis from U.S.
O.S.S. H.Q.[1] which we had inadvertently intercepted telling him to ensure that all Kachins and Burmese realized that
all the help that they were getting was from American
money. I therefore made a speech in Gurkhaywa to a thousand or more headmen and hangers-on, including Burmese,
Shans, Kachins, Indians and Burmese Gurkhas, descendants
of the Gurkhas who had fought for us in our conquest of
north Burma, and to whom we had granted land. The gist of
this talk, which was interpreted in turn into Burmese, Gurkhali and Urdu, was that we had been driven out of Burma
while our backs were turned, fighting against Germany;
that we were now returning; that the granting of so-called
'Independence' by the Japanese was a trick to make things
awkward for us on our anticipated return – where was their
independence in any case under the Japs? – that after the
reconquest of Burma, Britain would rule as before until
order was restored; that independence would be granted
when they had proved that they were capable of enjoying it,
and would not relapse into inter-racial strife; they must not
fight each other, but fight the common enemy.

I also, as usual, exempted them from all taxes. I allowed
them to cut down as much timber as they required, and
stated that no arrears of taxes would be charged against
them. These were real fears in their minds, and they needed
alleviating. I then bade them God-speed, and told them that
they must give all the help that they could to our allies,
including the Chinese whom they feared because of their
looting, rape and arson during the retreat in 1942.

After my speech, leaving my headquarters to take their
place in the line of march, I rode on fast to get to Kamaing.
The path was atrocious. There would be mile-length

[1] United States Office of Strategic Supply, a clandestine organization.

stretches where a marching man would never see his feet in the mud, which often came up to his waist or higher. Men would disappear into weapon pits hidden in the mud and water and be dragged out by their comrades. Two of the Lancashire Fusiliers died of exhaustion on the march. One was found by the Americans dead at the side of the track. Halts were caused by Chinese columns advancing in the opposite direction. I pushed on fast with Ginger, my groom. We slept at Tumbongkha and had a wonderful meal at a wayside American medical station. We then came into an area completely flooded by the Mogaung river. We walked for miles in the floods, guessing where the path was, our horses loaded with rifles in rifle buckets, our bedding, their feed and each of us with our heavy packs.

Finally we had to swim in the gaps between the trees, and Ginger, who was no swimmer, could not go on, nor control his horse, which tried to reach down to touch ground with its hind legs, and leap up again, getting entangled in the shrubbery below. Jean behaved very well, but was tiring. I had to prop both horses' heads in forks of trees, and let Ginger rest on a tree. His horse had swallowed so much water that it had given up and was lying on its side. Leaving them, I swam off into the jungle with my heavy pack weighing me down. There was no danger – one could always grasp a branch. Thorns and brambles below, which caressed and entangled one, were frightening, but not dangerous. I eventually found dry land. I was more exhausted than I realized and lay down for a while. Then having taken off my pack and boots and other encumbrances, I swam back for Ginger. I helped him to the bank, which was only about 100 yards away. I then went back for his gear. I swam Jean out. She was docile, putting her trust in me. Ginger's horse was more of a problem as he lay on his side and made no effort to help. I had to tow him holding his nostrils out of the water, resting now and again on branches. When we did reach the bank he leapt about and got well entangled in a thorn bush, from which it took all our combined strength to pull him. Once out, he at once started to graze, as horses and mules do after a difficult experience.

We rested for a while in the rare sunlight. Then we made our way along what proved to be the bank of the Mogaung river, to find half the brigade in a tented camp on the bank.

That stormy night our veterinary officer heard a mule struggling in the torrential water of the Mogaung. He went in to rescue it, and was drowned. Death was still following us, as men still died of disease.

I went up the Mogaung with Lieut.-Col. Howell, R.E., who was running the 'Chindit Navy' on the Mogaung river to the Indawggyi Lake. He took me to where General Stilwell had his H.Q., and where Joe Lentaigne also had his Advance H.Q. I was welcomed with whisky by Henry Alexander, who was now Lentaigne's Colonel (Operations), and a harassed Joe. I had caused General Lentaigne a great deal of worry over my march to Kamaing, as he had been refuting charges by Stilwell to General Slim, that our brigade was refusing to obey orders. Here was a flagrant and obvious case. I was to see Stilwell in the morning. There was the possibility of a court martial. I was still stunned by the reaction of those long months of striving, and was too tired to mind. I slept in comfort in a hut for the first time in four months.

After a good night's sleep, we jeeped along to General Stilwell's simple office in the jungle, with Alexander telling me to give him hell, and Joe entreating me to be careful what I said, and to think of the Force. I had decided that I would briefly tell the whole story from our fly-in until the capture of Mogaung, and let Stilwell judge.

Stilwell sat at a table between two of his staff officers, General Boatner and his son, Lieut.-Col. Stilwell. We shook hands. 'Sit down.' I was given the chair in the centre opposite him, with Joe and Henry either side.

'Well, Calvert, I have been wanting to meet you for some time.'

'I have been wanting to meet you too, sir.'

'You send some very strong signals, Calvert.'

'You should see the ones my brigade major won't let me send.'

General Stilwell roared with laughter, hitting his staff officers on the back. 'I have just the same trouble with my own staff officers when I draft signals to Washington.'

By a fortunate remark I had hit on exactly the right approach. From then on everything was easy. I told him of our fly-in, our casualties, of the chart we had kept at White City of his progress, how we had had to take it down as it was too depressing, how we had not fully destroyed the railway, waiting for him to come down it, how we were nearly flown out, how we could not help at Aberdeen, how we anticipated his orders to take Mogaung, our long struggle there, our casualties, all our casualties, how battalion commanders had wept at their casualties, how Brigade H.Q. had been put into the attack, the B.B.C. bulletin, Colonel Li's message, our return. 'I am sorry, sir, if I disobeyed orders, but I think you will realize the strain that we were put to.'

Throughout Stilwell kept saying to his staff, 'Check that. Is it correct?' 'Yes, sir.' 'Why wasn't I told?' He had not realized that we were the brigade flown in four months before. He had not believed our casualty lists – he had been so used to false ones. His staff knew of his anti-British feelings, and had therefore told him of any failures and defeats, but had concealed from him our victories and successes. He was too great a soldier to allow his natural antipathy of the British to overcome his fighting instincts; but his staff weren't.

'You and your boys have done a great job. I congratulate you. Give me the names of five officers or men to whom I can award the Silver Star.'

'Yes, sir.'

I later wrote out five citations. He ruled out one as most of his gallantry had occurred while we were not under General Stilwell's command. He was kind enough to add my name to the five.

I got permission for some thirty of my best mules, and my pony Jean, to be flown out to form a cadre for the training of our new intake. The remainder were marched back by the mule-leaders via Mogaung to Myitkyina and handed over to 36 Division. They had arrived in Kamaing in surprisingly good condition, which gave rise to much favourable comment amongst the Americans.

I flew back to Kamaing in an L5 plane fitted with both floats and wheels. I navigated the American pilot to the spot, and he started to go on. 'Where are you going?' 'I am looking for a landing ground.' 'There isn't one, you land in the water.' 'I have never done that before.' 'Now's your chance.'

He asked which way, and where to land. I directed him to land up-stream, and near some boats so that if we capsized we were near succour. We landed beautifully. A boat came alongside. I got out. He asked me, 'Which way do I take off?' I pointed upstream, and said, 'That way.' I had under-estimated the distance, and he had to go round a bend in the river before he left the water.

That incident was typical of these fine American pilots. They would always have a go.

I gave out the necessary orders for our withdrawal, writing up recommendations for decoration with my battalion commanders, and returned to Shaduzup. After a few days there, I flew out to Assam. As we flew north in the Ledo direction, I saw below the straight line of the flooded Ledo road glistening between the green sea of the surrrounding jungle. It was of this road that the story goes that Lord Louis, flying to visit Stilwell, said, 'What is that river? I can't see it marked on my map.' 'That is the Ledo road, sir.' It was described by an American magazine as the tarmacadam highway to China.

We landed in the dark, and were taken to a very well-run reception camp, but it was all a bit of an anticlimax. All ranks in Burma had shaved and polished themselves up on my orders. I knew from my experience in 1940, 1942 and 1943 that the appearance of troops as they came out makes a lasting impression on the minds of those who greet them. Next day I visited the hospital and met some of our wounded. One man was coming round out of an anaesthetic. He gripped my hand and thanked me for everything. It was an embarrassing, but gratifying, moment in that crowded ward.

As arrangements were in hand to transport the brigade to Dehra Dun, I took the train to Calcutta to visit Francis. Our troops on the train were greeted en route by at least two Governors of Provinces, in one instance in the middle of the night. I thank them.

I found Francis in hospital and, for the first time, learnt that he was dying. He was propped on pillows, thin, hollow-cheeked, hollow-eyed. We talked of the campaign. He said that he would not have missed it for anything. I told him, 'You must get better quickly and help me write up the account.' He showed me some of his poems. He had a book in which he copied anything beautiful he came across in his reading. He often used to show it to me in the jungle. He also wrote little poems himself, some poignant, some merry. He had written one or two poems in hospital.

I now knew he was dying. I think he knew too. I think that he knew all along that he had T.B., before he joined the brigade. I had met him in Simla recuperating from a 'chest complaint'.

He had summoned up his last strength to see Stilwell on his way out, and to tell him of our situation. After our victory at Mogaung reaction set in, and people let themselves go. They had lived on their spirit, and when they relaxed, many died. I think that, but for Francis's talk to Stilwell, I would have been placed under arrest for disobedience of orders. Francis had paved the way. This is not important, but shows his spirit and loyalty.

Next morning I went to see Mr. Casey, Governor of Bengal. I had read in *Reader's Digest* of some new drug, diasone, which had cured T.B. I was desperate, and refused to believe Francis was dying. I had reasoned with the doctors, but they said that there was no chance. However, Mr. Casey, whose mother I had known in Australia, and who had been Australian Ambassador in Washington, agreed to cable for this drug. There was only one place in America which had it. The drug was flown out. It made no difference.

I went and saw Francis once more and told him that he had been awarded the D.S.O. (He was in fact awarded the M.C. – we had used up our ration of D.S.O.s.) We talked again until I was ushered out.

I then went and got drunk, and joined in quite a nice fight in a Chinese restaurant. Francis died a week later.

I flew to Delhi and motored on to Dehra Dun, where I was to hear of my mother's sudden death.

We motored up to our resting place tired and weary. There was no difficulty about accommodation. We were now so few. As we drew near to the camp, I saw a large yellow banner draped from tree to tree right across the road. On it was written in black lettering:

CHINDITS! WATCH YOUR SALUTING!

POSTSCRIPT

Since I wrote *Prisoners of Hope* in 1950 many new facts have come to light. Unfortunately many foolish and ignorant things have also been written in the intervening years, the main object of which seems to have been to belittle the achievement of Wingate and the Chindits. By recording here the composition of the various forces involved I hope that the facts will speak for themselves and help to set the record straight.

The total Chindit force in Central Burma, before 16th Brigade was flown out, consisted of:

Thirteen British battalions (including one converted artillery regiment) Four Gurkha battalions (3/4th, 3/6th, 3/9th, 4/9th)

Three West African battalions (6th, 7th and 12th Nigerian Rifles)

Three British, one West African, and one mixed British/Indian engineer field squadrons.

Four troops, 160th Field Regiment, R.A. (totalling eight 25 pounders)

Four Troops, 69th. Light Anti Aircraft Regiment, R.A. (totalling twenty-four bofors L.A.A. guns)

The equivalent of one Burma Rifle Regiment distributed throughout the brigades

Three R.A.S.C. air-supply companies

Medical, veterinary, R.A.F., etc., detachments.

In all, this would be the equivalent of twenty battalions with attached troops, or just over two light divisions without armour and little artillery.

Between March 6th and May 2nd (before Wingate's plan was changed and Fergusson's 16th Brigade was flown out) these Chindits, numbering about 20,000 men and 4,000 mules, defeated in detail, and partially destroyed, the following Japanese battalions:

(The first numeral is the battalion number, the second the regiment)

Battalion	Formation and original location	Where destroyed
2nd/146th	from 56th Division on the Salween	Broadway
3rd/114th	18th Division facing Stilwell	1st and 2nd attacks on White City
2nd/29th	from 2nd Division in South Burma	
2nd/51st	from Mutaguchi's 15th Division	Attacks at Indaw
3rd/15th Artillery Regt.	attacking Imphal	and White City
138th		
139th	24th Independent Mixed Brigade from	Attacks at Indaw
140th	South Burma	and second attack
141st		at White City
1st/4th		
2nd/4th		
3rd/4th	4th Infantry Regiment from Malaya	
3rd/4th		
1st/146th	from 56th Division on Salween	Morris force attacks on Bhamo–Myitkyina Road

The 5th Railway Engineer Regiment and numerous light anti-aircraft, engineer, motor transport, mule and signal companies also suffered heavy casualties in the Indaw–White City fighting.

After the abandonment of Wingate's plan, from May 2nd to August 27th (when the last Chindit was flown out to India) the Chindits helped to destroy the 53rd Japanese Division, newly-arrived in Burma and intended to be Mutaguchi's reserve for his attack on Imphal-Kohima.

At Blackpool, and at and around Mogaung, the 128th Regiment of the 53rd Division was virtually destroyed by the Chindits with the help of U.S. air support. The Japanese also state that their 1st/151st battalion was completely wiped out at Mogaung by air and ground operations. The 1st Artillery Battalion lost all its guns except *two* at Mogaung. These troops were being sent by General Honda to relieve Myitkyina but were diverted to the defence of Mogaung when 77th Brigade started its attack. The other two Japanese regiments of 53rd Division were diverted from the Imphal front to operate against the Chindits and oppose Stilwell, so Mutaguchi never received the reinforcements he expected.

Besides this one half of the Japanese 5th Air Division was used against the Chindit airborne landings just when Mutaguchi wanted it at Imphal. They received heavy casualties at the hands of the Chindits anti aircraft artillery and Cochran's Air Commando.

The Chindits captured Mogaung, one of the two Allied objectives laid down at the Quebec Conference and materially assisted in the capture of the other, Myitkyina.

14th, 16th and 111th Chindit Brigades were responsible for the destruction of a large number of Japanese dumps assembled for Mutaguchi's offensive against Imphal/Kohima, and for the virtual eradication of two out of three of the Japanese lines of communications supporting these offensives. The 31st Division attacking Kohima lost its umbilical cord to Burma altogether when its lines of communications were destroyed by 14th and 111th Brigades. This was a decisive factor in its failure to capture Kohima.

At no time did the Chindits use more than ⅕th of the Allied Air Supply effort in any one month, and it was usually much less than that. However, the four Dakota squadrons asked for by Wingate from Churchill and Roosevelt were received by Slim (who had supported this request) after Wingate's death and made possible the defeat of the Japanese and the subsequent re-conquest of Burma as Wingate had predicted.

The Japanese under Mutaguchi attacked the British 4 Corps on the Imphal plain with three infantry divisions (15th, 31st and 33rd) totalling twenty-seven battalions. 33rd Division, which had the advantage of a fairly good road, had some heavy artillery and tanks, but the two others were mainly on a pack artillery and animal transport basis. Mutaguchi also had an 'Indian National Army' brigade which was quite useless and which he would have preferred to do without as it just cluttered up his administration without adding to his striking power.

To oppose this attack 4 Corps under General Scoones had initially three and a half divisions with tanks and armoured cars, plenty of artillery and a large consignment of engineers. In support were about 15 to 20 squadrons of R.A.F. fighter-bombers of 3rd Tactical Air Force. Scoones was reinforced by air with approximately 1½ divisions. The open Imphal plain, which was the battlefield sensibly chosen by Scoones, was comparatively good tank country in the dry season and could be covered by the heavy artillery at his disposal.

33 Corps under General Stopford, consisting of two divisions (2nd British and 7th Indian) plus four good brigades complete with tanks and armoured cars, was sent to relieve 4 Corps from the north.

So the eventual victory at Imphal/Kohima was won by the equivalent of 8⅔ British/Indian infantry divisions supported by good armour and heavy artillery with overwhelming air superiority, against three undoubtedly excellent Japanese divisions with a few obsolete tanks, mainly pack artillery, completely inadequate air support, operating in unfriendly country at least one hundred miles from their bases (some of which had been destroyed by the Chindits) and across a 400-yard-wide river. Yet the Chindits, only about the equivalent of two light divisions with little artillery, destroyed the equivalent of one Japanese division and helped to divert and destroy another (the 53rd) although they were operating amidst the Japanese communications and close to the Jap supplies. The 14th Army units were receiving regular reliefs and reinforcements. The Chindits were starved of reinforcements when they needed them, the reserve brigade (23rd) being given to General Stopford as the policy appeared to be to let the Chindit Brigades waste themselves away.

In 1948, when on the C.I.G.S. Exercise Planning Staff at the War Office, I was shown a report of a meeting held in 1945 on the policy to be adopted in regard to the problem of Wingate and the Chindits. The meeting appeared to have been composed of the military representatives of the Army Council with at least one senior Air Force officer present. The conclusion reached, with the R.A.F. strongly dissenting, was that although Wingate had achieved many tactical successes throughout his career in Palestine, Abyssinia and Burma, he had, on the whole, had a disruptive and divisive effect on the British Army so that the total value of his services was negative. It was agreed that the policy in the future would be to write down Wingate and the Chindits. 'We don't want every company commander going off and growing a beard, thinking he is a Wingate and so can do what he likes.' 'We don't want any more Wingates, so we must write down the Chindits.' It became so that ambitious officers who had served with the Chindits concealed the fact for fear that it might prejudice their promotion.

But the fact remains that Wingate and the Chindits undoubtedly had a decisive effect on the war in Burma in 1944 by breaching the wall of mountains around Burma, preventing the Japanese from using interior lines to defeat each threat (British, American, Chinese) in turn and letting in the Allies from the north on to the Burma plain behind the Japanese facing 14th Army. Yet neither Wingate nor the Chindits have been given their military due for their sacrifices and tactical and strategical successes. One reason was that, after the war, when Britain was trying in vain to retain her Empire, it was a considered policy to give the kudos for any successes in the East almost solely to the Indian Army.

We, in the Chindits, were partly to blame for this state of affairs. Initially, perhaps, we received too much publicity and some of us behaved badly when on leave in India, and did not give sufficient thought for those who had borne the heat and burden of the day for two years or more on the Chindwin River and in the Arakan. Unfortunately, a force which sees itself as changing the history of war tends to be arrogant. However, this should not prevent the military historians from getting at the truth and seeing it in its proper light the sustained and venomous propaganda to which Wingate and the Chindits have been subjected.

MICHAEL CALVERT

October, 1970

APPENDIX I

REPORT BY LIEUT.-COL. R. P. FLEMING ON LOSS OF GLIDER 15 P ON MARCH 5th, 1944

To: Comd: 77 Ind. Inf. Bde.
From: Lieut.-Col. R. P. Fleming,
       Gren. Gds.
       G.S.I. (d)

Report on loss of Glider 15 P on 5.3.44

(Note: Owing to the facts that

(a) the party's War Diary was lost in the Chindwin crossing;

(b) the party had no maps of the area traversed other than 1 / 1,000,000 'escape' maps on handkerchiefs

all times and distances are approximate and the route followed is largely conjectural.)

A.—Take-Off

1. Glider 15 P (P for Piccadilly, the code name of the southerly of 77 Bde.'s two original landing areas in the Okkyi valley) was the short tow (port side) glider of the 15th pair in the first flight of operation Emphasis. With her opposite number on long tow (14 P) she was allotted to personnel of 77 Bde. H.Q. who were going in on D Day from Lallaghat L/G.

2. Her complement as shown on the manifest was 6 offrs., 7 B.O.R.s, 1 I.O.R., and 1 pony in addition to the American pilot. This was slightly altered before take-off. (See para. 7 below.)

3. Very shortly before 1800 hrs. when the 4 leading gliders containing the 2 'Blitz' parties for Piccadilly and Broadway were due to become airborne, a U.S.A.A.F. pilot (Lieut.-Col. Gatey) arrived on the scene with some excellent photographs of Piccadilly taken 3 hours earlier. (For obvious reasons of security there had been no air recce of Piccadilly since it was originally photographed some weeks before.)

4. These photographs showed that the whole of that part of the clearing which it was intended to convert into a landing strip had been liberally obstructed by the enemy with tree trunks and that the whole clearing was profusely marked with tracks. (These precautions may have been attributable to the detailed publicity given last year, in *Life,* to a successful Dakota landing on Piccadilly during the Longcloth ops.)

5. This development, which for dramatic value could hardly have been improved upon by Hollywood, necessitated a change of plan. This was made with great alacrity, the whole of the first night's sorties being switched to Broadway, the northern landing area, which it was hoped had not been compromised. The take-off began only a few minutes behind schedule, and the first tugs and gliders were soon circling over our heads, gaining altitude before heading east into Burma.

6. It cannot be said that at this stage 15 P gave her passengers the impression of being a lucky glider. Her original pilot had become a casualty 2 days previously as a result of a jeep crash; and now, when we jacked up her tail in order to load Jean (the Bde. Comd.'s pony), one of the supports slipped and the glider sustained minor damage which made her unserviceable.

7. This necessitated replacing her with another glider which was duly fed into the line in the same station. The new 15 P was not fitted with a stall and accordingly Jean and Cpl. Dermody had to stand down, their place being partly filled by Pte. Young Man-sun ('Automatic'), my Chinese orderly.

8. By approx. 2005 hrs. we had worked our way to the head of the double queue and at 2015 hrs. we became airborne without mishap.

9. F/O. Williams, the pilot, had asked for one man to be detailed to come forward if it proved necessary to trim her, and this man was ordered forward immediately after take-off. It soon, however, became apparent that the glider was not behaving satisfactorily and at ominously frequent intervals the pilot called 'another man forward' until all the passengers were wedged into a sort of pâté immediately behind the pilot's and co-pilot's seats.

10. From a very relatively enviable position in the latter, I (and nobody else) was able to see 14 B, the long-tow glider on our starboard quarter. Or rather, I had been able to see her for at an early stage in the flight I realized that she was no longer with us. At this point I made a serious error of judgment in not informing the pilot that 14 B had 'cut' for it I had (he afterwards told me) he would have cut too – owing to the danger of 14 B's loose tow-rope removing our starboard wing – and we should have landed on or near our base at Lallaghat.

11. My reasons for suppressing the information were (apart from ignorance of its full implications):

  (a) the pilot appeared to have quite enough on his mind already;
  (b) I considered it essential to take no action which might lessen the Bde. Comd.'s chances of getting at any rate part of his staff into Broadway that night. (The Bde. Staff in 14 B were at any rate temporarily out of the running; and we had on board his Signal, Medical and Intelligence officers, as well as ciphers, maps and other essential documents.)

12. 15 P reached an altitude of 8oooft. and proceeded on her way with every sign of reluctance. It had become early apparent that the controls – operated by 3 small handles above the pilot's right shoulder – were not in working order, and nothing we could do would induce them to turn in the required direction. Spells of relatively smooth flying alternated with mild but disturbing aerobatics, during which the glider shuddered convulsively and the blue lights on the tug see-sawed up, down and sideways across our field of vision. F/O. Williams afterwards told me that he was expecting the tail to come off and I consider that he showed commendable

determination in maintaining his objective in these circumstances. I assume that the defects in the controls were due to the glider not having been checked before replacing the original 15 P at the last moment.

13. We crossed the Chindwin at 8000 ft. approx 1 hour after take-off. At about 2140 hrs. 15 P had a fit of recalcitrance which culminated in (according to the pilot) an attempt to loop the loop. She banked steeply, causing all loose objects in the cockpit and elsewhere to come adrift. The pilot struck the release mechanism above his head, and we found ourselves diving fairly steeply and in comparative silence, the rush of air having decreased from a roar to a more soothing note without reduction in speed. I do not remember seeing the tug (with which, incidentally, we had never had means of inter-comn.).

B.–LANDING

14. For what must have been several minutes we spiralled unsteadily towards a point where a stream bed in a gully splayed out in an irregular patch of white sand. On this restricted and uneven space, missing a number of tree tops by a margin which was almost certainly greater than it seemed, F/O. Williams put the glider down with extreme skill and a resounding bump which broke open the forepart of the cockpit. Impelled partly by tactical considerations and partly by a sense of self-preservation (for the pilot and I, at the bottom of a groaning and blasphemous pile of soldiery, were now most unfavourably placed), I ordered all ranks to deplane with their arms.

15. No one was more than very slightly injured, though several were pardonably dazed. (We were lucky not to have had the pony with us as she could hardly have failed to have caused casualties.) Six men were ordered to form a perimeter round the glider within a radius of 50 yards, and we took stock of the situation.

16. Ciphers and all secret documents were burnt, a process which took some time and made the glider on the moonlit sandbank even more conspicuous than it was already. Major Faulkner returned from a short recce downstream to report that we had had the ill-luck to land within 100 yards of a

road used by wheeled traffic (the only road we saw in Burma), that a telephone ran along the road, and that dogs were barking in the vicinity.

17. It was obvious that the sooner we got clear of the glider the better, and I accordingly ordered all personnel to withdraw N. into the edge of the jungle and wait for me. While this move was in progress, the glider, which was still illuminated by burning documents, was attacked from about 300 ft. by one single-engined fighter with a burst of cannon fire (or m.g. fire using explosive bullets: the bursts were seen on the ground 80 yds. away). The attack was not repeated. The aircraft may have been attracted by a flare fired, just before landing, to illuminate the sandbank. At the time we thought the aircraft was hostile but Adv. 3 Ind. Div. assume it to have been a Hurricane.

18. Capt. Massey and I supervised and stoked the bonfires, slightly discouraged by the sound of an approaching M/T vehicle, which however stopped some distance away. We had in the glider 2 dummy buffalo wallows made of hessian and dassootie which had been intended to make the Piccadilly airstrip appear unserviceable, and these we spread out prominently on the sandbank as a ground-to-air signal in the form of an arrow pointing S. We then withdrew in a northerly direction.

19. I did not burn the glider as it was clearly impossible (owing to the steel framework, etc.) to conceal from the enemy that it had been a glider, and I was not anxious to advertise our position any further than had already proved necessary. I also decided against booby-trapping it with No. 36 grenades, as I felt that the chances of killing Japanese (as opposed to Burmese) were not sufficient to warrant the risk of reprisals on any personnel who might be taken prisoner.

20. Nothing of value except bulk rations was left in the glider and all ranks moved off complete with their arms and equipment.

C. FIRST NIGHT (*Mar. 5/6*)

21. Before leaving the edge of the clearing I impressed on the party:

(a) That if we behaved sensibly we had practically nothing to fear from the Japanese, who were almost certainly in a greater state of alarm and confusion than we were ourselves;

(b) that none was to think of himself as a 'survivor' or an 'evacuee' but rather as a member of an unusually well-found fighting patrol, inserted in the enemy's rearward administrative areas and perfectly capable of seeing off the small parties from L. of C. units which were all we were likely to meet at this stage;

(c) that we had been damned lucky so far.

(Mention is made of these, and will be made of later exhortations because I am convinced that the party was able to extricate itself unaided because of the confident attitude, based on a sense of proportion and an appreciation of the enemy's difficulties, which all ranks displayed under conditions which were on paper discouraging.)

22. We then climbed a low escarpment overlooking the chaung, struck a little-used path running slightly W. of N. through the jungle and followed it at a brisk pace for approx. 3 hours. This was the only time we travelled on a path and we did so for the sake of speed, which appeared at the time desirable. Two men without nails in their boots marched in rear with a view to partly obscuring the marks of hobnails.

23. At approx. 0130 hrs. we reached a further escarpment overlooking a small valley. Immediately below us (but not visible) was a village or settlement of sorts and from this came loud and for the most part petulant voices in Japanese as the local post turned itself out, presumably on receipt of news of our landing. There were some sounds of animal transport but none of M/T.

24. We moved off the path and lay up for a short time, then doubled back a short distance and attempted to detour to the W. This brought us to a boggy and frequented open glen with a stream in it. I recced a crossing without incident and the party moved across, walking backwards and leaving tracks so heavily down by the heel (owing to the weight of packs) that they would not have deceived Lestrade, let alone Sherlock Holmes.

25. There followed a frustrated interlude in a series of overgrown quarry-like cavities (typical, as we later found, of all

escarpments in the area) during which while on a recce, I stumbled on 2 supply dumps in deep natural pits. (The stores were partly hutted over though unidentifiable from above.) We seemed to be closer to the village than was healthy and accordingly withdrew to the glen, worked our way up it, and eventually struck S.W. into the jungle, halting for the night about 1 mile in a direct line from the village when the moon set about 0330 hrs. All ranks were by this time tired.

D. SECOND NIGHT *(Mar. 6/7)*

26. The following day we lay up in a patch of elephant grass and carried out various admin. tasks. We carried 8 days' K. rations and I put the party on $\frac{1}{2}$ rations (i.e. 1$\frac{1}{2}$ units per man per day) in case of accidents, such as having to lie up for several days or having our rate of march cut down by having personnel wounded or injured.

27. Everyone had either a T.M.G. [Thompson sub-machine gun], a Sten, a .303 rifle or a .300 carbine, the 6 officers also carried pistols, and ammunition (incl. grenades) was plentiful. There were several compasses in the party.

28. Non-essential possessions were sorted out of packs and buried. All ranks were ordered to shave daily when the water situation permitted. (This was part of the 'anti-survivor' campaign and, in my opinion, paid.)

29. The party was organized into an H.Q. and Recce Gp. (myself, Capt. Massey and 1 B.O.R.) and 2 sections under Major Pringle (2 i/c) and Major Faulkner. We moved always in the above order of march, the leading section throwing out a point to give the Recce Gp. more elbow room on the comparatively rare occasions when there seemed to be need for additional precautions.

30. Our position was on paper complicated, but in practice simplified, by the fact that we did not know where we were and had no map of the area other than the escape maps referred to above. Opinions differed as to our flying time E. of the Chindwin and the pilot did not know the course on which we had been flying. It was, however, fairly clear that we were between 30 and 50 miles E. of the Chindwin and almost certainly S. of the Uyu river.

31. I accordingly made and gave out a plan which can be summarized as follows:

Intention. To return all personnel to the theatre of 77 Bde's ops. as quickly as possible.

Method. Of the various methods open to us the following were ruled out:

    (a) to march E. and rejoin 77 Bde. on the railway. Impracticable owing to lack of maps and probable inadequacy of rations;

    (b) to march N.E. and join 16 Bde. in the field. Impracticable for the same reasons;

    (c) to find a landing ground for light aircraft, lie up, attract attention by ground to air signals and evacuate by air. Unenterprising, uncertain and calculated to cause an unjustifiable diversion of air support.

We would accordingly march W., cross the Chindwin and rejoin by air after making contact with our forces.

32. No sounds were heard from the village during the day and the jungle in our vicinity appeared unfrequented. At 1700 hrs. the Recce Gp. went out to have a look at the first leg of the night's march, a smooth getaway from the lying-up area being good for confidence. Half a mile W. we came to the edge of a large and as far as we could see oblong open space. While spying this through field glasses I observed a Japanese in an elaborately camouflaged uniform (incl. a silly sort of hat and – as far as I could see – a mask) proceeding across my front at a range of approx. 300 yds. His gait was one of exaggerated stealth and he was moving so slowly, with what appeared to be a machine carbine at the ready, that I at first assumed he was stalking a deer or buffalo (there had been several single shots in the area during the day, which sounded as though some one was shooting game).

33. I then noticed, on the far side of the clearing, what appeared to be a camouflaged hide and near it the legs of a man whose body was concealed by a bush. I accordingly sent the remainder of the Recce Gp. back to halt the main body, who would by this time be moving up.

34. Meanwhile I had lost the exponent of slow motion eurhythmics but on moving forward found him again up a tree, in a 'machan' the base of which appeared to be improvised from some form of metal plate, presumably with a view to protection from S.A. fire. He was gazing intently towards the centre of the clearing and his buttocks offered, at 250 yards, a target which it required the strongest sense of duty to forgo.

35. I withdrew, picked up the main body and made a short detour to the S.W. It appeared however that the clearing curved and that we were on the inside of the curve, for very soon we bumped the edge of it again, at a point where another Japanese, in an attitude of exaggerated vigilance, was peering through a loophole in a kind of camouflaged stockade.

36. This necessitated another slight detour but this too brought us back to the perimeter immediately behind another sentry crouching in a tunnel-like basha and sedulously watching his front. It was now nearly last light. We shifted off and halted for a few minutes. I took the opportunity of pointing out to the party that conditions locally were much more favourable to us than we had supposed. All the evidence available suggested that:

(a) the local commander was in a state of flap;
(b) his troops, who appeared to be thin on the ground, were committed to a static defensive role;
(c) he was obviously expecting an airborne landing in the clearing and had made careful arrangements to ambush it;
(d) there were bound to be other similar clearings in the area which he would have to watch;
(e) he had misappreciated our role and probably exaggerated our strength;
(f) we had the initiative.

37. By this time the Dakotas had begun to drone overhead on the Broadway run, lending colour to the local commanders's (alleged) fears. I do not consider that the above appreciation was far wide of the mark and it had a noticeable effect on the morale of all ranks (including my own)

and the march continued in an atmosphere of discreet truculence.

38. After proceeding for perhaps a mile and a half and almost bumping a small group of tents in or near which ducks were quacking we reached, recced and crossed a narrow neck of the clearing which at this point appeared to be unsuitable for glider landings and was watched either not at all or inefficiently.

39. I rested the party inside the jungle on the far side and encouraged the men to smoke and boast. We then marched due W. through the jungle for 3 or 4 hours, crossing several more small clearings, with dried-up wallows in them in some of which we tried unsuccessfully to dig for water. We halted for the night about 2330 hrs. In the course of the night there were 2 single shots not far away.

3. THIRD MARCH (*Mar. 7*)

40. The whole of our route lay through teak jungle and across uneven, rather broken country. The going was relatively easy. From the point of view of cover, teak looks more open than in fact it is, and by day the party had only to lie down to become virtually invisible at 50 yds. or less, while by moonlight – as long as we kept off the paths, which we always did – it would have been an unenviable task to search for us, even after contact had been made. Owing to the large dead leaves teak is noisy to move through, but it absorbs the noise far more quickly than the noise-maker realizes. Our only worry at this stage of the march was water.

41. On the 7th we had a major slice of luck in this aspect. After marching W. for an hour I altered course to N.W. so as to cut slantwise across the general westerly trend of the water-shed. Had this alteration been made 5 minutes or so earlier we should not have struck (as we immediately did) a large pond of sweet water in a clearing which subsequently proved to belong to the headwaters of the Nathan Chaung.

42. Down this admirable and deserted water-course we marched for the remainder of that day without incident. At 0900 hrs. we heard what sounded like a Diesel engine 1 or 2 miles to the S.W. and in the course of the morning we

crossed an old path with one fresh set of naked footprints on it. Otherwise there was no sign of life. It may be pointed out that a disused water-course offers an ideal axis of advance for tactical as well as admin. reasons in circumstances such as ours were. No community however small and however primitive can live on a river or stream without leaving traces both up and downstream of its location; and as long as these are absent the danger of bumping either enemy or natives is for practical purposes nil. Moreover, paths running across the water-shed in arid country generally offer, at the points where they cross the stream, a good opportunity for assessing the nature and density of the traffic on them, since parties generally halt and often bivouac at such crossings, leaving tracks and other clues. The upper Nathan Chaung offered a very high degree of security and we made slow but steady progress before halting for the night.

FOURTH MARCH (*Mar. 8*)

43. This progress was maintained during the next day, the only incident being the discovery of the fresh footprints of a small Japanese party on the only N.S. path crossed. The jungle now began to get dense and the chaung to wriggle about convulsively, both factors which lowered our net rate of advance.

FIFTH MARCH (*Mar. 9*)

44. Part of this day was lost owing to the main body losing touch with the Recce Gp. in thick cover, causing a certain amount of counter-marching to previous R.V.s. The valley was now opening up and all ranks were cheered by glimpses of the mountains on the W. bank of the Chindwin.

45. Early in the afternoon we crossed (obliterating our tracks), a much used N.S. path and left the chaung which henceforward ran through open country on the floor of the valley. Here the wooded spur which we were following petered out and at 1630 hrs. we lay up on the edge of the open ground. A recce revealed more signs of life than we cared for. To the N. was a house and some cultivation, to the E. sounds of a village and immediately ahead of us to the W. many wood-cutters were working on both sides of the

chaung. (The fact that there were no voices of women and children and that the work continued after dark suggested that this activity was under Japanese or B.T.A. (Burma Traitor Army) supervision.) One of the wood-cutters, walking past us inconveniently close, emphasized the fact that we were in a dangerously congested area with too much open ground about.

46. All observable signs of permanent habitation were on the N. bank of the Nathan Chaung and I therefore decided to stick to the S. bank and if possible by-pass the activity ahead of us in the course of a night march.

SIXTH MARCH (*Mar. 9/10*)

47. The party had a few hours' sleep, a detachment was sent out across the open without incident to fill water-bottles and chaguls, and we moved S. at midnight, veering S.W. after a mile or so. This brought us into some pony lines in the middle of the jungle, either ill- or unguarded. (Approx. 20 ponies: no Japanese chargers seen.) We sheered off and at the end of another short detour again bumped a similar number of ponies in a hollow.

48. A further detour brought us to a small, partly dried-up chaung, evidently a tributary of the Nathan Chaung. We struck it at a point where there was some cultivation and, on the opposite bank, a palisade with a gate behind which somebody was moving about. We waited until he quietened down and moved off S. up the side of a narrow open space. This we presently crossed, halting at a moonlit pool in the middle, partly to drink and partly to restore any confidence which the party might have lost as a result of our recent encounters and evasions. We then did 2-3 hours' march due W. through fairly easy jungle, halted and slept heavily till dawn.

F. SEVENTH MARCH (*Mar. 10*)

49. This was a short one which brought us to the edge of a large open space running S.W. and crossed by a well-marked footpath, short of which we prudently lay up about noon. At 1600 hrs. the only I.O.R. in the party (Pte. Dattu Bhosle of the Mahrattas), who was on guard, saw a patrol of 15 Japan-

ese marching very fast S.W. down the path, which ran just inside the jungle on the opposite side of the open ground. (This was an extremely creditable sighting under difficult conditions.) They crossed to our side and as their tracks later showed carried on S. down the path. The day being 'Army Day' the party was encouraged to believe that the patrol was going to get drunk with a post nearer the river. ('Lying-up' periods tend to impose more strain on the nerves than even the most alarming incidents on the march, and while lying up the more grounds for optimism or even complacency men have the better they will rest.)

G. EIGHTH MARCH (*Mar. 10/11*)

50. At 1900 hrs. I gave out that it was my intention to cross the Chindwin within 48 hours and we moved off, crossing first the track followed by the patrol and then the open space without incidents but not without disappointment for there was no water in the old chaung that ran down the middle. We then marched W. for about 2 hours through easy unfrequented jungle to reach the top of a steep escarpment below which, and not far away, flowed the Chindwin.

51. The escarpment at this point appeared to consist of a series of over-grown pits or shafts down which teak had formerly been dropped after felling. With Sgmn. Angus and making a noise like a small avalanche, I reached the bottom and found a grass glade separated from the river bank by a considerable belt of swamp and jungle. A little way to the W. we found a steep track leading up the escarpment. We climbed this, brought the main party down, and drew water at a point where we unfortunately had to leave unmistakable tracks in the mud beside a well-used path.

52. We were ill placed here, cramped between the escarpment and the path, and for the first time since the night of Mar. 5/6 our large and hobnailed feet had advertised our presence. We accordingly had a few hours' sleep in one of the quarry-like pits, then climbed the escarpment again before first light and moved S.W. along the lip of it, breakfasting in an old Jap O.P. directly overlooking the Chindwin.

53. We spent some time in observation, directly above what appeared to be a 5-rooster village of which nothing was visible except a patch of cultivation. The Recce Gp. then worked its way down the escarpment to a point – ideal for an ambush – overlooking the main Chindwin path at easy gun shot range. The main party was brought up, covering parties were put out, the footbridge and path were crossed without incident and the E. bank of the Chindwin was reached by 0900 hrs.

54. We found ourselves in an equilateral triangle of jungle, the sides – 100 yds. long – being formed by the path, the river bank and a small stream running into the river. The banks on both sides were 50 ft. high and steep, and on our side there was a short muddy foreshore. No boats were to be seen on either bank and there was no movement on the river. We were, though we did not know it at the time, somewhere near the village of Kyaingkyaing (SF 2248) approx. midway between Homalin and Thaungdut, where 15 (Japanese) Div. was to effect crossing in strength a few days later.

55. The absence of boats was a disappointment, for we had always assumed – in the light of 77 Bde.'s experiences last year – that it would be possible to beg, borrow or more probably steal some kind of craft, either beached or in passage. The river appeared to be 650 yds. wide, we had only 6 Mae Wests and we were under the delusion (which ceased to be a delusion 3 or 4 days later) that the W. bank was at any rate partly dominated by Japanese, B.T.A. and I.N.A. patrols, which meant that we should continue to be responsible for our own defence and administration and must therefore get our packs and arms across the river at all costs.

56. In the circumstances there seemed nothing for it but to build a raft, and to this task all ranks addressed themselves with enthusiasm under the ingenious direction of Major Faulkner, the Bde. M.O. Our scope as shipwrights was limited by the fact that we were working in or on the outskirts of a village and only a few yards from the main land L. of C. in the area, and cutting or hammering were therefore out of the question.

57. This in no way deterred Major Faulker. All packs (14

British, 1 U.S.) were emptied and repacked with empty water-bottles and K. rations (which we believed incorrectly to be watertight) at the bottom, the remainder of the contents being stowed on top of this supposedly buoyant foundation. The packs were then divided into 3 lots of 5, each of which was enclosed in a groundsheet (we had 4 of these: the 4th was to be used as deck covering). The 3 floats thus formed were to be lashed together within a framework made of half a dozen lengths of dead bamboo, the extremities of which would, it was hoped, be kept buoyant by inverted chaguls. Two paddles were improvised, and would each be wielded by a non-swimmer seated on the raft. The remainder of the party, sustained where necessary by Mae Wests, would hang on to the bamboo framework and propel the raft swimming. After the raft had been assembled, all ranks rehearsed their various tasks – lashing and stowing arms, supervising stores, etc. The raft was far too heavy and fragile to be carried down the bank and would have to be assembled in the water after dark.

58. These novel and pleasantly absorbing tasks were interrupted throughout the day by various alarms, which grew frequent towards evening but were all caused by Burmese passing along the path behind us or along the foreshore immediately below us. (It is a measure of the good luck which had attended our stealthy progress that, after 6 days and nights in Burma, none of us had yet set eyes on a native of the country, and when one was sighted it was necessary to form a queue at the relevant O.P. to avoid too conspicuous a display of curious faces.) No enemy were seen, and I am sure that if there had been any in the village we should have heard them. The appearance of Burmese women and children on the foreshore about a mile to the S. also suggested that there were no Japanese in the area.

59. At last light sentries were withdrawn, I gave out my orders and we moved down to the beachhead and took off our trousers and boots. All three floats were placed in the water; all three floated. Tremendous activity ensued amongst the shipwrights, accompanied by a good deal of splashing and the creaking of bamboos. In a surprisingly short time the raft was assembled, and the arms, clothing and equipment loaded on to it in that order.

60. At this point it was discovered:
  (a) that the raft had been aground for some time,
  (b) that all the groundsheets were full of water and the
       packs waterlogged.
I ordered the raft to be unloaded and dismantled.

61. Our situation at this stage appeared so unpromising as to be almost comic. Fifteen officers and men, in nothing but their shirts and by this time extremely cold, were engaged in dismantling, by the brilliant light of the moon, a contraption which had hitherto seemed their only hope of escape. For an hour and a half we had been making a good deal of noise in the immediate vicinity of a village, the whole foreshore was plastered with our tracks, our waterlogged packs were too heavy to be carried away, and we were dominated at less than 100 yds. by a steep bank carrying a track on which even an optimist had to admit the probability of patrols.

62. However, nobody lost heart, the B.O.R.s in particular showing great spirit and ingenuity in repacking the floats into units based on our 4 groundsheets, some of which, to everyone's surprise, floated. My main worry was the four non-swimmers and at Major Pringle's suggestion I sent these across forthwith in Mae Wests under his charge. They were accompanied or closely followed by Capt. Hepburn, Lieut. Mallory, F/O. Williams, and one or two others all carrying arms, Lieut. Mallory's Mahratta orderly put on his pack and equipment, slung his rifle and marched thus accoutred into the river, which was wadeable for 150 yds. He soon however discovered that swimming was something different from what he had supposed and returned to the E. bank, shivering and much discomfited. Some of the swimmers pushed units of 3 packs tied up in groundsheets.

63. Major Faulkner, Ptes. Kemp, Kennedy and 'Automatic' (my Chinese orderly) and I remained with the arms and equipment that the first flight could not take waiting for Major Pringle (who in happier days had swum for the Royal Military Academy) to bring back the Mae Wests and groundsheets necessary to transport them. After some time we heard screams which made it clear that someone was in difficulties on the far side and later learnt that Sgmn. Angus had been drowned. Although a non-swimmer he had been making excellent progress in a Mae West and was in fact

ahead of the others when they lost sight of him. We had tested all Mae Wests in the stream during the day and I can offer no explanation of the casualty. Angus was an excellent man and had shown himself throughout our experiences resourceful, intelligent and cool.

64. A little after this Lieut. Mallory recrossed with a Mae West for his orderly. Before leaving once more the W. bank he gave a very discouraging account of the crossing, which he said was far more difficult than anyone had supposed. He did not know whether Major Pringle was returning.

65. We had now been active on the foreshore for more than three hours and although reluctant to abandon anything I did not feel justified in risking the rear party (who were beginning to suffer from exposure and had a long swim before them) much longer in a situation from which, if the enemy did appear, there was virtually no hope of escape. I accordingly waited for 15 minutes more and then gave orders for the rear party to cross, leaving the packs on the beach in case Major Pringle returned with groundsheets, carrying all the arms and equipment they could, and throwing the remainder into the river.

66. I was influenced in making this decision:
- (a) by Lieut. Mallory's report, though I discounted most of it as alarmist,
- (b) by the belief that the packs and arms already floated across would be adequate to equip and ration the party for the remainder of the march (about half of these had sunk).

67. The rear party, who all claimed and indeed turned out to be strong swimmers, insisted on my using the only available Mae West and we got across, fairly heavily encumbered with arms, without incident. Pte. Kennedy, however, was missing on arrival at the far bank (he belonged to the 'I'll manage, sir' school of military swimmers and looked as though he would go straight to the bottom on immersion). I swam most of the way back without locating him. He turned up shortly afterwards explaining that the 2 Sten guns round his neck had choked him and he had returned to the shallows to 'cast up'. 'Neptune almost 'ad me,' he confessed, giggling. The crossing was completed by 2300 hrs.

68. We lit large bonfires and sat over them most of the night, too cold to sleep and trying to dry our clothes. Major Pringle, who had crossed the rear party on his return to the E. bank, turned up with another invaluable 'float' containing packs. Even so, we were seriously short of certain stores, particularly boots, and Major Pringle volunteered to cross again before first light and salvage outstanding essentials. I accepted this gallant offer and Major Pringle, accompanied by Lieut. Mallory, returned to the W. bank at 0700 hrs. with practically all the arms which we had thrown into the shallows as well as other valuable items. Both officers had thus swum the Chindwin five times in the course of a night. Apart from one or two revolvers which were left in the shallows I believe that no arms or equipment of any value fell into the enemy's hands, though of course we lost a good deal from sinkings in midstream.

69. In the morning after sorting ourselves out and drying everything in the sun, we found that by pooling our resources all ranks could be provided with clothing and a weapon (in some cases only a grenade) and that by reducing our ration scale from $\frac{1}{2}$ to $\frac{1}{3}$ we had food for 3 more days. No movement was seen in our beachhead area on the E. bank before we moved off at 1030 hrs. A search for Angus's body was made but was unsuccessful.

70. During the last 48 hours we had heard desultory gunfire to the S. We knew that the going on the W. bank was much harder than on the E. and that we should probably have to use tracks. We accordingly marched N. along the river bank (which we believed to be partly under enemy control), intending to strike west at the first opportunity and get well inland before closing on the sound of gunfire.

70. After less than a mile, at a place called Awya, we walked unobserved into an O.P. manned by a patrol of the 9/12 F.F. (Frontier Force) Regt. who treated us with some reserve (one sepoy up a tree removing the pin from a grenade), but informed us that there were British posts all along the west bank to the south.

72. We accordingly turned about and marched S. and after 2 hours fell in with a patrol of the 1st Bn. Seaforth High-

landers under Sgt. Merritt. They provided us with guides
who led us (at a breakneck pace which they possibly
imagined to be our normal gait) to their Bn. H.Q. some miles
away behind Tabaw. Here we were most hospitably enter-
tained by Lieut.-Col. Jamieson and his officers, who in spite
of our protests (we were still self-sufficient as regards rations)
regaled all ranks with large quantities of food and drink.

73. On the following day (Mar. 13) we marched 12 miles
over the pass to the roadhead in the Kabaw valley (Thanan)
and proceeded to Tamu by M/T under 1 Ind. Inf. Bde. arrangements. I got a light aircraft and reported to Adv. 3 Ind.
Div. at Imphal that night, the remainder of the party following by Dakota the next day. Responsibility for them was
thereafter assumed by Rear H.Q. 77 Bde.

J. CONCLUSIONS

74. The main factor contributing to the successful extrication of a party consisting almost entirely of staff officers
and their batmen was of course luck. Our luck, both positive
and negative, was consistently good. Perhaps the most outstanding example of it was fluking the headwaters of the
Nathan Chaung but for which we should almost certainly
have been delayed by the need to search for water. In view
of the extremely narrow margin by which we beat 15
(Japanese) Div. to the W. bank of the Chindwin any delay
would have been a serious matter.

75. The incidents of this 6-day march, though devoid of
operational significance, have been described at some length,
partly owing to the natural prolixity of the writer, but
mainly in the hope that they may prove of interest and possibly of value to those concerned in future airborne ops. over
enemy-occupied territory, in the course of which small
mixed parties are liable to find themselves in similar pre-
dicaments to our own.

76. Apart from luck and a certain amount of tactical
common sense, my personal opinion is that morale played an
important part in getting the party out. Both Major Pringle
and Major Faulkner agreed that all ranks came out full of
self-confidence and genuinely anxious to rejoin their Bde. in
the field and there is no doubt that practically everybody

keenly enjoyed a great many of their experiences after the somewhat alarming first night.

77. I attribute the high level of morale, which was reflected in the good standard of efficiency and endurance, to the doctrine laid down by Brigadier Calvert (Comd. 77 Ind. Inf. Bde.) and inculcated by him in training. This doctrine consists in effect in maintaining a sense of proportion with regard to the Japanese, the jungle and other real or supposed hazards which beset a small isolated detachment in enemy occupied territory. The feeling of being hunted is an unpleasant one and personnel who become oppressed by it are liable to act, should a crisis or irksome delay arise, in a foolish and unsoldierly manner. Though I never felt justified in attempting any offensive action, I think we managed to avoid this hunted feeling or at any rate overlay it with a firm (and at least partially valid) belief in:
   (a) our ability to look after ourselves,
   (b) the enemy's difficulties, preoccupations and capacity to making mistakes.

78. The leader of a party of this kind has perpetually to choose between security and
   (a) speed (while on the move),
   (b) convenience (while lying up).

Rightly or wrongly, I almost always decided in favour of (a) or (b). An opposite policy would have entailed endless and unexplained halts while on the march, frequent stand-to's while in bivouac and – most damaging of all to morale and endurance – less brewing of tea. Deliberately taking minor risks undoubtedly saves much delay and lessens the nervous strain on the party, who are seldom aware that a risk is being taken.

79. Another practice which seemed worthwhile, judging by results, was to explain very fully to all ranks what the plan was before making a move, what obstacles or dangers might be encountered and in general how our chances stood. This tended to lessen the exasperations, uncertainties and minor hardships which a detachment moving cautiously through jungle, particularly at night, is bound to encounter.

80. Certain admin. rules which we evolved (but did not always keep) when lying up are perhaps worth recording:
   (a) Split the day up as far as possible by fixing times for

eating, cleaning arms, etc. This prevents worried men from curling up under a bush and brooding on the worst possible case.

(b) Trample a path leading to the sentry's O.P. This allows you to move up to his position quietly on a signal. If this is not done the leaves crackle horribly.

(c) Make everyone write down the address of everybody else's next-of-kin. I ordered this to be done on the third day, explaining that while some of us might by bad luck become casualties, it was most unlikely that we all would, and survivors could write home and tell the bereaved that we had at least given the Japanese a run for their money, etc. This order was popular and had a marked effect on morale.

81. The work and devotion to duty of all ranks was of a very high order, but I consider that the following were outstanding:

(a) *Major G. Faulkner,* who displayed throughout coolness, good judgment and resource.

(b) *Major C. Pringle,* who displayed marked courage and endurance in swimming the Chindwin five times, on three occasions transporting arms and equipment.

(c) *F/O. Bruce Williams, U.S.A.A.F.,* to whose skill in landing his glider the party owed their lives and who thereafter showed both equanimity and enterprise in a high degree.

(d) *Capt. G. Massey* and *Pte. McMurdoch,* who did valuable work with the Recce Gp. often at the end of a long and tiring march.

(*Signed*) R. P. FLEMING
Lieut.-Colonel,
Grenadier Guards

APPENDIX II

MOST SECRET

SPECIAL FORCE COMMANDER'S TRAINING NOTE NO. 8

THE STRONGHOLD

Turn ye to the Stronghold, ye prisoners of hope

OBJECT OF THE STRONGHOLD

The Stronghold is a machan overlooking a kid tied up to entice the Japanese tiger.

The Stronghold is an asylum for L.R.P.G. wounded.

The Stronghold is a magazine of stores.

The Stronghold is a defended airstrip.

The Stronghold is an administrative centre for loyal inhabitants.

The Stronghold is an orbit round which columns of the brigade circulate. It is suitably placed with reference to the main objective of the brigade.

The Stronghold is a base for light planes operating with columns on the main objective.

The Stronghold is designed to fulfil a definite function in the employment of L.R.P.G.s; a function which has hitherto been neglected. In all our recent contacts with the Japanese it has been apparent that any dug-in defended position sited in remote areas where it is almost impossible to assemble a concentration of artillery and extremely difficult to make accurate reconnaissance without heavy losses is capable of a most obstinate and prolonged defence against greatly superior force. In fact, no single large and well-constructed position has as yet been taken by assault. Yet none of the Japanese positions we know of possess the advantages it is proposed to give the Stronghold. They are all accessible to wheeled transport although in some cases artillery can only be brought up to attack them with great difficulty.

From this I draw the inference, firstly, that it is foolish to direct attacks against defended enemy positions if by any means he can be met in the open, and, secondly, that we should induce him to attack us in our defended positions. It is obvious that columns of L.R.P. have un unrivalled chance of meeting him in the open and that, therefore, they should even more rarely need to attack him in his positions. In fact, it may truly be said that they should do so only when the position concerned has already been isolated by the action of columns for a considerable time, or there is other reason to suppose that the position will put up a weak resistance.

We wish, therefore, firstly to encounter the enemy in the open and preferably in ambushes laid by us, and secondly to induce him to attack us only in our defended Strongholds.

Further, to make sure of our advantage, and in view of the fact that the enemy will be in superior force in our neighbourhood we shall choose for our Strongholds, areas inaccessible to wheeled transport.

For convenience sake such Strongholds should clearly be used to cover (but not to include) an airstrip. The ideal situation for a Stronghold is the centre of a circle of thirty miles radius consisting of closely wooded and very broken country, only passable to pack transport owing to great natural obstacles, and capable only of slow improvement. This centre should ideally consist of a level upland with a cleared strip for Dakotas, a separate supply-dropping area, taxi-ways to the Stronghold, a neighbouring friendly village or two, and an inexhaustible and uncontaminatable water supply within the Stronghold. Such an area can then be organized in the manner indicated in the accompanying sketches.

The motto of the Stronghold is 'No Surrender'.

The questions of how the garrison should be equipped, how organized, what additional measures are required, such as making dummy strongholds, dummy guns, organizing artillery, O.P.s, laying minefields, constructing keeps and stores either in the Stronghold or in hiding places outside, and many others are all matters for study. They will not be fully dealt with here, both for lack of space and lack of study.

In emergency the Stronghold may become the storehouse of the L.R.P.G. and for this reason every opportunity will be taken of stocking it with rations and material of war of every description. Owing to its fixed nature S.D. (supply-dropping) planes will be thoroughly acquainted with its exact location and will be capable of a heavy drop each bright moonlight night. If all the S.D. planes available are turned on each moonlight night three such visits a month should not only stock for the equivalent of five columns using the Stronghold as base, but a reserve should be built up for the remaining six columns and H.Q.

In order to make the stocks as ample as possible, the two floater columns will farm the neighbourhood and employ purchasers of rice and cattle up to a considerable distance from the demesne, in order to subsist as far as possible on local resources. The catching of fish and slaughter of buffalo will not be neglected.

The Stronghold will be regularly used by up to ten planes of the light plane force. Splinter-proof pens must be built for these in the protected bay under the lee of the Stronghold. Normally, columns in the field will receive their S.D. direct but in emergency these planes, which will seldom be more than forty miles from the columns in the field, will feed the columns with rations and ammunition. Using the strip with discretion the planes can flit to and fro, doing several round turns apiece on moonlight nights, or perhaps a couple at dawn and dusk on moonless nights. The distances involved are so small that the danger period is reduced to a minimum. On each trip the plane takes 700 lb. of supplies and can evacuate a wounded man or a prisoner. In this way wounded and prisoners and captured war material will accumulate in the Stronghold, whence they will periodically be evacuated either by light plane from Kabaw valley or by Dakota, by night.

NATURE OF THE STRONGHOLD

The Stronghold proper is a fortification or earth-work large enough to be occupied by a battalion or two columns, plus two troops of artillery, a stores depot, and an asylum for

284

personnel to the number of two hundred at a time. At the same time, it must be small enough to give the necessary compactness in defence. It aims to hold out against all attacks whatsoever and, to accomplish this, relies upon earthworks and minefields for immediate defence from the enemy's weapons, with a well-co-ordinated and thoroughly tested fire-plan for the employment of its own weapons.

To assist in its local defence one company will invariably be employed outside the Stronghold as a floater. The function of this company is to perambulate the country within a few thousand yards of the Stronghold with the object of getting news of any enemy intrusion and attacking him before he reaches the Stronghold. It will also prevent the enemy digging-in, cut off his supplies and generally harass him. To enable it to exist while the Stronghold is closely invested a certain storage of supplies in hiding places well clear of the Stronghold (at least one mile away), is advisable.

This floater company, detailed by the day, will also find the local garrison for the L.M.G. pits giving immediate local protection to the airstrip.

Owing to the need for compactness it is wrong to attempt to include an airstrip within the Stronghold. The latter must be sited close enough to the strip to afford direct protection to aircraft using it. That means the strip must be within artillery range of the Stronghold and that a taxi route leads to a harbour immediately under the Stronghold. Normally the strip is protected by three or four L.M.G. posts whose crews are found from the floater company on duty. It is, of course, further protected both by the Stronghold and by the perambulating floater company. Protection may also be improved by the organization of local inhabitants into an intelligence corps to give early warning of enemy approach from any direction.

These measures ensure that the strip can always be used with confidence of freedom from enemy interference except when a large enemy force has succeeded in reaching the Stronghold and is engaged in attacking it. Owing to the nature of the Stronghold defence it will presently be seen that such force will have no power to remain for longer than a week or so at a time in the region and demesne of the Stronghold.

The use of the artillery in the garrison, which will consist of one troop of 25-pounder guns and one troop of ½-inch Vickers m.g.s, or possibly of a Bofors troop, is indicated in the attached sketches and in the notes thereon. The fact that this artillery must normally be loaded on Dakotas makes it desirable that the Stronghold shall be sited near a Dakota strip. Provided, however, gliders can be put down, this is not essential. It is essential, however, that it be sited to cover a light plane strip.

The location of the Stronghold is a matter of such importance that it has been dealt with in a separate paragraph.

Additional points dealt with in the notes to the sketches are, booby traps and minefields, supply-drop area apart from the strip which might be otherwise employed, water storage, sanitation, storage of warlike stores, weapons and equipment, patrols, lifebuoy fuel, and rations.

HOW THE STRONGHOLD WORKS

When the Stronghold is first introduced and long before its construction is complete a visit by enemy patrols to its neighbourhood may be expected. These patrols are unlikely to be much more than a platoon or company in strength but it will be essential to drive them off without permitting near approach or any attempt to dig-in near the Stronghold. This will call for vigorous activity, firstly on the part of the floater columns who should get the first information of the enemy's approach, and secondly on the part of the Stronghold floater company which must, therefore, be detailed and capable of functioning correctly from the very first.

It will be undesirable to unmask the artillery in the Stronghold on this first visit of the enemy but this may be done of course in case of need.

The enemy's recce planes will meantime have found the strip and will pay it constant attention. For this reason the construction of a dummy strip is necessary. The ideal would be for the strip used for putting down the force to become the dummy and another secretly constructed a few miles away for serious use, with the Stronghold standing guard over it. It will not, however, always be possible to fulfil this ideal.

The enemy, on learning that something is going on in the

area and that his light patrols are driven off while his air action against the dummy strip does not appear to have put an end to the activity, will fit out an expedition to reduce the Stronghold. Whatever weapons this force may be provided with, they will not be able to reach the Stronghold unless on a pack basis. It will be the business of the nearest floater column to obtain early news of the approach of this force and then to attack it continuously, affording it no time to rest. Coolies for road construction can be driven off in the first encounter. Bivouacs will be attacked by night. Suitable points in the tracks will be skilfully ambushed by day.

Unless the floater column has failed to do its work this first enemy column, which is unlikely to be more than a battalion in strength, will be driven back without ever getting near the Stronghold, much less attacking it. Should the column reach the immediate area of the Stronghold the latter's floater company joined to the dummy strongholds and the artillery plan should completely discomfort it, and the subsequent action of the floater columns, which will have closed in from the rear, will complete the effect.

Thus failed, the enemy will have to consider whether to launch a really powerful attack with a greatly reinforced column or to accept the presence of the Stronghold in his midst and endeavour to render it as innocuous as possible by air attack. His decision will depend upon the general situation.

Let us assume that he decides on a full attack. He will allot a regiment with artillery and light tanks, a coolie contingent to build the road, or roads, and air support.

The brigade commander who will have anticipated the possibility will have made arrangements for reinforcing the floater columns to a greater or less extent in accordance with the general situation. If the task he is doing is of vital importance and must not be interrupted he may tell the two floaters and the Stronghold to manage by themselves until he is free to come to their aid. This they should be perfectly capable of doing. But it will normally be possible for him to reinforce them with an addition of another two or more columns. In this way the enemy is met under ideal conditions; making an approach whose route can be foreseen through country with which we are more familiar than he, and compelled to move slowly to cover his road construction.

Under these conditions two columns should find little difficulty in cutting up a regiment.

Some of the enemy force may, however, reach the Stronghold area. He is now under the necessity, with which we have become so familiar, of pushing in costly probing attacks to find out the exact location and extent of the Stronghold and the nature of its defences. It will be well to conceal these as far as possible in the opening stages. Meanwhile the columns will close in from without, completely cutting off whatever force has succeeded in reaching the Stronghold, and preventing it from digging-in in the neighbourhood of the Stronghold. Thus this force should share the fate of the others and dissolve, yielding both prisoners and booty.

The enemy will now consider whether to renew the assault, and if so, how. It will be clear to him that only a sustained assault with powerful air forces, combined with great superiority on the ground, will be likely to succeed. He must therefore project a division or equivalent force into the attack under the same unfavourable conditions. This time the brigade commander must devote all his resources to repel the assault. In doing so he should have an excellent chance of success, especially if he has taken the precaution and found opportunity to store supplies in hiding places in the demesne. (The demesne may be defined as the area under the aegis of the Stronghold.) The enemy will seldom be able to stage such a large-scale operation in the middle of the embarrassments inflicted on him by the operations of columns. If he is able to do so he affords an ideal opportunity for the full use of an L.R.P. brigade.

APPENDIX III

SOME STATISTICS

The number of troops and animals of 77 Brigade flown into Burma during campaign:
March 5th to August 1st, 1944 (exclusive 3/9 Gurkhas)

UNIT	INITIAL FLY-IN				REINFORCEMENTS	
	Officers	Other ranks	Ponies	Mules	Officers	Other ranks
Bde. H.Q.	23	354*	6	34	4	35
1 King's..	44	804	24	117	4	96
1 Lancashire Fusiliers ..	40	751	19	112	2	40
1 South Staffords ..	42	791	18	124	13	63
3/6 Gurkhas	26†	861	24	120	8	106
267/69 L.A.A. Regiment	2	63	—	—	—	—
'R' Tp. 160 ⎱ Field Regiment ⎰ ..	3	45	—	—	—	—
Total	180	3669	91	507	31	340

* Includes Brigade Defence Company, Chinese, R.E., Royal Corps of Signals, Burma Rifles and Royal Air Force.
† British officers only.

The total numbers who served with 77 Brigade, exclusive of 3/9 Gurkha Rifles, was 211 officers and 4,009 other ranks.

This does not include 3/4 and 4/9 Gurkhas who were initially under my command, and who later became Morris Force under Brigadier Morris on the other side of the Irrawaddy. I omit the 3/9 Gurkhas only because I have not their statistics. They were an intrinsic part of the brigade until they joined Jack Masters' 111 Brigade at Blackpool.

The Gunners later served at Myitkyina where they saw further action. All their officers except Major Cox, I think, were killed. Major Cox, who was a very fine officer, received the M.C.

At different periods I had 12 different battalions under command.

SUMMARY OF CASUALTIES

This is divided into two periods, 'A' and 'B'. 'A' is March 5th to May 17th before Mogaung. 'B' is May 18th to August 1st. Viceroy and Governor commissioned officers (Gurkha and Burma Rifles) are included in the column 'Officers'. Six of them were killed and 11 wounded. None went sick.

UNIT		KILLED OR DIED OF WOUNDS		DIED OF SICK-NESS		WOUNDED EVACUATED		WOUNDED NOT EVACUATED		MISSING		SICK EVACUATED	
		Officers	*O.R.s*	*Officers*	*O.R.s*	*Officers*	*O.R.s*	*Officers*	*O.R.s*	*Officers*	*O.R.s*	*Officers*	*O.R.s*
1 King's	A	2	25	—	3	3	32	1	4	3	58	3	55
	B	1	17	—	1	3	88	2	11	—	70	Figures not available	
1 Lancashire Fusiliers	A	1	23	—	—	3	34	—	—	1	8	3	119
	B	3	54	—	8	5	83	—	18	—	6	1	77
1 South Staffords	A	6	52	—	—	6	77	5	19	—	—	1	140
	B	7	88	—	—	8	116	2	19	—	2	2	35
3/6 Gurkha Rifles	A	10	33	—	—	5	113	5	23	—	—	3	10
	B	6	68	—	—	6	28	3	45	—	—	2	4
Bde. H.Q. including everyone else except R.A.	A	9	29	—	1	6	41	1	4	1	2	5	26
	B	2	14	1	4	5	35	3	9	1	5	3	23
Grand Total	..	47	403	1	17	50	747	22	152	6	151	23	489

Total casualties including sick evacuated totalled over 50 per cent of the entire brigade. About another 25 per cent went to hospital after return to India to get rid of malaria, jungle sores, dysentery and other insidious diseases.

* Total killed in action or died immediately afterwards, after recount, numbered 884.

APPENDIX IV

THE JAPANESE TESTAMENT

After the war it was possible to obtain some of the views of high Japanese commanders on various aspects of the campaign. As yet, however, there has been no 'Other Side of the Hill' book published giving the Japanese viewpoints on some of the more controversial aspects of the Japanese War. This has probably been due more to the fact that interested parties do not wish to expose the falseness of some of their claims, both of the quantity of the Japanese who defeated the Allies at the beginning of the war, and the hollowness of certain so-called allied victories later. Two of the most controversial aspects of the campaign in Burma were the two Wingate operations and the results that they achieved. Could the thirteen British (I exclude 23 Brigade which was used in an outflanking role on the Kohima front), four Gurkha and three West Africa battalions and their attendant ancillary forces, bases, and R.A.F. and U.S.A.A.F. effort have been of greater use to the Burma campaign if employed elsewhere in a more stereotyped role?

This subject had been discussed beforehand at the Quebec Conference, during which Mr. Churchill and Admiral Mountbatten supported this different approach from that of ploughing straight through Burma, but were opposed by many very senior officers, both British and American.

It would need someone more objective and unbiased than myself to assess all the evidence and make a considered judgment. Here I can only state some of the views given by senior Japanese generals in interrogations made immediately after the campaign. Mogaung is not mentioned much as I do not think the interrogator knew much about what happened there. I came across these interrogation reports after I had finished the narrative of this book which itself is based on a 60,000 word narrative report I wrote immediately after the operation and which, in its turn, was based on all the signals, both operational and administrative, that I had received and sent during the campaign. Dates should therefore be correct.

There must necessarily be a certain amount of repetition as I give the views of the various officers concerned at different levels, from the exalted Chief of Staff, Southern Army, the army which was responsible for most of the South-east Asia area, down to the commanders of brigades and junior staff officers who take a more subjective viewpoint. It must be remembered that their views cover the operations of all the brigades, whereas my narrative deals almost exclusively with the activities of 77 Brigade. Where the operations can be identified I name them and also give our names of the places concerned such as White City and Blackpool in order to see how the narrative fits.

I begin with the Japanese views on the 1943 expedition because of the effect that it had later on Japanese thought and tactics.

Lieut.-General Mutaguchi held the appointment of G.O.C. 18 Division in north Burma in the spring of 1943 and later became G.O.C. 15th Army at the time of the Wingate airborne landings. This is what he says of the first operation:

> Following the capture of Mandalay on May 1st, 1942, 18 Division was employed in mopping-up operations against remnants of the Chinese Forces in the southern Shan States in East Burma.
> In the winter of 1942 15 Division relieved 55 Division and took over the defence of North Burma. Division H.Q. was at Maymyo and I had units under command stationed at Maymyo, Mandalay, Sagaing, Indaw, Mogaung and Myitkyina. As there had been many cases of misunderstanding between the local people and the Japanese forces, I planned to dispatch units under my command to the Sumprabum area to the north, to the Bhamo area to the east, and to the Chindwin area to the west for propaganda and pacification purposes. I was engaged in the execution of this plan for about one month after the end of February 1943.
> The Wingate expedition's land counter attack of spring 1943 happened to coincide with the time of the above

scheme. I had never anticipated such a risky plan of counter offensive on the part of the British Forces and I was therefore handicapped by the lack of the reserves with which to meet this threat. I had sent two companies which were in the Chindwin area at the time across the Zibyu Taungdan range. Both companies encountered units of the Wingate Force unexpectedly on the way. Units forming the main strength of the Wingate Force were encountered unexpectedly by the Nasu Battalion of 33 Division and Major Nasu, O.C. Battalion, was killed in the ensuing action.

The place which the enemy had chosen as his crossing point of the Chindwin, opposite Sittaung, was the borderline of the defence sectors of 18 and 33 Divisions and was not carefully watched. For this reason the Wingate Force crossed the Chindwin unopposed. Native reports overestimated the strength of this Force and it was therefore difficult to forecast its plans.

The question whether or not the British would send more counter-attacking forces of this type on a large scale caused me grave concern at that time. Fortunately, such was not the case, and I was able to reduce my disposition to the east.

Since the area that we had to defend was very large in proportion to our strength and consisted mainly of jungle where the enemy could infiltrate freely during the dry season, we abandoned any idea of holding fixed defensive positions and devised measures to meet attacks in any part of the defence area.

General Numata was Chief of Staff Southern Army which comprised most of South-East Asia. His views are therefore more from the strategic standpoint of the overall campaign.

He states that the Japanese reaction to the first Wingate expedition was the offensive-spirited one of carrying out similar operations against Imphal since

(a) it was found as a result of the Wingate campaign and the Japanese operations in opposition thereto, that the terrain in North Burma was favourable for guerrilla warfare by small bodies of crack troops, but it was very difficult to defend the territory because the enemy could not easily be engaged. And,

(b) under the circumstances, it would therefore be best to give up defensive tactics and resort to an offensive to destroy the enemy's bases for counter operations, such as Imphal, Kohima, Tinsukia, etc.

[I had laughed at the gloomy foreboding of some of the officers of the Indian Division through which we had marched on our way to the Chindwin 'that all you will do is to stir them up against us', never realizing that it would turn out true.]

General Numata said that the Japanese Army did not consider it likely that the enemy would henceforth resort regularly to such expeditions. While a section of the staff held the view that such another expedition would be probable, the majority adhered to the view cited above. Consequently the second Wingate expedition in March 1944 took the Japanese by surprise.

There was no special preparation to meet the expedition. He added that because of this lack of preparation, the second Wingate operation threw the units in the rear into confusion, and that the higher command, without sufficient information, could only gather local units together more or less indiscriminately. Such time-saving measures resulted in the Japanese forces being repulsed everywhere. It was not until the beginning of April that the Japanese command realized that the enemy was engaged in a serious and large scale penetrating operation with a powerful corps.

General Numata, on being questioned about the effect of the airborne landings, stated that

> The reaction of the Japanese Army to this operation was so great that the Japanese 15th Army (the Army which included the three divisions detailed for the Imphal offensive) even thought of sparing from the force attacking Imphal a substantial force to annihilate the enemy unit and thus secure the safety of its rear. This plan was not carried out. Instead railway units and line of communication guards were collected and deployed against the British troops; while on the other hand 24 Independent Mixed Brigade, which was guarding the Moulmein area south-east of Rangoon against a possible sea landing, was ordered to proceed north at all speed.

All those units were ordered to advance against the Allied airborne troops around Mawlu.

15th Army decided that the airborne forces' intention was

(a) To interrupt Japanese supply lines by cutting the Mandalay and Myitkyina railroad;

(b) To disturb the rear of the Japanese forces attacking Imphal;

(c) To counteract Japanese propaganda among the Burmese.

We became aware of the main landings on March 9th [four days after 77 Brigade had taken off] but information available then was insufficient, and we did not think that it was on a large scale. We became aware of its serious proportions only after the Japanese attacks were repulsed.

General Naka, who was at the time Chief of Staff Burma Area Army and was later to become G.O.C. 18 Division, also gave his rather more detailed views. In this connection it would be wise to define these terms as an 'Army' in the Japanese military set-up does not mean quite the same as 'Army' in British and American military parlance. In the Japanese military forces the chain of command is section, platoon, company, battalion (usually named after the battalion commander), regiment (approximating to our brigade), division. There are engineer and artillery battalions and regiments within the division. Above a division they go straight to a 'numbered' army which can either approximate to our Corps with two or three divisions or to our Army with eight or ten divisions without a Corps headquarters in between. If only a few divisions of the Army are taking part in an operation, a special headquarters for that operation is formed and the force is named after the commander, e.g. Také Force.

Above 'Army' they have an 'Area Army' which is named after the area of operations and approximates to our 'Army Group'. The area army takes as much administrative burden as possible off the 'Armies' to let them get on with the business of fighting. Beyond that again there is a 'Regional Army' similar to our 'Commands', e.g. SEAC, SHAEF, MELF. The whole organization is much more flexible than ours and there is thus a very great saving in staff compared with the British and American forces.

General Naka said:

Our reactions to the airborne landings were as follows.

First Stage (beginning of March to mid April)

We immediately sent one infantry battalion of 56 Division [facing the Chinese], two infantry battalions of 24 Independent Mixed Brigade (then in Tenasserim, South Burma) and one battalion from 15 Division Field Artillery to attack the British troops.

Second stage (from April to August)

The main force of 53 Division was increased and its commander put in charge of operations; and, when 33 Army was formed, its commander was put in overall command of operations againt airborne forces.
We judged the airborne force's intentions to be

(i) To secure important points on the Myitkyina railway, and to cut off the rear of the Japanese 18 Division;
(ii) To draw the Japanese forces in strength into the Indaw area to facilitate the attack by the main body of British troops which was expected from Central Assam. [This was what General Wingate had always hoped for.]
(iii) To establish link-up points for the British advance into Burma.

We knew of the landings only by March 9th.

General Hayashi, who was G.O.C. of the 53 Division which came up from Kuala Lumpur in Malaya and was reserve Division on the Imphal front, has a few words to say about his initial defeat.

We were unsuccessful in our attack against the British airborne forces through lack of reliable intelligence. We attacked Mawlu [White City] from April 11th, but owing to our troops being cut off in the northern part of the Naba area [this was the effect of my counter attack from White City to behind the Japanese forces] we were

296

unable to send the fighting troops supplies. We therefore had to suspend battle. We were weak, also, in that we used mixed units and not a single force. We judged the enemy strength in the Mawlu area to be about 1,000 and thought that they would be able to resist for a considerable time. There were also expected to be reserve mobile units around Mawlu about 2,000 or 3,000 strong, to help secure the position at Mawlu and cut off our troops from the rear. [This shows very clearly the effect of General Wingate's teaching of having a 'floater' unit outside the 'stronghold'. But it must be as strong or stronger than those holding the stronghold, as we had found.]

Now comes the question on which the whole Chindit case hinges. This was the question asked of General Numata, Chief of Staff Southern Army, of General Naka, and of Lieutenant General Mutaguchi.

To what extent, if any, did the airborne forces upset the Japanese plan for operations on

(i)   The Central Assam front (14th British Army)
(ii) The Northern Combat Area Command front (General Stilwell)?

General Numata answered:

The advance of the airborne forces did not cause any change in Japanese operational plans on either the Central Assam front or the Northern Combat Area front. Operations continued according to plan but these airborne forces proved to be a devastating factor in cutting lines of communication. The difficulty encountered in dealing with these airborne forces was ever a source of worry to all the headquarters staffs of the Japanese army, *and contributed materially to the Japanese failure in the Imphal and Hukawng operations.*

General Naka's answer was:

This airborne operation had no direct effect on the Central Assam Front, but it shortened our supply of reserves, and made the supply road Wuntho-Pyinbon-Pinlebu-Homalin useless. It completely cut off 18 Division's (opposing General Stilwell) supply route, thereby making impossible that division's holding operation against the enemy in North Burma.

A further interrogation of General Naka, who also had with him his General Staff Officer Operations, Major Kaetsu, confirms this.

The big effect of the airborne operations was on the administrative situation of the main offensive into Assam. There were three main supply routes for the Imphal, operation reading from south to north

Mandalay-Shwebo-Kalewa
Mandalay-Pinlebu-Sittang (on the Chindwin)
Indaw-Homalin (on the Chindwin)

The first was the most important. The second, because of bad roads, was not used. The third became of no use as it was 'wiped out by bombing and ground raids'. (Evidently large supplies were wiped out by the bombing.)

[16th, 111th and 14th British and Indian Chindit Brigades must take credit for this. The supply dump hidden in the jungle was found by one of Bernard Fergusson's R.A.F. officers who had lost his way and spent the night in this enormous dump in the jungle. Later he found 16 Brigade again at 'Aberdeen' and reported his find to Bernard Fergusson who then asked for all the air support available. While the R.A.F. officer in a light aircraft marked out the extent of the dump with smoke flares, U.S.A.A.F. Mitchells and Mustangs came again and again to wipe it out.] Consequently, supplies intended for the Indaw route had to be brought up the Chindwin to Sittang – a very difficult task. The Shwebo route was already congested.

31 Division Infantry Group used the northern route on its initial advance on Kohima. It carried twenty-one days' supplies initially. This Group came through Ukruhl and cut the Kohima road to the south.

The result of the northern line going out and the consequent lack of food and ammunition for all 31 Division had a vital effect on the Kohima operation. [Comment by the interrogator – a Major-General in the British Army: The expressions used were 'the situation was very, very bad' and 'it was the absolute vital point'.]

Now for the testimony of Lieut.-General Mutaguchi when asked this vital question. He was G.O.C. 15th Army which was responsible for both the Hukawng and the Imphal fronts until mid March 1944 when 33 Army was formed.

> The airborne landings were made during the night previous to the day on which we were to begin the Imphal operation.
> [It turned out well that we did go in the night we did in spite of the blocking of Piccadilly as otherwise we should have been drawn into the Imphal operation and General Wingate's plan and theory of war would never have been proved. The blocking of Piccadilly was not intentional but was done by Burmese foresters who pulled the teak logs out into the open space to dry out their sap, thus making them light enough to float down the Irrawaddy.]
> As already stated, some staff officers in Burma Area Army were of the opinion that the Imphal operation should be temporarily suspended, but my resolution remained unchanged and I carried out the operation as planned.
> At the time I judged the situation as follows:
> (a) The recapture of Burma by one airborne division was absolutely impossible. I had been informed that the unit was *not* more than one division.
> (b) It was believed that an overland operation would be put in operation from Ledo in North Assam to coincide with the airborne assault, but I did *not* think that General Stilwell could reach the Irrawaddy for at least two months.
> I was therefore *not* immediately concerned with this airborne threat and I devoted myself to my previous intentions. It was a matter of great regret and concern to me that Burma Area Army switched one entire division (53 Division) to cope with the enemy airborne force, especially *at a time when the provision of one regiment of 53 Division for the Imphal front might well have ensured the success of that operation.*
> In mid-March, 1944, 2nd Battalion 146th Regiment,

and in mid-April Regimental H.Q. and 3rd Battalion 146th Infantry Regiment, together with a mountain gun battalion and engineer, signals and medical personnel were sent to Mogaung on order of Burma Area Army and came under command of 18 Division. These units returned to 56 Division about June 1944, having suffered almost *one third casualties*.

There the Chindit case rests. But it should be remembered that it was *not* the original task as laid down at Quebec for General Wingate's force to assist the British Indian forces forward from Assam. The role given was to help General Stilwell with his Chinese American forces to take Mogaung and Myitkyina and an area south in order to allow communication through to China by road and thus keep China in the war.

The remainder of this 'other side of the hill' viewpoint consists of extracts from the more detailed histories of the Japanese 15th Army, the Japanese 33rd Army, 53rd Division, 24 Independent Mixed Brigade, as they apply to the operation against the Chindits. There are also interesting extracts from an essay by Lieut.-Col. Fijiwara Iwaichi who was an extremely capable and intelligent staff officer. He was Staff Officer (Intelligence) for the first part of the campaign and Staff Officer (Operations) for the second half.

These histories in some instances do not quite tally, as is to be expected of histories from different levels of command, but they are compiled by the Japanese commander, or his staff officers and the more closely concerned they are with the fighting the more they seek to minimize their own faults.

HISTORY OF JAPANESE 15TH ARMY

Operations against paratroops

At the beginning of March 1944, there were reports that enemy paratroops had landed in the Katha area. Immediately 3rd Battalion 114th Inf. Regt., 3rd Battalion 15th Arty. Regt., 3rd Battalion 51st Inf. Regt. and 1st Battalion 213th Inf. Regt. were sent to the Katha-Indaw area to seek out and destroy them. On March 18th it was reported that the paratroops had also moved to the Meza area. [111 Ind. Inf. Bde. Meza is just south of Indaw.]

Meanwhile, it was also reported that paratroops were advancing towards the Bhamo-Namkham area [Morris force at the time under command 77 Bde. Later separated] and 1st Bn. 146th Inf. Regt. was immediately sent towards Bhamo to deal with them.

24 I.M.B., dispatched by Burma Area Army to attack Mawlu, met with no success and was compelled to sit tight in its defensive positions. *The number of deaths from disease and in action reached 3,000.*

BRITISH DEFENCES

The British defences were effectively constructed against infantry and artillery attack. For instance, in May 1944 when the Wingate Div. captured Mawlu and 4 Corps was defending Kohima and Imphal, the Japanese suffered heavy losses in attacking enemy positions, which were nicknamed 'beehives'. The British were well acquainted with the Japanese methods of attack and the defences were constructed in such a manner as to exploit the Japanese weaknesses.

We gained the impression that the British forces were generally not concerned about camouflaging their positions, probably because of the lack of danger of observation from the air. Enemy positions in the hills round Mawlu [due to parachutes stuck in the trees] and Imphal were easily visible from the air and would have been open to attack if we had possessed more aircraft. We did, however, obtain information of large-scale use of camouflaged barricades in the Palel area and according to a report from 31 Div. the fortifications in and around Kohima merged perfectly into the landscape and were very difficult to locate. Japanese losses from all these positions were heavy.

ENGINEERING EQUIPMENT

One of the engineering feats that surprised us most was the rapid construction of airstrips in the middle of the jungle. It was the Wingate Airborne Division that dropped the first construction parties from the air and, to our great surprise, airstrips were completed within a few days. [American engineers with mechanical equipment, helped by British sappers, labour and explosives.]

301

CLOTHING

As a result of long experience and scientific study, clothing issued to the British forces appears to be well suited to the climatic conditions in the operational area. Japanese clothing was found unsuitable.

MEDICAL SUPPLIES

Among many things for which we envied the British forces, were their medical services and their facilities for the evacuation of sick and wounded from operational zones by air. Many of our casualties, who, with similar facilities, would have recovered, had to be left to die.

DISCIPLINE AND MORALE

It was observed that the British forces maintained their traditionally high standard of discipline throughout a most difficult campaign. The high standard of morale and discipline of the Colonial forces surprised the Japanese troops.

HISTORY OF JAPANESE 33RD ARMY

(a) *The Hukawng Operations*

1. This was a supplementary campaign in support of the main operations carried out by the Japanese Burma Area Army, namely 15th Army's advance into India. The object of 33rd Army's operations was to check the Allied southward advance from Ledo and to distract the attention of the Allies from the operations being carried out by 15th Army.

2. The forces involved consisted of 18 Div., which was slowly withdrawing from the North Hukawng area, the main body of the newly arrived 53 Div., and a part of 2 Div. At this time the line held by 18 div. to the north of Kamaing became untenable and it became necessary for the division to withdraw and shorten its line. A new front was therefore formed to the south of Kamaing, a move which increased the difficulties facing 33rd Army in carrying out its operations. The main body of 53 Div., which was then coming up, was ordered to Mawlu to clear up Allied airborne troops in that area, after which they were to proceed as soon as possible to the Mogaung area.

3. In the middle of May Allied airborne troops landed in the Myitkyina area [American Merrill's Marauders] and 114th Inf. Regt. plus an infantry bn. and a mountain gun coy. from 18 Div. under command of Colonel Maruyama, was dispatched to Myitkyina to strengthen the garrison. The Allied forces, however, rapidly reinforced their strength and mounted an attack on Myitkyina. To meet this threat an infantry group from 56 Div. under command of Major General Mizukami was dispatched to Myitkyina to reinforce the garrison again. Major General Mizukami assumed command of all troops in the area and made every effort to defeat the Allied troops, but by the beginning of August, the Japanese had been completely defeated. Colonel Asano in command of 119th Inf. Regt. from 53 Div. was dispatched to Myitkyina together with a bn. of field artillery to try and save the situation. In the meantime other Allied forces had advanced towards Mogaung [77 Bde., 14 Bde., 111 Bde., West African Bde.] and were threatening to cut the rear L. of C. of 18 Div. and the Asano detachment was recalled to Mogaung where it rejoined its parent formation. 53 Div. had from the end of July been gradually handing its commitments to 18 Div. in the Sahmaw [west of Mogaung] area, and at the beginning of September 1944 had left the command of 15th Army. By the end of September 18 Div. had completed its concentration in the Namkham area. ['retreated to' would be better. Namkham is east of the Irrawaddy.].

(b) *Operations in the Myitkyina Railway Corridor*

1. These operations were planned to defeat the Allied troops which landed in the vicinity of the Myitkyina railway corridor and threatened to cut the L. of C. and disrupt the rear areas of 15th Army which was engaged in the Kohima/Imphal operations. These landings also threatened the L. of C. of 18 Div. which was operating at that time in the Hukawng area.

2. 24 I.M.B. which hitherto had been operating against the Allied airborne troops under command of 15th Army was put under command of 33rd Army. As it became apparent that the Allies intended to cut the Myitkyina railway line and were concentrating in the Mawlu area for this purpose, the newly arrived 53 Div., with 24 I.M.B. under its

command, mounted an attack and succeeded in capturing Mawlu. They claim that considerable casualties were inflicted on the Allied troops at Namkwin [Blackpool, held by 111 Bde.] forcing the Allies to retreat northwards. This campaign opened 18 Div.'s L. of C. to the rear.

First Dispositions in Burma

2nd and 3rd Bns., 151st Inf. Regt., with 1 Coy., 53rd Engr. Regt. were now ordered away to the Imphal campaign and came under the command of 33 Div. The rest moved north and came under the command of 33rd Army in time to be ordered to 'snuff out' the airborne landings in the railway corridor.

This was 53 Div.'s first battle experience and to the disappointment of the divisional commander about half the troops under his command did not belong to his formation, but were a motley crew gathered together for the operation under the blanket form 'Také' Force.

The Japanese Order of Battle against airborne troops was as follows:

> 53 Div. H.Q.
> 128th Inf. Regt.
> Part of 53rd Engr. Regt.
> Part of 53rd Tpt. Regt.
> Div. Sigs.
> Four bns. of 24 I.M.B. (about 2,800)
> 4th Inf. Regt., 2 Div. (about 1,800)

The total number of troops was 7,500. 'Také' Force had no tanks and no support from 53rd Fd. Arty. Regt., as it had not yet arrived.

On May 14th, 1944, Lieut.-General Takeda Kaoru took over command as Kawano was sick. (Kawano was evacuated to Japan and later in the year died in a military hospital there.)

One regret voiced by the officers interrogated was that they never really came to grips with the airborne forces. A grand attack was arranged against their positions at Mawlu, but the airborne forces removed themselves before it materialized.

Airborne Forces' attack at Namkwin [111 Bde. forming Blackpool] caused the 53 Division to leave Mawlu on May 16th, 1944. It arrived at Hopin on May 19th and attacked at Namkwin on May 22nd. The attack was mounted by 128th Inf. Regt. and by 1 Bn., 151st Inf. Regt., which had meanwhile arrived from Rangoon.

Casualties during these operations were not numerous but the first signs of serious weakening of this new division, with its high content of reservists who were past their prime, began to show, in the amount of daily sickness. Malaria was the main trouble. Anti-malaria tablets were scarce. [Major Lockett's capture of a whole dump of these at Kyusunlai Pass was probably the cause of this.]

Myitkyina and the Railway Corridor Battles

A new menace came from the Allied attacks down the Hukawng valley and on Myitkyina. 18 Div. had one regiment on Myitkyina and 53 Div. was ordered to break off its action near Namkwin and go to the south side of Myitkyina. The division moved to the '715' metre bridge on the railway about 5 miles from Myitkyina on May 29th, 1944. Roughly this date marks the end of the old 'Také' Force, although other units of it besides 53 Div. continued the struggle for a time in the railway corridor proper.

The rapidity of the advance by the Allies from the Hukawng direction, and the threat to Mogaung and Kamaing, caused the division to be moved to Mogaung to strengthen the position. After some losses the deterioration in the north led to 53 Div.'s being ordered to Sahmaw and Taugni on June 20th, whereupon the division 'advanced back' (literal reading) to those places and was in position there by June 30th. (This was after our capture of Mogaung.)

The division was told that the divisions in North Burma must at all costs try to prevent the American-Chinese Army from opening a direct route from India to China. It was ordered to persevere in its attempts to defend the railway corridor.

Better positions were available at Mawhun and 53 Div. removed there on August 10th and established positions. [36 British Infantry Division continued south after being flown into Myitkyina and relieving the Chindits at Mogaung.]

New Chief of Staff

In August 1944 Colonel Nakamura, C.O.S. until that time, gave way to Colonel Oyabe Shozo, who had been assistant C.O.S. under him.

Effect of the Monsoon and Malaria Season

The division suffered terribly from malaria. Supplies of quinine and other pills were insufficient. Although the officers interrogated can give no detailed figures, they say that the division's record in malaria incidence was probably the worst in Burma. A high proportion of the cases were fatal.

The War in South-East Asia

The Japanese impressions of the Burma theatre do not differ very much from the impressions of the average British soldier. Both officers and men have no love for the country, and throughout the campaign they were much preoccupied with thoughts of repatriation. Their worst enemy was the weather. The climate is much too hot and wet for the Japanese. After that the chief trouble was disease (the most disastrous being malaria), insufficient rations, inadequate mail, and in the latter stages of the campaign, anger at their lack of air support and general inferiority in weapons and ammunition. For the latter reason they preferred jungle warfare with its greater opportunities for concealment, rather than fighting in the open valleys.

They regarded the Burmese rather as ignorant children and were not surprised when they supported whichever side was winning. They lacked 'spirit' and were lazy. The Japanese were struck by the way the people seemed to spend all day sitting, sleeping and talking. Nevertheless, the ordinary soldier made friends with the Burmese easily and felt that they had racial characteristics in common.

The favourite station in the south was Java on account of its climate and food. The most unpopular was Burma.

HISTORY OF 24 INDEPENDENT MIXED BRIGADE

Operation against Wingate's forces in North Burma

In the middle of March 1944 Allied airborne landings

took place in North Burma. A force composed of 24 I.M.B. H.Q., 138, 139, 140, and 141 Bns. plus supporting Arty. Engrs. and Sigs. was ordered to proceed at once to Indaw. Their task was to clear rail and road obstacles and protect the lines of communication which were under attack.

A series of unsuccessful attacks were made on the Mawlu roadblock in March. Subsequently the brigade moved northward, occupying airstrips during the Allied withdrawal in May and June 1944. In August when the northern area was being evacuated by Japanese forces, the I.M.B. moved south again and eventually reached Moulmein in October.

Original Organization as on January 8th, 1944

	Officers	Other ranks	Civilians Attached	Total
24 I.M.B. H.Q. ..	19	190	2	211
138 Inf. Bn. ..	28	853	—	881
139 Inf. Bn. ..	Figures not available (approx.)*			900
140 Inf. Bn. ..	,,	,, ,,	,,	900
141 Inf. Bn. ..	28	853	—	881
Arty. Regt. ..	16	256	—	372
Engrs. Coy. ..	3	179	—	182
Sigs. Coy.	5	173	—	178

Total 4505

* Figures showing distribution of personnel of 439 and 140 Bns. are not available as these later came under a different command.

In addition to these units on establishment above mentioned, the following units were attached; strengths shown are approximate only.

70 A.A. Bn.	300 all ranks
M/T Unit from B.A.A.S.	30 all ranks
20 Special M/T Coy.	40 all ranks
211 Special M/T Coy.	120 all ranks
94 Mule Coy.	300 all ranks
Indian National Army A.A. Bn.[1]	100 all ranks
Burma Defence Army A.A. Unit	80-100 all ranks

[1] We found these were mainly men from the British Hong Kong and Singapore Brigade R.A. After severe casualties they surrendered to us at Mogaung and became our stretcher bearers.

Including attached units, the strength of the I.M.B. came to approximately 5,500.

North Burma Operation

(a) *Situation:* Towards the middle of March 1944 intelligence was received to the effect that enemy airborne troops had landed in north Burma and were harassing communications in the area north of Indaw.

24 I.M.B., H.Q., 138, 139, 140 and 141 Bns. plus Arty., Engrs. and Sigs. units were dispatched immediately and established a base at Indaw on March 25th, 1944. Their object was to guard rail communications between Indaw and Hopin and wipe out the invaders. The I.M.B. at this time had come under the command of 15th Army.

(b) *Indaw:* Operations commenced immediately; 3 Inf. Bns. and two bns. of Arty. attacked enemy positions in the Indaw Lake area. A four-day battle ensued, March 26th-30th, resulting in the withdrawal of the enemy forces to the north. Japanese casualties estimated that 100 dead, 150 wounded. [This was Lieut.-Colonel Wilkinson's action when commanding 1st Leicesters of 16 Brigade. In my opinion it was one of the finest battalion actions of the war and deserves detailed study as long as battalion actions are studied.]

(c) *Mawlu:* On April 2nd the I.M.B. moved north and established H.Q. at Sepein (south of Mawlu) preparatory to making an attack on an enemy roadblock at Henu. The enemy's main positions were on two heights immediately east of the railway track; their airstrip just west of the track.

Between April 6th and 17th 24 I.M.B. carried out repeated assaults on this block from the direction of east and south-east but were repulsed each time by the overwhelming resistance of the enemy. On April 20th the I.M.B. retired south to Tonlon, having sustained heavy casualties.

On April 25th they fought a one-day battle, engaging an enemy column south of Tonlon. [I do not know to what action they refer.] They routed this force and completed mopping up next day. From Tonlon the I.M.B. returned to base [retreated?] at Indaw. Here they joined forces with 53 Div. which had moved up from Mandalay.

(d) *Second Attack on Mawlu:* The combined strength of

these two formations advanced to Sepein on May 8th for the second attack on the Mawlu block. Two days were engaged on recce and preparation for the assault. At dawn on May 11th the I.M.B. plus 4th Inf. Regt. advanced as planned only to find that the position had been evacuated only a few hours earlier.[1]

53 Div. now moved north in pursuit of the enemy while 24 I.M.B. proceeded east of Henu to attack two airstrips at Nami [Piccadilly] and Karat [Broadway]. These had also been evacuated and, after rendering them useless, Bde. turned southward, arriving at Indaw on May 23rd.

(e) *Garrison Duties:* It now became the role of the I.M.B. to guard that section of the railway from Wuntho to Mohnyin and maintain communications. The engineers set to work rebuilding bridges and clearing the track.

Early in June 1944 the I.M.B. moved north again, setting up H.Q. at Hopin. Bde.'s task now was to protect railway communications south as far as Indaw.

Apart from occasional skirmishes with enemy patrols no action took place in this area. On June 10th one coy. of 138 Bn. was sent to guard a landing strip south of Indaw against a possible enemy relanding.

(f) *Withdrawal:* During the general southward withdrawal of the Japanese forces in August, 24 I.M.B. moved south to Indaw and eventually arrived back in Moulmein in October.

THE ESSAYS OF LIEUT.-COLONEL FUJIWARA IWAICHI

Reasons for expecting an Allied Counter-Attack

(i) British and Indian forces in the Mayu peninsula had made persistent and determined counter-attacks between December 1942 and February 1943.

(ii) A Chinese expeditionary force under the command of Chen Shin was assembled in Yunnan province. This force was being trained and supplied by officers and men of the U.S. Army. The size of this force was daily increasing and

---

[1] This brilliant operation under the eye of the enemy was carried out under the command of Brig. Ricketts, who had taken over command West African Bde. at White City 10 days after leaving England. All guns and nearly all equipment were flown out at night. Major Lockett was the last to leave after booby trapping White City extensively.

Chungking was continually emphasizing the need for a counter-offensive in Burma in order to reopen the Burma road.

(iii) The Chungking Army which had retreated into Assam in May 1942 had there been reorganized into a powerful operational unit with U.S. equipment.

Development of Operational Plans by 15th Army up to about June 1943

Lieut.-Col. Hayashi, who had been Staff Officer (Operations) in Southern Army H.Q., began, from about June 1942, to advocate the advantages to be obtained from an attack on Imphal. He considered that Imphal would become the main base for a British and Indian counter-offensive against Burma. He also emphasized the advisability of exploiting the successes achieved in the Burma operations in the spring of 1942 before British and Indian preparations for defence were completed. Southern Army and Imperial H.Q. concurred in this plan and 15th Army was ordered to make preparations for the proposed operation.

However, the plan was opposed by the Staff Officer (Intelligence) for the following reasons:

(a) Scarcity of good roads in the India-Burma frontier area.

(b) Ignorance of enemy strengths and of topographical conditions.

(c) Incomplete preparations for supplying forward troops.

(d) Danger that the advance of the Japanese Army into Indian territory would provoke political ill-feeling against Japan among masses in India. Further, Lieut.-General Mutaguchi, commanding 18 Division, and Lieut.-General Sakuri, commanding 33 Division on the front line in Burma, showed great reluctance to undertake the task. They pointed out the difficulties caused by topography, communications and disease in the India-Burma frontier areas. This, they considered, rendered operations in these areas almost impossible for either side. For these reasons and for those given above, the plan for an attack on Imphal was abandoned about December 1942.

As a result, it was decided to strengthen the defence of

Burma by occupying strategic positions and constructing defence works. However, the plan for an attack on Imphal was reconsidered about April. Lieut.-General Mutaguchi, commanding 18 Division, who had previously been opposed to the plan, now gave his support. He had been very impressed by the exploits of Major General Wingate's British and Indian 77 Brigade, which had broken through the Jupi mountain range. This range had been previously considered impassable for operational troops. 77 Brigade had caused confusion in the 18 Division area and had also engaged powerful forces from 33 and 56 Divisions.

Mutaguchi now recognized that operations were possible anywhere in north Burma frontier area in the dry season, if proper preparations were made. He preferred rather to attack and destroy the Allied base for a counter-offensive than to stand on the defensive and attempt the impossible by defending a front several hundred kilometres long with one division. He was appointed commander of 15th Army in March 1943 and thereupon began to advocate this plan strongly. Against this view were, however, Major General Obata, his staff, and the staff of Burma Area Army H.Q., who were in favour of defensive tactics, because of scarcity of operational troops and the difficulty of supply.

But Lieut.-General Mutaguchi, who happened to be the only officer who really knew the topography of north Burma well, was adamant, and as all the members of his staff had been only recently appointed and were ignorant of the area they were unable to dissuade the G.O.C.-in-C. Thereupon the Chief of Staff decided to send staff officers to the front to reconnoitre the area. Major Fujiwara was to go to the left bank of the Chindwin and Colonel Kinoshita and Major Takahashi to the Jupi mountain area.

When Lieut.-General Mutaguchi's opinion was reported to H.Q. Southern Army and to Imperial H.Q., some of the staff agreed to the plan.

As a result of the reconnaissance of the Chindwin, it was learnt that the area was suitable for mule transport and that five or six battalions could obtain supplementary rations locally. It was further observed that the Chindwin river was easily passable by rafts in the dry season. It was decided therefore to advance the front line to the east bank of the Chindwin, though the main plan was still defensive in accordance with the orders of Burma Area Army H.Q. When the advance line had been pushed forward to the Chindwin the G.O.C.-in-C. became even more convinced that the offensive against Imphal should be undertaken immediately.

The Chief of Staff, Major General Obata, as mentioned above, was strongly opposed to the G.O.C.-in-C. on the question of the Imphal offensive and when Lieut.-General Mutaguchi pushed his line to the mountains on the western bank of the Chindwin about May 1943, disregarding the approach of the rainy season. Major General Obata expressed strong opposition to this plan and was finally removed. However, Burma Area Army were still against the plan and the idea had to be dropped.

Major General Kunomura was appointed Chief of Staff in June 1943.

Meanwhile, Lieut.-General Mutaguchi's plan was gaining support at Southern Army H.Q and at Imperial H.Q. One reason for this was the low state of morale in Japan owing to the adverse situation in the Solomons. The Tojo Government tried desperately to combat this depression. A second reason may have been the influence of Subhas Chandra Bose who in a recent visit to Tokyo had strongly emphasized the need for action by Japan for the liberation of India.

Because of these tendencies at H.Q. Southern Army and Imperial H.Q., 15th Army began to make preparations for possible offensive operations in the following dry season.

Invasion of the Wingate Air-Corps Commando Div. into North Burma and its Effects

On March 9th when the Army had launched the attack after so many months of waiting, Army H.Q. received information that British-Indian Army airborne troops of unknown strength were landing in the neighbourhood of Katha. The L. of C. troops in the Wuntho area were in a state of panic, and it was impossible to obtain any information about the location of the landing, its strength, and objective of its operations. The Army at first underestimated the strength of these units at two or three thousand and judged them to be nothing more than guerrilla troops. However, by the beginning of April it became clear from frag-

312

mentary information that they constituted a powerful operational unit, and the Army attempted to find counter-measures. First of all, it ordered the L. of C. troops and a part of 15th Division in the neighbourhood to deal with the situation, but they were repulsed.

Results of Wingate Operations

Army H.Q. for the above reason was unable to advance to Indainggyi till the end of April. Owing to poor liaison be-tween Division and Army H.Q., ill-feeling and disagree-ments increased.

While making preparations for operations, the main part of the M.T. units was employed on the Wuntho-Homalin Road. These were to be transferred immediately after the commencement of operations, but the road was cut by the Wingate force and these vehicles could not be transferred to other areas. *This was one of the reasons why supplies for the troops in the Imphal area became more and more difficult.*

Part of 15 Division, 53 Division and an Independent Mixed Brigade which were to be employed as re-inforcements for the Imphal operations were absorbed by the operations against the airborne division.

5 Air-Division which was to have employed its full strength in the Imphal operations was transferred to take part in operations against the airborne division.

The supply-line of 18 Division was cut, and as a result this division, which had been fighting under difficult conditions, was faced by ever-increasing trials. All this had a very bad effect on the morale of Army H.Q. and of the divisions con-cerned.

INDEX

315

Mawhood, Colonel, 13
Medally, Pte., 171–3
Merrill's Marauders, 17, 38, 230, 303
Merritt, Sgt., 279
Mizukami, Major-General, 303
Monteith, Major David, 34, 43, 55, 106, 108–9, 111, 117, 183, 185, 203, 242
Morris, Brigadier, 95, 100, 289
Morris Force, 95, 142, 230, 289, 301
Mountbatten, Lord Louis, 14, 15, 38, 214, 291
Musgrave, Lieut.-Col., 13
Mutaguchi, General, 7, 108, 185, 257, 292, 297, 299, 310–12

Naka, General, 245–8
Nakamura, Colonel, 306
Nasu, General, 293
Nigeria Rifles, 6th, 19, 78, 97, 110–11, 256
Nigeria Rifles, 7th, 19, 122–4, 126–7, 149, 256
Nigeria Rifles, 12th, 19, 127–8, 256
Numata, General, 12, 293–4, 297

Obata, Major-General, 311–12
Old, Brigadier-General, 23, 32–3

P'ang, Major, 223–4, 243, 250
Parachute Battalion, 1st British, 43
Parachute Brigade, 50th, 101
Park Captain, Mungo 133–4
Parker, Lieut., 117
Patterson, Captain H. N. F., 50
Perry, Sgt., 54
Pringle, Major, 73, 169, 267, 276–9, 281

Quebec Conference, 291, 300
Queen's Royal Regiment (West Surrey), 2nd, 19

Railway Engineer Regiment, 5th Japanese, 257
Rebori, Major, 32, 75
Reconnaissance Regiment, 45th, 19, 109, 123–33, 135–6, 139, 145
Richards, Lieut.-Col., 43, 50, 60–2, 144, 152, 160
Ricketts, Brigadier Abdy, 157–8, 309
Rogers, Captain, 122, 137
Rome, Colonel Claude, 17, 22–3, 29, 34, 42–3, 75–83, 102, 105, 155–7, 166–7, 170, 178, 180, 190, 213, 218, 231–2
Rooke, Lieut., 129, 175, 182
Roosevelt, Franklin D., 65, 258
Royal Artillery, 126
Royal Corps of Signals, 25, 289
Royal Engineers, 25, 289
Ryan, Captain Paddy, 60, 62, 73, 127, 144, 151–2

Sakuri, Lieut.-General, 310
Satrai, Lieut., 62, 198
Scholey, Lieut., 54
Scoones, General, 258
Scott, Lieut.-Col., 13, 21, 23, 28–9, 31, 34, 43, 66, 89, 105, 246
Seaforth Highlanders, 1st Battalion, 278–9
Serjeant, Cpl., 171–3
Shaw, Major Freddie, 43, 50–3, 68, 108, 113–14, 129, 155, 206, 235–6, 238, 242
Shozo, Colonel Oyabe, 306
Shuttleworth, Major, 21, 30, 43, 49, 55, 64, 67, 68, 106, 108, 112–13
Singh, Bahadur, 191
Skone, Lieut.-Col. Hubert, 43, 50, 52, 67–9, 103, 105, 108–9, 118–19, 122, 128, 132–6, 138, 144, 155
Slim, General, 8, 14, 22, 38, 65, 85–6, 100, 102, 105, 143, 176,

319

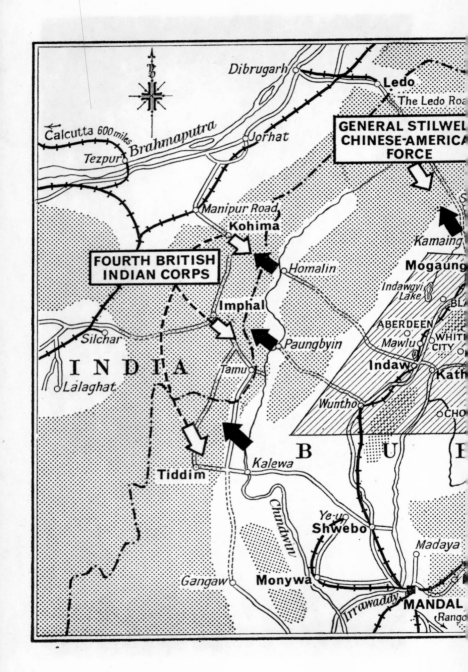